WITHDRAWN

PRINCIPLES OF ECONOMICS
Micro

THE IRWIN SERIES IN ECONOMICS

Consulting Editor
LLOYD G. REYNOLDS
Yale University

AMES *Soviet Economic Processes*

ANDERSON, GITLOW, & DIAMOND (eds.) *General Economics: A Book of Readings* rev. ed.

BALASSA *The Theory of Economic Integration*

BEAL & WICKERSHAM *The Practice of Collective Bargaining* 3d ed.

BLAUG *Economic Theory in Retrospect* rev. ed.

BORNSTEIN (ed.) *Comparative Economic Systems: Models and Cases* rev. ed.

BORNSTEIN & FUSFELD (eds.) *The Soviet Economy: A Book of Readings* 3d ed.

BUCHANAN *The Public Finances* 3d ed.

CARTTER *Theory of Wages and Employment*

CARTTER & MARSHALL *Labor Economics: Wages, Employment, and Trade Unionism*

CHAMBERLAIN *Contemporary Economic Issues*

DAVIDSON, SMITH, & WILEY *Economics: An Analytical Approach* rev. ed.

DAVIS, HUGHES, & MCDOUGALL *American Economic History: The Development of a National Economy* 3d ed.

DOLL, RHODES, & WEST *Economics of Agricultural Production, Markets, and Policy*

DRUMMOND *The Canadian Economy: Organization and Development*

DUE *Government Finance: Economics of the Public Sector* 4th ed.

DUE & CLOWER *Intermediate Economic Analysis* 5th ed.

FELLNER *Probability and Profit: A Study of Economic Behavior along Bayesian Lines*

FERGUSON *Microeconomic Theory* rev. ed.

FISHER *Money and Banking*

GAMBS & KOMISAR *Economics and Man* 3d ed.

PRINCIPLES OF
ECONOMICS
Micro

WILLIS L. PETERSON, Ph.D.
University of Minnesota

1971

RICHARD D. IRWIN, INC.   Homewood, Illinois   60430
Irwin-Dorsey Limited, Georgetown, Ontario

Library of Congress Catalog Card No. 72–149899

Printed in the United States of America

PREFACE

The general philosophy of this book probably is best expressed by Alfred North Whitehead in *The Aims of Education and Other Essays:* "Whatever be the detail with which you cram your student, the chances of his meeting in afterlife exactly that detail is almost infinitesimal; and if he does meet it, he will probably have forgotten what you taught him about it. The really useful training yields a comprehension of a few general principles with a thorough grounding in the way they apply to a variety of concrete details. In subsequent practice the men will have forgotten your particular details; but they will remember by an unconscious common sense how to apply principles to immediate circumstances."

In line with this philosophy, the book strives for three main objectives. The first is to help the student improve his understanding of how a market economy operates. How are prices and wages determined and why are they continually changing? Who determines what will be produced and how much? These are some of the questions that the book addresses itself to. The second objective is to help the student acquire an understanding of the major tools or principles that have proved useful in making economic decisions or solving economic problems. The third and most important objective, but also the most difficult to attain, is to help the student acquire a skill in using these tools or principles to conduct economic analysis.

Hopefully, the student will not be so unfortunate as the economist who decided to build his own house. After acquiring the necessary tools—hammer, saw, level, etc.—he proceeded to go about his task. After finishing the house, it didn't look quite right to him so he asked a carpenter friend to take a look at his accomplishment. A quick glance at the structure prompted the carpenter to reply, "Of course it doesn't look right, you've built it up-side-down"; to which the economist replied, "Oh, I thought something was wrong, I kept falling off of the porch." Unfortunately, "up-side-down" answers to economic questions are much less recognizable than up-side-down houses. To avoid such answers, it is necessary to be able to use the tools of economic analysis as well as just to learn of their existence.

This book is a twin. It is related to my *Principles of Economics: Macro* in style and is complementary to it as far as content is concerned. Yet the book is capable of standing alone, or it can be used with any other principles text. Also, both the micro and the macro books were written with the objective in mind of their being used interchangeably. Some instructors prefer to teach macroeconomics first, others micro. In addition, the many new "current economic issues" books that have come on the market in recent years can serve as excellent complements to either book.

No book, of course, is the product of just one person's thinking, least of all this one. Credit must go to all those who have influenced my thinking in economics—my teachers, my colleagues, and my students. I am especially indebted to Professor Conrad Caligaris of Northeastern University for his perceptive comments and suggestions on the first draft of the manuscript. Also, I have benefited from discussion with my colleagues and fellow principals, teachers—Dale Dahl, John Helmberger, Emiel Owens, Jerome Stam, and John Woelti. Special thanks also go to Mrs. Norma Raske and Mrs. Kay Perry for their long hours of typing the manuscript, and to Dorothy Peterson for her help and cheerful endurance as a "writer's widow."

March, 1971   WILLIS L. PETERSON

CONTENTS

CHAPTER
1
INTRODUCTION TO MICROECONOMICS

"MICRO" VERSUS "MACRO" ECONOMICS

As economics developed into a discipline, two major areas of study emerged: micro and macro economics. As the name implies, microeconomics is concerned mainly with the economic activities of individual consumers and producers, or groups of consumers and producers which are known as markets.

Macroeconomics, on the other hand, is concerned mainly with economic aggregates, or the economy as a whole. The two major problem areas of macroeconomics are unemployment and inflation. To be sure these problems are of great concern to individuals. But they are problems that the individual has virtually no control over. Rather the cause and/or solutions to these problems lie in the realm of government action; action which affects the entire economy.

It would be a mistake, however, to conclude that the micro and macro areas are distinct or unrelated fields of study. There is a certain amount of overlap between the two. For example, we will see in later chapters that much of what the government does in terms of enacting laws or levying taxes directly effects individuals and markets, and that these effects can be analyzed with the tools of microeconomics. By the same token, the actions of large groups of consumers or producers, such as the increased desire to save on the part of many people, are analyzed with macroeconomic tools.

Because of the impossibility of completely separating the micro from the macro, some economists argue that a more appropriate division would be price theory versus monetary and income and employment theory. In more advanced courses, particularly at the graduate level, microeconomic principles are generally referred to as price theory, mainly because the material deals with the determination of prices and the effect of prices on the output and input mix in the economy.

Rather than try to offer a formal definition of microeconomics or price theory, whichever you prefer, let us begin our study.

THE PROBLEM OF SCARCITY

In studying economics, as in any other activity, we like to have some reason for exerting our effort. We attend the theater or go to a ball game because it is enjoyable. We attend school to learn or hold down a job to earn a living. But why study economics?

There may be a few people in this world who would be willing to study economics purely for the enjoyment it brings. For most of us, however, learning economics is not 100 percent entertainment. To be sure, mastering a subject provides a certain amount of intellectual satisfaction. But it is hard to justify economics only on this basis. Crossword puzzles or chess might do just as well or better on this score. No, the social science known as economics must rest on a different foundation.

I have posed this question to my students and so far all have been too kind (or too smart) to say that we study economics because it is a required subject. But this would beg the question, why is it required?

The answer we are looking for can be simplified down to a single word —scarcity. In other words, human wants are greater than the resources available to satisfy these wants. Because resources are scarce we have to economize. If all resources, including time, were unlimited, we would have no need for economics. We could be as wasteful as we pleased and still satisfy our wants.

ECONOMIC DECISIONS

Each of us from the time we are aware of the world around us are forced to make economic decisions, or to economize if you wish. This harsh reality of the world soon becomes apparent the first time a child stands in front of a candy counter clutching a nickel or a dime. The coin will buy a candy bar, a package of gum, or a roll of "lifesavers," but not all three. An economic decision must be made.

It would be misleading, though, to conclude from this example that economic decisions all involve money. They do not. Probably the best example of a nonmoney economic decision is how we allocate our time— a scarce resource that seems to become even more scarce the older we become. For example, the student must decide if he shall spend the evening studying, say, mathematics or history. Or, perhaps even more fundamental, whether he will devote the evening to study or to leisure. Allocating our time to the best use is one of the most important economic decisions we have to make. And it could well be one of the most important things we learn in school.

More traditional types of economic decisions involve the operations of households and firms. For the household, a continuing array of economic decisions must be made on how to allocate the weekly or semimonthly paycheck. How much goes to housing, how much to food, clothing, transportation, entertainment, etc.? Managing just a modest income for a family requires thousands of economic decisions each year.

Considering the complexity of a household's economic decisions, we can fully appreciate the decisions that must be made in managing a business firm. What kind of things should the firm produce? Should it specialize or diversify? Should it produce a large volume and sell at a low price or produce less and charge more? How do the decisions of rival firms affect each firm? Should the firm employ more labor and save on machines or should it substitute machines for labor? These are some examples of economic decisions that each manager must make. How well he makes them largely determines the success or failure of his firm.

The need to make economic decisions, of course, does not stop at the level of the household or firm. Indeed economic decisions must be made as well at the governmental level, ranging from local governments such as townships and municipalities to the states and federal government.

Perhaps the most basic of economic decisions here is to decide how much of the total production of society shall be provided through the public sector and how much through the private sector. In a democracy governmental decisions tend to reflect the broad wishes of society, but of course they cannot please everyone. People of a more conservative philosophy tend to desire a greater share of production in the private sector while those of a more liberal bent stress the need for more public goods and services.

Once society decides the mix between public and private goods it must then decide what kind of public goods and services should be produced. For example, what is the appropriate mix between military and nonmilitary public goods? Should we have less weapons and more public expenditure on slum clearance, public parks, pollution control, etc.? You might have noted that economic decisions involving governments or nations have much in common with those made by the child at the candy counter. Both require making a choice among alternatives, although one may involve a nickel or a dime while the other may run into billions of dollars.

THE USEFULNESS OF THEORY

Unfortunately, economic theory has suffered from a bad press for many years and not entirely without justification. Students tend to be turned off by theory because they visualize dry, abstract material that has little relevance to their world. But theory does not have to be dry or irrelevant. In fact there is little to be gained by theory if it cannot help us make day-to-day economic decisions or resolve economic problems.

How is theory useful? The main value of theory is that it provides us with a framework for thinking. We need such a framework because the world is by far too complex to take into account every bit of information that bears upon a decision or problem. Thus we have to sort out the important from the unimportant. But as we know, information does not come in neat categories labeled "important" and "unimportant" nor is it always obvious which is which. Theory, then, is formulated to help us identify the important bits of information for making decisions or solving problems.

Essentially, a theory is an idea or a concept. Another alias for theory is principle. Thus the title of this book could as well be theories of economics. But because theory has become somewhat of a bad word, authors shy away from using it in titles, fearing that it will reduce the sale of their books.

Of course, studying theory for theory's sake is a waste of time. If theory cannot help you make decisions your time would be about as well spent reading a sex novel. Hopefully you will not find this book a waste of time. Each theory, principle, or idea that is presented is accompanied by an application or example. It is hoped that these applications will help you to use economic theory correctly and more effectively. It is a mistake to believe that only economists use economic theory; everyone uses it every day, although not everyone uses it correctly.

PRODUCTION POSSIBILITIES

We know now that economics exists because we cannot have everything we would like and thus we are forced to make economic decisions. These decisions take the form of choosing among alternative goods or services that will best satisfy our wants. Thus society must decide what to produce out of an almost infinite range of possibilities. Economists have traditionally represented this range of choices by what they call a "production possibilities schedule" (Table 1–1). Or this schedule may be represented by a diagram (Figure 1–1) and called a "production possibilities curve." Figure 1–1 is just a representation or picture of the relationship expressed by numbers in Table 1–1.

As we go along you will find that in economics we use diagrams a great deal. Essentially these diagrams are just pictures of ideas. If "one picture is worth a thousand words" then a diagram is a relatively efficient and concise way of explaining an idea or concept.

The production possibilities schedule or curve is a way of illustrating the idea that a nation or individual faces limits on what can be produced and must make choices between many possible combinations of goods or

TABLE 1-1.   Production possibilities schedule

Wheat (Million Bushels)	Corn (Million Bushels)
0	80
10	75
20	65
30	50
40	30
50	0

FIGURE 1-1.   Production possibilities curve

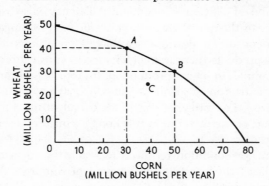

services. In the simple example used here we see that if this nation devoted all its resources to the production of corn it could produce 80 million bushels of corn and nothing else. Or if all resources were devoted to wheat, 50 million bushels could be produced but no corn. It may like to have 50 million bushels of wheat *and* 80 million bushels of corn, but this combination is not possible because the nation does not have the resources to produce both.

It would be more realistic, of course, to believe that the country would choose some combination between the two extremes, say 40 million wheat and 30 million corn, or 20 million wheat and 65 million corn. We will postpone for now just how a country goes about making this choice. The important point here is that such a choice must be made.

EFFICIENCY AND FULL EMPLOYMENT

Let us focus our attention for a moment on the production possibilities curve, noting some of its characteristics. First, we should be aware that the very best that can be achieved is to be on the surface of the curve. Any point outside the curve is by definition not possible. Essentially the curve bounds or defines what is possible to achieve. But it would be a mistake to believe that a nation or an economy always achieves the possible. To be on the surface of the curve, say at point *A* or *B*, requires two conditions: (1) all production is carried on in the most efficient manner possible and (2) all resources are fully employed.

We might stop at this point and ask, what do we mean by efficiency? Essentially there are two types of efficiency and both are required to be on the surface of the production possibilities curve. One type, engineering efficiency, requires that maximum output is obtained from a given amount of resources, i.e. resource waste is kept to a minimum. In economics we generally do not concern ourselves with engineering efficiency, leaving this to engineers and physicists.

The other kind of efficiency, economic efficiency, also is required to reach the surface of the curve. By economic efficiency we mean producing products which consumers desire at the lowest possible cost. In the production of most products there is some chance to substitute one input for another. For example, in wheat production, if labor is high priced relative to machines, as is true in the United States, wheat production should be highly mechanized, i.e., utilizing machines to substitute for high-priced labor. A large part of the material in this book is concerned with achieving economic efficiency.

The second major condition required to reach the surface of the production possibilities curve is full employment of resources. The resource that we are most concerned with is the human resource. If there are people who are unemployed but would like to be working, the economy is not getting the goods or services these people could produce. Thus unemployment is wasteful for society. And, of course, for the individual who is unemployed the loss of income is a critical problem. Much of the material in macro economics deals with achieving full employment.

It would be an extremely unusual economy that would be able to achieve both maximum efficiency and full employment. Most economies probably operate below the surface of the production possibilities curve. This does not prevent them, however, from striving to reach the maximum production possible subject to environmental constraints and conservation needs. Much of the work of economists deals with helping society move towards its maximum possible output.

OPPORTUNITY COST

Let us assume for the moment that our simple economy is achieving maximum production so that we are now on the surface of the curve, say at point *A* in Figure 1-1. At this point it is producing 40 million bushels of wheat and 30 million bushels of corn per year. Suppose it wished to increase its production of corn, say up to 50 million bushels per year. To do this the nation would have to reduce its production of wheat from 40 to 30 million bushels. In other words, it would have to give up 10 million bushels of wheat to obtain the extra 20 million bushels of corn. This 10 million bushels of wheat, then, is the opportunity cost of the extra corn. Thus we can define opportunity cost as the amount of a good or service that must be given up to obtain more of another good or service.

If all resources are employed, everything that is produced has an opportunity cost. By producing one good or service, the opportunity to produce some other good or service is given up. The idea of opportunity cost applies as well to the individual firm, household, or person. The firm that uses its plant to produce shoes cannot produce belts or basketballs. The family that spends its vacation at the seashore must forego the opportunity to spend this time in the mountains. When you are reading this book you cannot be doing something else such as reading a novel, studying mathematics, or sleeping. Thus the opportunity cost of studying economics is the novel you did not enjoy, the mathematics you did not learn, or the sleep you lost. Everything you do has a cost—nothing is absolutely free.

The mark of good management, regardless if it be managing a business, a household, or a person's own time, is whether what is being produced or gained is of more value than the opportunity cost of the next best alternative. The good manager is always asking, is there anything that I can do different that will give more profit or satisfaction than what I would have to give up?

The idea of opportunity cost applies particularly well to the choice between labor and leisure. The opportunity cost of going fishing or to a baseball game on a weekday afternoon is the wages foregone from your job. For a person who highly values his income or what it will buy, there is little chance that he will take off to go fishing because its opportunity cost is too high.

Another person, however, might place a high value on his leisure. The person, for example, who not only values freedom and leisure highly but through lack of skills can earn only a low wage will likely choose more leisure. Of course, we must remember that a man who supports a family must take their welfare into account too when deciding whether or not the value of his leisure is greater than his income foregone.

It is sometimes argued, for example, that people in underdeveloped countries or areas are lazy because they have been known to quit work projects once they have earned a little money. What is often forgotten is that the choice of consumer goods available to these people is very limited because of an underdeveloped production and marketing system. Moreover the goods that are available tend to be high priced relative to income because of high transportation and marketing costs. If there is not much that your income can buy then the opportunity cost of staying home is relatively low. Before we criticize people for being lazy, therefore, we should first ask, what is the opportunity cost of their leisure?

INCREASING COSTS

The idea of increasing costs also is illustrated by the production possibility schedule or curve. You will note from Table 1-1 that in order to get the first 10 million bushels of wheat, this country had to give up 5 million bushels of corn (80 down to 75). Or for each extra bushel of wheat obtained, one-half bushel of corn was given up.

Suppose we go one step further and see what happens when this economy increases its wheat production from 10 to 20 million. Now corn production is reduced from 75 down to 65 million. In this step, for each extra bushel of wheat obtained, 1 bushel of corn was given up. At the range where we approach the maximum wheat, 3 bushels of corn is given up for each bushel of wheat obtained. Thus we see that the opportunity cost of a bushel of corn increases from one-half bushel of wheat to 3 bushels of wheat.

The same thing would be true if we start at the bottom and move up. At first only one third of a bushel of wheat is given up per bushel of corn. At the top two bushels of wheat must be sacrificed to obtain an extra bushel of corn.

This idea is illustrated also in Figure 1-1 by the concave nature of the production possibilities curve. Notice that close to the vertical axis the curve is very flat. This means that as you began to produce corn, the production of wheat declines relatively little. Then as you move down along the curve and approach the horizontal axis the curve becomes very steep. This means that in order to obtain an extra bushel of corn a relatively large amount of wheat must be sacrificed.

The slope of this curve tells us, therefore, how easy or how difficult it is to transform one good into another. For this reason the production possibilities curve is sometimes called the "transformation curve." In this example, when we move down the curve we transform wheat into corn, or moving up, we transform corn into wheat. As we move along the curve the rate of transformation changes because of increasing costs. With little or no corn, it is easy to transform wheat into corn; with almost all corn it becomes more difficult to make this transformation.

Does it make sense to believe that the idea of increasing costs really fits reality? Economists have argued that it does because they believe that resources are more productive in some uses than in others. In our example, it is reasonable to believe that some land is better suited for wheat than for corn. In the United States the arid Great Plains area would provide an example of this idea. If all of this land were planted to corn it would not yield very much. Taking this land out of corn and replacing it with wheat would not reduce corn production greatly because of the low corn yield in this area but would increase wheat production considerably if wheat grew relatively well here.

In the production of other products, the idea of increasing costs is less clear. For example, consider the case of devoting all our resources to the production of automobiles or airplanes. Would you expect increasing costs here? Both use steel, aluminum, plastic, rubber, semiskilled and skilled labor, etc. In this case the rate of transformation probably would not change very much as you moved down along the transformation curve. In this situation we would come closer to case of constant costs. In other words, the opportunity cost of an additional airplane (in terms of automobiles given up) would not be expected to change very much over the range of production.

But you might argue, if you reach the point of all airplanes and zero automobiles, surely there will be a shortage of specialized people such as test pilots, aeronautical engineers, etc., which in turn will lead to increasing costs because less qualified people will have to do these tasks. True. And this brings up an important point. If resources are *rapidly* shifted from automobiles to airplanes, we would likely run into increasing costs of airplanes. On the other hand if the move was very gradual and people anticipated the shift so that more would receive training in the needed skills, there would likely be less evidence of increasing costs.

This example brings out the importance of time for adjustment. Allowing little or no time for adjustment, a large and rapid change to different combination of products means that many resources will have to be employed in other than their intended purpose. Automobile factories must be turned into airplane factories, mechanical engineers into aeronautical engineers, etc. Allowing a longer time to adjust, however, will allow resources to become better adapted to new uses. New factories that are built will be designed for airplane production; more people will train as aeronautical engineers, etc. Thus, the transformation curve would not exhibit as much curvature allowing a long time for resources to adjust than is the case when forcing a rapid adjustment. Figures 1–2 and 1–3 illustrate this difference.

A related point, but also important, is the need to realize that no economy ever moves the entire distance along the transformation curve from one axis to another. Most changes are relatively small, say from A to B or B to A in Figures 1–2 and 1–3. And you will note that even though the transformation curve has a pronounced curvature, especially in Figure 1–2, the segment of the line between points A and B is close to a straight line. You might check this by running a straight edge through points A and B. A perfectly straight line represents constant costs.

Thus, it is reasonable to believe that in the range where you would expect changes to take place, there would not be as much evidence of in-

FIGURE 1–2. Transformation curve al-   FIGURE 1–3. Transformation curve allowing one year to   lowing ten years to
adjust   adjust

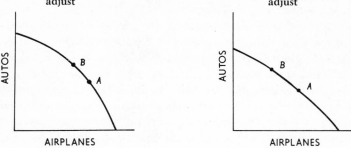

creasing costs as over the entire range of the transformation curve. And the more time allowed for adjustment the closer this segment would come to a straight line as illustrated by segment of the line between *A* and *B* in Figure 1–3.

PUBLIC VERSUS PRIVATE GOODS

The production possibilities curve is useful to illustrate, among other things, that total output for a nation is limited and choices must be made. Because it is simpler to use a two-dimensional diagram we are restricted to considering the choices between only two different goods at a time, e.g., wheat and corn, autos and airplanes, etc. Of course, it is possible to aggregate products and use the production possibilities curve to represent the choice between one good such as wheat and all other goods.

Another classification that is useful to make is between public and private goods. It is perhaps simplest to think of public goods as goods which society buys collectively such as public parks, highways, national defense, law enforcement, public education, etc. Typically these goods are not bought and sold in the marketplace but rather are financed through taxes or special fees and are distributed through a governmental agency. Public goods can be further classified as consumption goods (public parks) or investment goods (hydroelectric dam), or some combination of the two.

Society finds it necessary to produce public goods because it would be largely impossible, or at least uneconomic, for individuals to acquire these goods for personal use. Could you afford to build the highways and streets you use each day? It would be a mistake to conclude, however, that public goods are produced by governments. Although these goods generally are financed through public funds the actual production is carried on largely by private firms under contract to the government.

In a democracy the amount of public goods produced depends largely on the wishes of society. Almost everyone would agree on the need for at least a minimum amount of public goods and services such as law enforcement, highways, and streets, etc. But the optimum amount of public goods and services to be provided is not so well agreed upon. The more conservative members of society stress the ability of the individual to provide for himself what he deems best. More liberal individuals stress the dependence of people on one another and the need for more public goods and services. The actual amount of public goods is therefore a compromise between the wishes of different groups in our society.

Private goods, the other major classification, include the normal items that we purchase and use in our daily lives: food, clothing, shelter, entertainment, etc., are the standard examples. We shall devote a large share of this book discussing how society goes about allocating resources to the production of private goods and services.

PUBLIC UTILITIES

There is a class of goods and services that falls somewhere between the public and private goods categories. These are called public utilities. Some examples include your local power and light company or telephone company. Goods and services provided by these companies generally are purchased by individuals in the marketplace, so in this sense they resemble private goods. But for reasons that will become clear in a moment, society has decided that the normal production of these goods by many firms in each area would not be desirable. Thus the government regulates their production. In this sense public utilities resemble public goods.

The main reason for having public utilities is to avoid a costly duplication of facilities and services. Suppose, for example, there were 10 telephone companies serving your area instead of one. Each of these companies would require its own lines, telephones, etc. Assuming comparable efficiency the cost under this system would be high compared to the present case where there are one set of lines and one telephone per subscriber. Also it is easy to imagine how difficult it would be to make calls. For example, you might buy telephone service from a different company than the person you wish to call. Thus in order to avoid duplication and unnecessary confusion the government gives exclusive right to just one company to operate in each city or area.

By giving a firm exclusive right to operate, however, the government makes a public utility a virtual monopoly free from the competitive forces in the market. In order to guard against excessive prices or inferior service to the public, the government also regulates these firms by setting the prices they charge and establishing standards of performance.

ALLOCATING RESOURCES: CAPITALISM
VERSUS COMMUNISM

It is important at this point to stress again the fact that the production possibilities curve only tells us the possible combinations of goods and services that can be produced—it does not tell which of these combinations a nation will choose at a particular time. Will it choose much wheat and little corn or vice versa? The need to make economic decisions of this nature is common to every nation. How nations go about making these decisions will vary according to their economic system.

Under capitalism or a free market economy, the allocation of resources is determined largely by the forces of supply and demand in the market. Much of the discussion in future chapters will dwell on how this takes place. For now we might convey an intuitive idea of the process by going through a simple example.

Consider for a moment how the market determines the number of loaves of bread and pairs of shoes that are produced each year. If bread is scarce and shoes abundant, the price of bread will tend to rise and the price of shoes will fall. This change in price has the effect of increasing profits in bread production and decreasing profits in shoe production. This in turn creates an incentive for owners of resources to move resources out of shoes into bread, thereby increasing the production of the former at the expense of the latter. If we can visualize bread and shoes on a production possibilities curve, the result would be a movement along the curve away from shoes towards bread.

The key information transmitter in a market system is price. A rising price of a good is a signal for producers to move more resources into its production. A major advantage of such a system is that producers acting through their own self-interest also serve the interest of society by providing more of scarce goods or services and less of things not so highly desired by society. It does not require any benevolence on the part of producers whatsoever.

The example we have just worked through was concerned with the product market. We could go through a similar example for the resource or factor market. For instance, in the production of shoes, a scarcity of leather and a resulting high price of leather provides an incentive for producers to economize on leather and use more of a substitute material. This lowers the cost of producing shoes from what it would otherwise be and provides more leather for other uses. Again consumers benefit from this action.

In a communistic system the resources or factors of production are owned by the government. Thus the government must decide where and how their resources are to be employed. It is an enormous and virtually impossible task to direct all resources to the use that benefits society the most. How does the government know if people desire more bread and less shoes? About the only way it can find out is to observe a large buildup of shoes in storage and empty bread shelves. Once the government decides that more bread is needed, it is another problem to move shoe factory workers to the wheat fields. People are uprooted involuntarily, enemies are made among shoe factory managers, etc. Thus, the decision to cut back on shoe production may be postponed or just not made.

In recent years some communistic governments have decided that the price system and economic incentives are more efficient methods of allocating resources than direct orders. If bread is scarce and shoes abundant, the government raises bread prices and lowers shoe prices. Also the wages of labor and prices of other resources in bread production might be increased which tends to pull resources into this activity. Under this system the only difference between the capitalistic and communistic methods of allocating resources is the way prices are set. In capitalism most prices are set in the market by forces of supply and demand whereas under communism most are determined by the government.

In summary, both capitalism and communism, or any mixture of the two political-economic systems, share a common characteristic; both are constrained by a production possibilities curve, and both must decide where to employ their available resources. In pure capitalism the choice of what to produce is largely determined by the people as they express their preferences through the forces of supply and demand in the market; in pure communism government officials must decide either what is to be produced and/or what price to charge.

Most economies, including the United States, fall somewhere between these two extremes. The U.S. economy is often described as mixed capitalism where a large part of available resources are allocated by the market but some public goods are allocated by government decision.

PREVIEW OF THINGS TO COME

We have now set the stage for a more detailed look at the basic ideas and concepts in economics. We begin by focusing in on the individual consumer or household to see how each of us can obtain the most satisfaction from the things we buy. We then extend what we know about consumer behavior to derive the concept of consumer demand. Next we take a similar look at the production side, first studying how resources can be combined in the most efficient manner and then extending our knowledge to derive producer supply. Next we combine the concepts of demand and supply to see how they interact in the market to determine the price paid and quantity sold of a good or service.

After making our acquaintance with demand and supply and how they work in the market, we take a more detailed look at different kinds of product markets from the standpoint of the degree of competition present. Specifically we will see why some firms have price determined for them by the market while other firms have some power to determine for themselves the price they charge. We will then turn to a discussion of the labor and capital markets. We will learn that these markets have much in common with the markets for consumer goods and services. Lastly we will turn to the topics of education and research and attempt to determine whether or not these represent a good investment for the individual or the economy.

MAIN POINTS OF CHAPTER 1

1. Economics has evolved into two major fields of study: macro and micro economics, although there is considerable overlap between the two.

2. Economics exists because of the basic problem of scarcity. Human wants are greater than the resources available to satisfy these wants.

3. Because resources are scarce, individuals, households, firms, and governments must choose among alternative goods or services. Everyone from small children to the largest governments must make economic decisions. Not all economic decisions involve money. Allocating our time is an important nonmoney economic decision.

4. Economic theory is useful because it provides a framework for thinking, enabling us to separate the important from unimportant information in making economic decisions or solving problems.

5. The production possibilities curve represents the idea that total output of goods and services is limited by the resources available, and choices must be made among possible alternatives.

6. The surface of the production possibilities curve is reached only with maximum engineering and economic efficiency, and full employment of resources.

7. With maximum efficiency and full employment of resources, more of one good or service can be obtained only by giving up a certain amount of another good or service. This is called opportunity cost.

8. Increasing costs occur if resources that are less well suited to the production of a good or service are shifted into its production from more suitable alternative employment.

9. Increasing costs become less prevalent when more time is allowed for resources to adjust to new uses.

10. Every advanced society produces both private and public goods. In general public goods are those bought and used collectively by society. Although in the United States, most of the public goods and services are actually produced by private firms.

11. Capitalism and communism both make similar economic decisions in that both are required to choose among alternatives. Under capitalism the market allocates most resources, whereas under communism the government does the allocation or at least sets prices.

QUESTIONS FOR THOUGHT AND DISCUSSION

1. It was stated in this chapter that economics exists because human wants are greater than the resources available to satisfy these wants. Do you think we will ever see the day when all human economic wants are satisfied so that we no longer will need economics? If we were all millionaires, would we need to economize?

2. List some economic decisions you made today.

3. What is your opportunity cost of the time you are now spending on economics?

4. Explain the idea of opportunity cost as you would to a friend or relative who has not had any economics.

5. Would you expect increasing cost to be important in your allocation of time? Consider for example spending all your time on economics versus spending a small amount on economics and the remainder on other subjects and leisure.

6. "Goods produced in capitalist countries are private goods whereas goods produced in communist countries are public goods." Comment.

7. Put yourself in the place of an economic planner in a communistic government. How would you go about allocating the thousands of different goods and services produced and all the resources at your disposal? Assume that the free market is not an alternative.

8. Continuing with Question 7, suppose you decided that too little salt was being produced in the salt mines. How would you get more people into the salt mines?

CHAPTER
2
CONSUMER CHOICE

CONSUMER SOVEREIGNTY

It is fitting that we begin our study of microeconomics with the individual consumer. Because without consumption there would be no justification for production. The ultimate aim of all production is to satisfy the desires of consumers.

In the U.S. economy and in all other reasonably free market economies, the consumer is king. It is in the interest of each producer to cater to the wishes of consumers because if he produces what is most highly demanded he is rewarded by higher profits and a better living for himself and his family. After all, producers are consumers too. Economists refer to an economic system where production is carried on to satisfy the wishes of consumers as one characterized by "consumer sovereignty."

Society has found it necessary to restrict the sovereignty of the individual consumer somewhat, however. If consumption of a good is thought to be harmful to either the consumer himself or to others around him, society may pass a law against such consumption.

The use of habit forming drugs is one example. The individual, as well as harming his own health, may also harm others if he drives an automobile under the influence of these drugs or turns to crime to obtain money for their purchase. Laws regulating consumption of alcoholic beverages are another example of restricting consumer sovereignty to a certain degree. Society would prefer that consumers have corn flakes for breakfast rather than bourbon. In general, though, consumers are free to choose what they most desire and producers respond to their wants.

TASTES

Since the consumer is such an important part of our economic system it will be useful to study him in some detail. The first thing we must realize is that no two consumers are exactly the same in terms of their likes and dislikes. One may like to spend his leisure time watching baseball on television while drinking beer and eating pretzels, another may prefer to attend the opera or a symphony concert and dine on champagne and caviar.

Even though most of us recognize that tastes differ between people, we have a tendency to forget this when we criticize others for liking things that do not appeal to us. Or we sometimes criticize others for spending their income on a different mix of goods and services than we ourselves do. One person may place an expensive home high on his list of priorities while another prefers to spend more on travel or a more expensive automobile. If we are the type that likes the expensive home, for example, we still do not have any justification for criticizing people who prefer the expensive auto. Who is to say which is the superior taste—the expensive home or the expensive auto? If we forced a person to sell his expensive auto and buy a higher priced home, his total satisfaction may be decreased considerably. For this person, the superior taste is the automobile. The main point to remember about taste is that there is no absolute standard—each person decides what he likes best and then tries to satisfy these wants.

UTILITY

Although tastes and satisfaction are common ideas to all of us, it is much more difficult to express these concepts in concrete terms. Suppose you had just eaten an apple and a candy bar. Could you tell someone how much satisfaction you received from each of these items? Possibly you could tell which item you liked best but could you tell how much better you liked one over the other. You might say "quite a bit," "just a little," or some such vague descriptive term. But how much is "just a little" or "quite a bit"?

It is evident, then, that we need a more quantitive measure of satisfaction. For this reason economists have developed the concept of utility. The word utility means about the same thing as satisfaction but for illustrative purposes economists have created the concept of a "util" which is a unit measure of utility. Taking our previous example, suppose you agreed to arbitrarily assign 100 utils as the satisfaction or utility you receive from the apple. If you liked the candy bar less you would then assign it a number smaller than 100, or if you liked it more you would give it a number greater than 100. If, for example, you assigned a 50 to the candy bar, we could then say that you liked the apple about twice as much as the candy bar.

Conceivably, if you wanted to take the time, you could assign utils to all of the things you consume or might possibly consume, using one of the items as a reference point. The important thing in assigning utils to each item is not the absolute size of the util measure of each item but rather its size relative to the other items. As we said, tastes are an individual matter, hence utility is not something we can compare from person to person. Taking an individual example, we might assign numbers to a partial list of the things we consume during one week in the following manner:

Items Consumed per Week	No. of Utils
Two pounds of steak...................	100
One-fourth pound of coffee.............	30
Two quarts of milk.....................	60
Shelter of the house...................	300
Transportation of auto.................	200

This example brings out two points that should be emphasized. First, consumption is measured as an amount per unit time. In this example, we used one week. It does not make any sense to say you consumed two pounds of meat. Is it per day, per week, per year, or per lifetime? As you can see the time dimension is necessary to know if you are consuming much or little. The second point is that we consume services as well as goods. In the above example house shelter and transportation from the auto are services. We could list many more, such as services purchased from your doctor, lawyer, dentist, barber, beauty shop operator, etc. In economics we treat a service just as if it were a good. For our purposes they are essentially the same; both yield satisfaction or utility to the buyer.

THE MARGINAL UNIT

In this section we shall become acquainted with a new concept that is used a great deal in economics. This is the idea of the marginal unit. Perhaps the easiest way to grasp this idea is to think of marginal as being the same thing as extra or additional. If you have 10 units of something, say 10 pencils, and you acquire one more, then the 11th one is the marginal pencil. Think of the marginal unit as the one that is added or subtracted off of the top of whatever you have.

The idea of the marginal unit is one of the most important and useful ideas employed in economics. This is because most economic decisions involve relatively small changes. For example, you do not decide whether to spend all your income on steak or none on steak. Rather you decide if you should buy a little more steak and a little less hamburger or vice versa. Thus the decisions that you make generally involve the marginal or extra unit.

MARGINAL UTILITY

Our concern now is with marginal utility. This is the extra or additional utility you obtain from consuming one more unit of a good or service per unit time. Or it can also be the utility you lose by reducing your consumption by one unit. Let us return for a moment to the utility example in the previous section. Recall that 100 utiles were obtained by consuming 2 pounds of steak per week. Now suppose, you were to increase your steak consumption to 3 pounds per week and receive 140 utiles in total from this amount. The utility received from the third, or marginal pound of steak in this case, would be 40 utils. Or we could take the same example and subtract 1 pound of steak from weekly consumption. If, for example, we received 55 utils in total from 1 pound, then the marginal utility of the second pound is 45 utils. The following table summarizes what total and marginal utility might for 0, 1, 2, and 3 pounds of steak consumed per week:

Pounds of Steak Consumed per Week	Total Utility (Utils)	Marginal Utility (Utils)
0	0	—
1	55	55
2	100	45
3	140	40

You will note that the utility of the marginal unit (marginal utility) can be calculated by subtracting the total utility obtained before the marginal unit is added from the total utility obtained including that unit. Another method of calculating marginal utility is to divide the *change* in total utility by the *change* in number of units consumed

$$\text{Marginal utility} = \frac{\text{Change in total utility}}{\text{Change in units consumed}}$$

You might also note that the total utility at any given unit is just the sum of all the marginal utilities up through and including that unit.

DIMINISHING MARGINAL UTILITY

The preceding example also illustrates the idea of diminishing marginal utility. This means that as you increase your consumption of one good or service, say steak, holding constant the other things you consume, beyond some point the extra or marginal utility you obtain from the last unit will begin to decline. Of course, you knew this all along. If you consume more and more steak, for example, you soon become filled up and tired of it and the utility or satisfaction you obtain from each additional steak declines.

MARGINAL UTILITY AND PRICE

The utility or satisfaction we receive from a good or service is, of course, a major reason why we buy the things we do. Generally if we do not like a product we do not buy it. But it is not quite this simple. For one thing, likes or dislikes are not all or nothing concepts. We all have varying degrees of likes and dislikes, as we saw in the diminishing marginal utility example. And there is still another problem we all have to face: the problem of price.

Many times when faced with the choice between two or more items that we could buy, we deliberately choose the item we like the least. Looking over a menu in a restaurant, for example, you may like the $5 T-bone steak better than $2 chopped beef (hamburger) but you choose the chopped beef. Why? Or when buying a car, you may like the $5,000 sports car better than any car in the showroom but you end up buying the $2,500 sedan. Why? Is your behavior irrational or inconsistent with the concept of utility? Not at all. In your purchasing decisions there are two vital factors to consider: utility and price.

When you choose an item that is less desirable but also less costly, you are implicitly deciding that the extra cost is not worth the extra satisfaction it brings. You decided, for example, that the additional satisfaction from the steak over the hamburger is not worth $3 to you. There are other things you can buy with the $3 that will give you more utility. So in deciding what things to spend your money on you really look at marginal utility per dollar rather than marginal utility alone. Using the chopped beef–T-bone steak example, suppose the marginal utility, price, and marginal utility per dollar (marginal utility divided by price) are as follows:

	Marginal Utility (Utils)	Price	Marginal Utility per Dollar
Chopped beef.........	30	$2.00	15
T-bone	50	$5.00	10

This example illustrates that choosing chopped beef over T-bone is indeed a rational choice. The marginal utility per dollar of the cheaper cut (15) exceeds the marginal utility per dollar obtained from the T-bone (10). Now, of course, this is only an example. We could have as easily created an example where T-bone would have been the best choice. We could have done so by raising its marginal utility or lowering its price. The point is that it is not always best to buy the cheaper item. But it can be.

MAXIMIZING SATISFACTION

So far we have just considered choosing between two items. We know, however, that life is a good deal more complex than this. During a normal shopping trip, to the supermarket for example, we have literally thousands of items to choose from. How do we decide what to buy?

The first thing we must realize is that our budget is limited; we just have so much to spend. Given this constraint our objective is to maximize our satisfaction or utility. The basic rule to remember here is to equalize, as much as possible, the marginal utility per dollar for all the goods and services you buy. Recall that marginal utility per dollar is obtained by dividing marginal utility by price. For example if the marginal utility of good A is 30 and its price is $5, then its marginal utility per dollar is 6. The general rule to follow for all goods and services A through Z is:

$$\frac{\text{Marginal utility of good } A}{\text{Price of good } A} = \frac{MU \text{ of } B}{\text{Price of } B} = \cdots = \frac{MU \text{ of } Z}{\text{Price of } Z}$$

In other words, to maximize utility, we should try to make the marginal utility per dollar of good or service "A" equal to that of good or service "B" and these equal to all other things we consume.

Why does an equalization of the marginal utility per dollar for all goods we consume result in maximum satisfaction for us? This is perhaps easiest to see if we look at a situation where they are not equal. Suppose the marginal utility per dollar spent on housing per month is 50 but the marginal utility per dollar spend on the automobile per month is only 30. In this situation you could gain 20 utiles per month by spending one less dollar on the automobile and one more dollar on housing. In this situation you are spending too much on your car and not enough on your house or apartment. You could increase your total satisfaction, therefore, just by rearranging your purchases without spending any more in total. This same idea applies to everything you buy. If certain goods or services are not giving you the marginal utility per dollar that other goods or services are providing, reduce your purchases of the low return items and increase your spending on those which give you higher marginal utility per dollar.

SOME COMPLICATIONS

Your reaction to the preceding discussion on marginal utility is likely to be, at best, one of incomplete acceptance. Certainly, you might argue, no one takes the time to think of the utils he obtains from consuming an item, much less writing them down and dividing by price. You are right, not even economists go through this laborious process. Rather the main value of marginal utility is to give you a framework for thinking about your purchases. If you know what you must do to theoretically maximize your satisfaction, you can use this knowledge to at least move in the direction of maximum satisfaction for each dollar you spend. In fact, most wise shoppers are already using the idea of marginal utility without realizing it, in an attempt to get the most for their money.

Even though we may try to maximize our satisfaction by striving to equalize the marginal utility per dollar for all our purchases, we are not likely to ever reach that theoretical maximum and stay there. The main reason is that our estimates of utility or satisfaction from each good and service is likely to be changing all the time. Our estimates of utility for each good or service changes for several reasons. First, we may just grow tired of something that we have consumed for a long while. Most humans like some variety in their lives. Thus the marginal utility of what we consume today depends somewhat on what we consumed yesterday. Second, new products or services may appear on the market that make old products or services less desirable to us. This phenomenon is most evident in products that change in fashion or style. How many times have we admired a certain model of automobile only to have a new model come out that made our former dream car seem ugly and old fashioned. Third, our tastes or estimates of utility may be changed by advertising. If a popular movie star or athlete uses a product it sometimes becomes more appealing to us.

A second major reason to change the mix of goods we consume is because prices are always changing. If the price of one item rises relative to other alternatives, its marginal utility per dollar will decrease relative to other things. We would then want to buy less of it.

As a final complicating factor, we should realize that the marginal utility of each good or service we consume may well depend also on the other things consumed along with it. Economists call this interdependence of utilities. Interdependence between goods can take the form of either a complementary or substitute relationship. Two goods are complements to each other if consuming one enhances the marginal utility of the other. Bacon and eggs are a good example. Most people find eggs more appealing at breakfast when accompanied by a strip or two of bacon. Or, take the woman who has just purchased a new hat; a new handbag, gloves, shoes, etc., generally makes the hat more desirable and the hat also complements the accessories. On the other hand, a substitute relationship between goods exists if consuming one good reduces the marginal utility of another. For instance, the marginal utility you obtain from consuming a glass of orange juice at breakfast would likely decline if you also consume a glass of grapefruit juice at the same meal.

Because of the many complications which have the effect of changing the marginal utility of each good or service we buy, or consider buying, the optimum bundle of goods and services that will maximize our utility is constantly changing. Therefore it is necessary for us to continually re-evaluate our purchase decisions if we hope to get the most for our money.

CONSUMPTION VERSUS SAVING

Thus far we have considered only how people decide what mix of goods and services will give the most utility for a given expenditure. But this does not imply that all income is spent. As you know most people attempt to save at least a small portion of their current income for various reasons. We may save "for a rainy day" in order to have something to fall back on in case we cannot work. Or we may save for retirement to supplement a pension. Most people save in order to make a large purchase such as a car, a downpayment on a house, etc. Others may save just for the sake of saving; they like to count their cash or watch the balance in their bank account grow. Still others wish to leave an estate for their heirs or some noble institution.

The decisions to save or not to save and what to save for are very much like the expenditure decisions we have just considered. The marginal utility of saving is the satisfaction we can expect to obtain when we eventually spend this extra dollar, or the satisfaction we now obtain from knowing that someone else will be able to spend it. There is also the utility obtained from accumulating wealth for its own sake.

Estimating the marginal utility of saving is somewhat more difficult than it is for the ordinary day-to-day purchases, however. Foremost, there is the problem of uncertainty. No one knows what the future may bring or even if there will be a future. The more uncertainty a person has about the future, the less utility he will expect from saving. In other words, he will discount the future heavily.

A person who discounts the future heavily is said to have a high rate of time preference. He prefers to consume now rather than later. The stereotyped soldier or sailor who epitomizes the "eat, drink, and be merry" attitude is a good example of someone with a high rate of time preference. His marginal utility from future consumption is low relative to current consumption.

In general everyone has some degree of time preference. We cannot postpone all consumption for the future; if we did there would be no future. The person who is relatively patient, however, having a low rate of time preference, will tend to obtain relatively more utility from future consumption than his "eat, drink, and be merry" counterpart, hence will likely save a larger fraction of his income, other things equal.

In estimating the marginal utility of future consumption, it is also necessary to take into account the interest or dividends we receive on our savings. If the rate of interest we receive on our savings is, say, 5 percent, one dollar saved today will be worth $1.05 one year from now. Assuming no increase in prices, the extra dollar saved will buy somewhat more in the future than it will buy today. Hence the interest return on savings compensate us for waiting to consume in the future. The higher the interest or dividend returns on our savings, the more each dollar saved at the present will buy in the future. In other words, a higher interest rate increases the price of present consumption compared to future consumption. For this reason people tend to increase their saving with an increase in the rate of interest.

Given our rate of time preference and the interest or dividend return on our savings, the proportion of our income we save will depend also on the size of our income. People with low incomes generally must spend a large share of their income on the immediate necessities of life—food, clothing, and shelter. The marginal utility of present consumption of these items is high relative to the marginal utility of their future consumption. Taking an extreme example, most of us would pay everything we owned for a drink of water out on the desert if without it we would not survive. Without any future the marginal utility of future consumption is low indeed.

As incomes grow and nonessential items make up a larger share of current consumption, the marginal utility of consuming at least some of these items currently declines relative to the marginal utility of giving some money away or of consuming more in the future. Thus as incomes grow, we tend to observe an increasing fraction of income saved, or at least not spent by the individual who earned the money.

THE PRICE OF PRESENT CONSUMPTION

We are now aware that the combination of goods we presently consume depend both on their marginal utilities and prices. The same basic idea applies in deciding to consume now or in the future. As we stated the price or opportunity cost of present consumption is what must be given up in the future. The higher the rate of interest, the more that a dollar saved will buy in the future, consequently the higher the cost or price of present consumption. For example if the interest rate is 5 percent, one dollar will buy $1.05 one year from now. With a 10 percent rate of interest, one dollar will buy $1.10 one year from now.

We can therefore consider the price of one dollar in present consumption as the dollar plus the interest return. If we specify the marginal utility that an extra dollar of present consumption will provide then we can divide this by price to obtain marginal utility per dollar. As an example, let us consider two individuals; one a spendthrift, the other a miser. In situation No. 1 both receive a 5 percent rate of interest on their savings as shown below. In the second case the interest rate is 10 percent.

	MU of an Extra Dollar Consumed at the Present	Interest Rate	Price of Present Consumption	MU per Dollar
Situation 1:				
Spendthrift	10	0.05	1.05	19.05
Miser	20	0.05	1.05	9.52
Situation 2:				
Spendthrift	20	0.10	1.10	18.18
Miser	10	0.10	1.10	9.09

The above example provides an explanation for different behavior of people with respect to saving. The eat, drink, and be merry spendthrift enjoys spending his money at the present more than does the miser. Thus, whatever the rate of interest, the marginal utility per dollar of present consumption is higher for him than for the miser. But at higher rates of interest, say 10 percent, the price of present consumption rises which results in a reduction in marginal utility per dollar of present consumption. Therefore we would expect both types of individuals to decrease present consumption (increase saving) because its price has risen.

The decision to save or to consume at the present, therefore, is very similar to the decision of what mix of goods to buy. This decision depends on tastes and on price. Again in this situation it is easy for us to criticize those who either spend or save a larger share of their income than we ourselves do. But this criticism is unwarranted if people do what they like best. If we forced a miser to spend a larger part of his income to "enjoy life," he would probably be truly miserable then because we would deprive him of the satisfaction of saving.

INTEREST AND PRICE CHANGES

In the discussion about the interest rate and saving we have assumed that prices remain unchanged. But in recent years we have experienced rising prices. How do rising prices, or inflation, influence saving? Consider the case where we receive 5 percent interest on our saving. A dollar saved will provide us with $1.05 worth of goods and services one year from now. But if prices rise by 5 percent during the year, then the $1.05 we receive next year will only buy one dollar's worth of goods and services in today's prices. In this case there is no incentive for us to save. The extra money we earned by saving is completely "eaten up" by inflation.

Thus whenever inflation is present, we should use what economist's call the "real rate" of interest in making a decision to spend or save. The real rate takes account of any change in the general price level. The real rate of interest we receive is equal to the money rate (the rate that is quoted by banks or other savings institutions on savings deposits) minus the percentage change in the price level, as we show in the following example:

	Money Rate	Percentage Change in Prices	Real Rate
1..........	5	5	0
2..........	10	5	5
3..........	5	10	—5

In the first case above, we see that a 5 percent money rate of interest will not provide us with any additional consumption in the future at all if prices rise by 5 percent. Here the price of an extra dollar of present consumption would just be one dollar. If we insisted upon a 5 percent real rate of interest on our saving with a 5 percent price rise, then we would have to obtain a 10 percent money rate of interest (case 2 above). We might find ourself in a situation where inflation is actually greater than the money rate of interest, such as is illustrated in case 3 above. Here we would receive a negative real rate which essentially means that you pay the person to borrow the money from you. It now becomes clear why people desire to reduce their rate of saving in times of severe inflation. The best thing to do then is to spend your income on goods that increase in value with the general level of prices.

SHORT-RUN VERSUS LONG-RUN SAVING

It is necessary to keep in mind that a person's rate of saving may fluctuate a considerable amount over time. For example, suppose you wish to purchase a new car next year. During the coming year you will probably attempt to save enough at least for the downpayment or possibly for the entire car. During the time you save for the car the percent of your income saved may be quite large—say 40 percent. But as soon as you buy the car all this is spent. Thus the length of time you consider generally influences the rate of saving you obtain.

The important point here is that your saving during a short period such as a month or even a year may not at all reflect your long-run saving habits. The stereotyped sea-faring man may save almost 100 percent of his wage during a six-month voyage but spend every cent when he arrives in port. It would be very misleading to measure the sailor's saving during the voyage and assume this is what he will save in the long run.

A similar situation exists with people whose incomes fluctuate a great deal. Farmers are a good example here. It is sometimes argued that farmers are thrifty folk who save much of their income. But the real reason might just as well be that farm incomes tend to fluctuate more than other people's and when incomes are high much of it is saved to provide for times when income is very low or even zero.

For college students it is not unusual to see people with a negative rate of saving. That is, they consume more than their income. The difference is made up either by consuming out of past saving, borrowing, or by gifts from relatives, friends, or benevolent institutions. There is nothing wrong with this behavior; indeed it is to be expected. But in the long run (a decade or more) the percentage of income saved by these same people may well be substantial.

INDIFFERENCE CURVES

So far in this chapter we have shown that the consumer maximizes utility, or gets the most for his money, by equalizing as much as possible the marginal utility per dollar of all goods and services he consumes as well as his saving. We will now take a slightly different route by developing the concept of the "indifference curve" which we shall see is another way of representing consumer choice. In the next chapter we will employ indifference curves to develop the concept of product demand.

Let us assume that you are given a collection of two different goods, say 10 tickets to see your favorite football team and 10 tickets to the theater of your choice. We can represent this combination by point A in Figure 2–1. Now ask yourself this question, if two football tickets were taken away from me, how many additional theater tickets would I have to be given in order to remain equally satisfied? Assume there is no chance to sell the tickets so you cannot exchange the extra theater tickets back to football tickets. Also do not be concerned, at least for the moment, about the price of the tickets. Assume they are being given to you or taken away without charge or compensation.

Your answer to this question will depend, of course, on how well you like football and the theater. For the sake of obtaining an answer with this one-sided conversation, suppose you decide that two additional theater tickets would compensate you for the loss of the two football tickets. In other words, you are indifferent between the combination of 10 football and 10 theater tickets and the combination of 8 football and 12 theater tickets. Let this combination be point B in Figure 2–1.

We might go through the same procedure again only this time taking away a total of eight fooball tickets. Now you only have two football tickets left. How many theater tickets would you have to be given to remain equally satisfied to the original combination of 10 of each kind of tickets?

Now, according to the idea of diminishing marginal utility, additional nights at the theater will provide less and less satisfaction. Moreover the closer you come to zero football, the loss of football tickets will mean losing more and more satisfaction. It seems reasonable to believe, therefore, that you will require more than eight additional theater tickets to compensate you for the loss of eight football tickets. Suppose you want 18 more theater tickets. We can say, therefore, that you are indifferent to the following combinations:

Combination	Theater	Football
A............	10	10
B............	12	8
C............	28	2

By now you probably see what we're doing. We are tracing out alternative combinations that make you equally well off. We could also trace out points on the upper part of the curve by taking away theater tickets in exchange for football tickets. For example, you might choose 8 theater and

12 football, or 2 theater and 24 football tickets as additional combinations, labeling these points D and E.

Assuming that the same general relationship holds between the points as on them, we can connect points A through E. We have now constructed what economists call an "indifference curve." From the standpoint of total satisfaction you are indifferent at all points along the curve.

FIGURE 2–1. An indifference curve   FIGURE 2–2. An indifference map

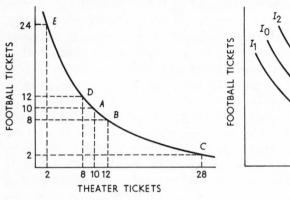
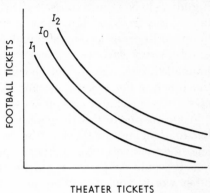

Of course, there are any number of curves that can be drawn, as shown in Figure 2–2. We started out with 10 tickets of each but we might have started with 6 of each. If you prefer more tickets to less, then the smaller combination would be on a lower indifference curve such as I_1 in Figure 2–2. Similarly, a larger combination such as 14 of each would be on a higher curve, say I_2. Economists call many such curves on a single diagram an indifference map. In a sense it is a picture of your preferences much like a contour map is a picture of the landscape.

We might pause here for a moment to note something about the shape of these curves. In this particular example, we have drawn them with a slight curvature, convex to the origin. This tells us that we consider football and the theater substitutes for one another, although imperfect substitutes. To see why, look again at the curve in Figure 2–1. Moving down the football axis and out along the theater axis, you will note that additional theater tickets will compensate you for less and less football tickets. In other words, the further you proceed, the greater the number of theater tickets it takes to make you willing to give up another football ticket.

If the two items were perfect substitutes for each other, then the rate at which you give up one in exchange for the other would be constant at all possible combinations. For example, nickels and dimes, or white and brown eggs (except in Boston) would be perfect substitutes. The indifference curve for perfect substitutes is illustrated in Figure 2–3. Generally economists are not very interested in goods that are perfect substitutes because for all practical matters they are the same good. That is, nickels and dimes are coins, or white and brown eggs are just eggs.

At the other extreme we have what we call perfect complements. These are goods that can only be used in fixed proportions with one another. The classic example is right and left shoes. Presumably you would not be any better off with one right and two left shoes than with just one of each. Thus the indifference curves for such products are represented by 90 degree angles as in Figure 2–4.

FIGURE 2–3. Indifference curves for   FIGURE 2–4. Indifference curves for
perfect substitutes   perfect complements

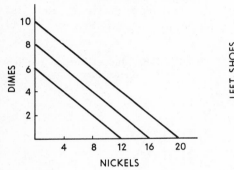

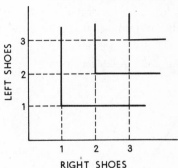

Most of the items we consume in our everyday lives are neither perfect substitutes nor perfect complements but rather the inbetween case—imperfect substitutes. You might have noted in Figures 2–3 and 2–4 that these indifference curves (lines) are parallel. In the case of imperfect substitutes, however, the curves do not have to run parallel to each other. The only restriction is that they do not cross, for if they did cross they could not be indifference curves (think about it).

THE BUDGET LINE

In a sense indifference curves are somewhat like the production possibilities curve. Both show alternative combinations of goods or services but neither indicates which alternative will be preferred. After we develop the concept of the "budget line," we will be able to say which of the many combinations shown on an indifference map will actually be chosen. The two items that enable us to make a choice are your income or budget and the prices of the goods represented.

To keep it simple, yet fairly realistic, let us continue to use the football and theater ticket example. We will assume you decide to spend $30 dollars on entertainment (football and the theater). How should you spend this $30 to maximize your satisfaction, i.e., get the most for your money? To answer this question we must know the prices of the tickets. Suppose football tickets are $2 each and the theater tickets sell for $3 per ticket.

We now have the necessary information to construct the budget line. Let us proceed by asking another question. How many football tickets could you buy if you spent your entire entertainment budget ($30) on football? Correct—15 tickets. Similarly if you spent the entire $30 on the theater you would be able to buy 10 tickets. Now we know the two end points of the budget line, i.e., the points where it crosses the vertical and horizontal axes (Figure 2–5). Any point on the line between the two end points also represent an expenditure of $30. Moving down the line you spend less and less on football and more and more on the theater. But the total amount spent is the same at all points along the line.

FIGURE 2–5. A budget line

FIGURE 2–6. Budget line on indifference map

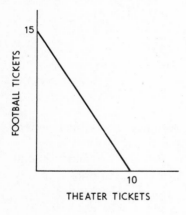

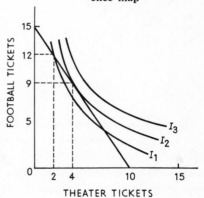

You might have noted by now that to have a continuous straight budget line, it must be possible to buy a fraction of a ticket. At first glance this may not seem realistic, but keep in mind that we are talking about consumption per unit time. For example $3\frac{1}{3}$ tickets per month would be equal to 40 tickets per year. Thus most items become divisible when you bring in the time dimension.

We are now ready to combine indifference curves with the budget line to find out what combination of tickets would give you the most satisfaction for your $30. In Figure 2–6 we have imposed an indifference map on the budget line from our example. This indifference map is just an example of what might be derived from an individual. As a first step let us choose any combination of tickets that cost $30, for example 12 football and 2 theater tickets. Will this combination give you the most satisfaction for your money? This question can be answered by looking at Figure 2–6.

You will note that the highest indifference curve that can be reached with the 12–2 football-theater combination is I_1. But you will note also that a higher indifference curve can be reached by moving down the budget line, that is, by choosing a different combination of tickets that will be worth $30. As you move down the budget line you reduce your purchase of football tickets and increase the number of theater tickets you buy.

Keep in mind that your overall objective is to reach the highest possible indifference curve within the constraint of the $30 you have to spend. By now you may have realized that the highest possible indifference curve you can reach is the one just tangent to the budget line, I_2 in this example (Figure 2–6). Indifference curve I_3 could not be reached unless you wanted to spend more than $30. Thus, the general rule to bear in mind is that your satisfaction will be maximized when you select that mix of goods on the budget line that enables you to reach the higher possible indiffer- .
ence curve.

In the example constructed above, the combination that maximizes your satisfaction is nine football and four theater tickets. The cost of this combination, $30, is the same as any other combination on the budget line such as 12 football and 3 theater, or 3 football and 8 theater; but your level of satisfaction is the greatest only at the 9 football–4 theater combi-
nation.

In later, more advanced courses it is shown that the marginal ultility per dollar is equal for the two goods under consideration at the tangency point of the budget line and the indifference curve. In other words, the two approaches we have considered (marginal utility over price and indifference curve–budget line) yield the same general results. However, we will see in the next chapter that the indifference curve approach is a bit more useful in constructing a demand curve.

MAIN POINTS OF CHAPTER 2

1. In a free market economy, production is carried on solely to satisfy the wants of consumers. This is known as a system of "consumer sov-
    ereignty."

2. Since everyone in society has his own unique tastes, there is no such thing as "good" or "bad" tastes. Hence we should not criticize others for liking things that we might consider distasteful.

3. Utility is a measure of satisfaction. Utils enable us to rank goods or services according to the satisfaction they provide.

4. The marginal unit is the last unit added or subtracted off of the top of whatever we are measuring.

5. Marginal utility is the utility or satisfaction provided by the marginal unit consumed.

6. Diminishing marginal utility means that as you consume more and more of a good or service, holding constant the consumption of other goods and services, the amount of satisfaction obtained from each additional unit consumed will, after a point, begin to decline.

7. When considering whether or not to buy an item, we should consider both its marginal utility and price.

8. In order to maximize satisfaction for the money we spend, we must equalize as much as possible the marginal utility per dollar for all the things we consume. Marginal utility per dollar is obtained by dividing the utility of the marginal unit by its price.

9. The combination of goods and services that will maximize our utility for a given expenditure is constantly changing for a variety of reasons. These include: (a) changes in how much we like the things we presently consume because of what we consumed in the past, what others are consuming, advertising, and new products appearing on the market; and (b) changes in prices of goods or services.

10. The decision to consume now or save for future consumption depends both on the utility of present consumption and on the price of present consumption.

11. The price of present consumption increases with an increase in the interest rate because with higher rates of interest each dollar saved at the present will buy more in the future if prices remain unchanged.

12. If inflation is present, the decision to spend or save should be based on the real rate of interest, which takes account of a change in the price level. The real rate equals the money rate of interest minus the the percentage change in prices per year.

13. The true picture of a person's saving habits is best reflected in his long-run behavior because much short-run saving may just be an accumulating of money to spend in a large lump sum.

14. An indifference curve traces out an alternative combinations of two goods all of which make you equally satisfied.

15. An indifference map is a collection of indifference curves. Curves further and further away from the origin represent higher and higher levels of satisfaction.

16. The shape of indifference curves depends upon the degree of substitutability between the products considered. Indifferences curves for perfect substitutes are straight, downward sloping lines; those for perfect complements (no substitution possible) are right angles. Most combinations of goods fall somewhere between these two extremes.

17. A budget line traces out alternative combinations of two goods that all cost a given amount.

18. To maximize satisfaction for a given expenditure, it is necessary to move along the budget line until you reach the highest possible indifference curve. This will be the curve that is tangent to the budget line.

QUESTIONS FOR THOUGHT AND DISCUSSION

1. "Because many people dislike long hair, society would be better off if the government passed a law forbidding males to grow long hair." Comment.
2. "The family that lives in a slum dwelling but owns an expensive car is irrational." Comment.
3. "If you consume two pounds of steak, your steak consumption is high." Comment.
4. Explain as you would to a friend or relative who has had no economics, what a marginal unit is.
5. "Most women prefer mink coats but buy cloth coats instead. This just goes to show that most women are irrational." Comment.
6. Suppose a shoe salesman attempts to sell me a $50 pair of shoes and I tell him that the shoes are very nice but I cannot afford them. What do I really mean when I say "I cannot afford" this pair of shoes?
7. Suppose the combination of food that maximizes my satisfaction for lunch today consists of one cheeseburger, one slice of apple pie, and one cup of coffee. According to economic theory I should continue to consume this combination for the rest of my life because this is what maximizes my utility. Comment.
8. "The more the merrier" contradicts the concept of diminishing marginal utility.
9. "Misers do not enjoy life." Comment.
10. A few years ago banks paid 3 percent on savings account deposits. Presently they pay 5 percent or more. We can conclude from this that it pays to save more at the present than in years past. Comment.
11. Explain as you would to a friend or relative who has had no economics, what an indifference curve is and what a budget line is.
12. Does the shape of the indifference curves between two goods tell you anything about how people view these two goods? Explain.
13. "Your satisfaction is maximized if you choose any combination of goods that corresponds to a point where an indifference curve crosses the budget line." Explain why or why not.

CHAPTER
3
PRODUCT DEMAND

THE CONCEPT OF DEMAND

Demand is a word that most everyone has used at one time or another. As a result there tends to be many interpretations of the word. It will be useful for us at this stage, therefore, to define rather rigorously the concept of demand as used by economists. You will probably find that the economist's concept of demand differs at least somewhat from the way it is used in newspapers, everyday conversation, etc.

The first, and perhaps most important, thing to recognize about demand, as used by economists, is that it is not a set or fixed quantity. Rather demand is a relationship between price and quantity. In order to know what quantity a person or group of persons will demand we must first know what price they will have to pay.

For example if I asked you what is your demand for football tickets, you would probably be a bit reluctant to answer unless you knew what price you had to pay. The number of tickets you would demand likely would be quite different if you had to pay $1 per ticket than if you paid $10 per ticket. And if we just appeal to common sense, we should agree that you will demand more tickets at the $1 price than at the $10 price. It does not take any formal training in economics to arrive at this answer.

It will be useful, though, to organize our thinking a bit more by illustrating the concept of demand with a diagram. As we said, at a high price less will be demanded than at a low price. This relationship between price and quantity is illustrated in Figure 3–1.

FIGURE 3–1.   Illustrating the concept of
demand, football ticket
example

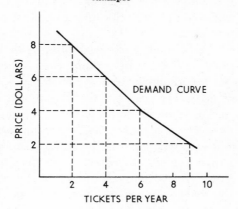

In the above example only two tickets are demanded per season if the price is $8 per ticket. At a $4 price, six tickets are demanded; and at the low bargain price of $2, nine tickets are demanded per season. By connecting the series of points on the graph we obtain a curve which is known as a demand curve. Essentially a demand curve describes a relationship between price and quantity. If we choose a price the demand curve will tell us what quantity will be demanded. Or if we choose a quantity, the curve will tell us what price will be paid.

It is important to distinguish between demand and quantity demanded. Demand, as we said, refers to the relationship between price and quantity. However, quantity demanded refers to a particular quantity or point on the demand curve. Thus when you wish to stipulate a particular quantity you will avoid confusion by calling it "quantity demanded" rather than "demand."

A second important characteristic to note about the concept of demand is that it reflects *wants* not *needs*. If you tell me that you need six football tickets if the price is $4 per ticket, it would be easy to take issue with your statement. That is, it could be argued that you do not need any football tickets because watching football is not necessary to sustain life. Or you might say you need a new car or a vacation trip to a distant city. Again, neither is necessary to sustain life. On the other hand, if you said you wanted six football tickets or a vacation trip, this could not be disputed. Only you can determine what you want, and these wants are at least partly satisfied by the things you buy.

A third item to note about demand is that quantity is measured as an amount per unit time. In Figure 3–1, the quantity football tickets is measured in number of tickets per year. However, there is no set time period that is always used. We can measure quantity as amount per week, per month, per year, etc. The time dimension that is chosen is often the one that is most useful to analyze the problem at hand. Of course, it must be recognized that when you change the time period you also change the scale on the quantity axis.

A fourth point to note about a demand curve is that it reflects what people actually would do if faced by certain prices rather than what they would like to do. My favorite make of automobile may sell for $6,000, and I would like a new one every year, but that doesn't mean I actually purchase one every year or even one in a lifetime. Demand only is useful if it reflects the actions of people, not what they would *like* to do.

It should be kept in mind, as well, that the demand curve shown in Figure 3–1 is only an example. In this diagram the demand curve is drawn with a slight curvature. This is not meant to imply that demand curves for all products look this way. Some may be straight, downward sloping lines; others may have more curvature. For the present our main concern will be with the downward sloping characteristic rather than with the extent of curvature of the line.

MARGINAL UTILITY AND DEMAND

So far we have appealed mainly to common sense in establishing the concept of demand; namely that people tend to buy more of an item when its price is reduced and less when its price rises. Let us now relate the concept of marginal utility to the concept of demand. Recall that a consumer maximizes satisfaction when the marginal utility per dollar of all goods and services he buys are equal. The following expression summarizes this idea:

$$\frac{MU \text{ of good } A}{Price \text{ of good } A} = \frac{MU \text{ of good } B}{Price \text{ of good } B} = \cdots = \frac{MU \text{ of good } Z}{Price \text{ of good } Z}$$

You recall also that marginal utility per dollar depends on both marginal utility and price. For a given marginal utility, the higher the price the lower is the marginal utility per dollar. As a very simple example, suppose a consumer is initially maximizing utility, as is illustrated in the expression above. Now consider just one of these goods, say good A, changes in price as shown below:

	Initial Situation	Price of A Rises	Price of A Falls
Marginal utility of A......	20	20	20
Price of A..............	$4	$5	$2
MU per dollar..........	5	4	10

In the initial situation, all goods consumed by this person yield a marginal utility per dollar of 5 utils. When the price of good A rises, this good

only yields 4 utils per dollar. In this case it will pay the consumer to reduce his purchases of good A. One dollar less spent on A will reduce his
satisfaction by 4 utils, but spending this dollar on something else that has
not risen in price will yield close to 5 utils. Thus the consumer can gain
one util of net satisfaction by spending one less dollar on good A and one
more dollar on one or more other goods.

As he continues to reduce the consumption of A, the marginal utility of
A will increase (raising marginal utility per dollar of A) and the marginal
utilities of other goods will decrease as more of these are consumed.
Eventually the consumer will reach a new equilibrium where marginal
utility per dollar is again equal for all goods. The important thing to note
here is that as the price of a good rises, marginal utility per dollar declines, and this creates an incentive for the consumer to reduce his purchases of the good. The end result, then, is consistent with the idea of a
downward sloping demand curve that we constructed in the preceding
section where a higher price leads to a decreased rate of purchase.

Exactly the same reasoning applies for a decrease in the price of A.
Here marginal utility per dollar increases, which in turn provides an incentive for the consumer to increase his purchase of A at the expense of
other goods. Again this is consistent with the concept of demand.

It ought to be pointed out at this stage that we have made one important simplifying assumption; namely that marginal utility of each good is
not influenced by the amount of other goods consumed. We have only
assumed that the marginal utility of each good is influenced by the quantity consumed of the respective good. In Chapter 6 we will drop this assumption when we discuss substitute and complementary goods.

INDIFFERENCE CURVES AND DEMAND

So far we have shown that the concept of a downward sloping demand
curve is consistent with the concept of marginal utility. Let us now proceed a step further by deriving a demand curve from an indifference map.
This will help clarify the relationship between indifference curves and
demand curves as well as giving a more rigorous definition of the concept
or theory of demand.

Let us begin by going back to the football-theater ticket example of
the previous chapter. Recall that we assumed the price of football tickets
to be $2 each and theater tickets $3 per ticket. At these prices the combination of 9 football and 4 theater tickets maximized satisfaction or utility
in this particular example (Figure 2–6). Let us now proceed by lowering
the price of theater tickets, first to a price of $2 and then to a price of
$1.50. What happens to the indifference map and budget line?

Since indifference curves, you recall, do not reflect prices, these do not
change as a result of changing the price of either good. On the other hand,
the budget line does depend on prices so this line will change with a

change in prices. The easiest way to see how it changes with a reduction in price is to ask where will this line cross the theater axis on the diagram if the total $30 entertainment budget is spent on theater tickets and each theater ticket sells for $2? The answer, of course, is 15. If the price is further reduced to $1.50, the budget line crosses the theater axis at 20. The budget line will continue to intersect the football axis at 15 tickets because the price of these tickets has remained the same. Thus the budget line rotates in a counterclockwise fashion with a fall in the price of the good on the horizontal axis. This is illustrated in Figure 3–2. Of course, an increase in the price of this good would have caused the line to rotate clockwise, or intersect the theater axis at points closer and closer to the origin of the graph.

FIGURE 3–2.   Indifference map and budget line, illustrating changes in the price of theater tickets

FIGURE 3–3.   Demand curve for theater tickets as derived from Figure 3–2

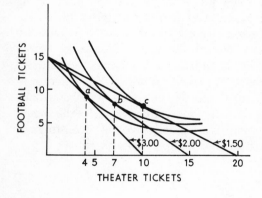

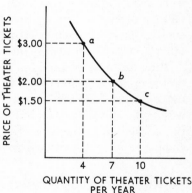

By now you probably are aware that a change in the position of the budget line will in turn change the tangency point with its highest possible indifference curve. With lower and lower prices it is possible to move to higher and higher indifference curves. In Figure 3–2 the tangency point moves from a to b to c with the reduction in price from $3 to $2 to $1.50. And you will note that because of changes in the tangency point the utility maximizing combination of the two goods also changes with a change in the price of theater tickets. Our main concern at the present is with theater tickets. At the original $3 price, four theater tickets per year maximizes utility. This quantity increases to 7 and 10 when the price falls to $2 and $1.50 respectively.

Turning our attention now to Figure 3–3 we can observe the relationship between the price of theater tickets and the quantity that will be purchased. This line tells us how many theater tickets will be demanded at various possible prices of theater tickets. And you will recall that this is none other than a demand curve. Thus we have just derived a demand curve from an indifference map and some budget lines. The purpose of this exercise is to make clear the relationship between indifference curves and a demand curve. Also it is a bit reassuring to learn that our common-sense notion of demand is consistent with economic theory.

INCOME AND SUBSTITUTION EFFECTS

So far in this chapter we have established that the demand curve of an individual consumer for a good is a downward sloping line. Let us now analyze this relationship more carefully. We might begin by asking, "Why do people buy more of a good when its price falls"? We are quite sure they do, but why?

Economists have identified two major factors or effects that help us understand why people behave this way. These are (1) the income effect and (2) the substitution effect. The income effect is so known because a change in the price of a good we buy changes the purchasing power of our income. It is as though we had experienced a change in income. For example, consider the decline in the price of theater tickets. As this price declines our $30 entertainment budget could buy a larger number of tickets. It is as if our income had been increased. The opposite occurs, of course, if its price would have risen. Now the $30 would have bought fewer tickets so it would be just like a decrease in our budget or income.

The substitution effect occurs because when the price of one good changes *relative* to another there is the incentive to buy more of the lower price good and less of the higher priced one. We all like to get the most for our money. But to really understand what the substitution effect is, we first must understand what is meant by relative prices. In the example used to construct the demand curve, the price of theater tickets fell relative to the price of football tickets. This is one example of a change in relative prices, but there are others.

If both prices had declined but theater prices had declined the most, then theater prices would still have declined relative to football prices. Or if both prices had increased but football the most, there would again be a relative decline in theater prices. The four situations below all illustrate a relative decline in theater ticket prices or a relative increase in football ticket prices.

1. Football the same, theater declines.
2. Football declines, theater declines more.
3. Football increases, theater increases less.
4. Football increases, theater the same.

Thus the income effect occurs because a price change has the effect of changing the purchasing power of our income. The substitution effect occurs because a price change has the effect of changing relative prices which in turn provides an incentive for us to buy more of the relatively lower priced good. A somewhat more exact definition of these two effects can be obtained using indifference curves and budget lines.

Figure 3–4 is a duplication of Figure 3–2 except that the $2 theater ticket price line has been deleted. At the $3 price, 4 theater tickets are demanded; and at the $1.50 price, 10 tickets are demanded. The question that we can now ask is: How many of these six additional tickets that are demanded because of the price reduction are due to the income effect and how many are due to the substitution effect?

We can measure the income effect by drawing in a hypothetical budget line parallel to the original budget line but tangent to the new indifference curve (the dotted line in Figure 3–4). This budget line illustrates the income effect because the price reduction provides the same effect as an increase in our income or our budget. Thus the hypothetical budget line will measure the increase in quantity that is due to the income effect. In the example illustrated by Figure 3–4, the income effect accounts for two additional tickets, i.e., the horizontal distance between A and B. The remaining four additional units of quantity demanded, shown by the horizontal distance between B and C, is accounted for by the substitution effect. The substitution effect is always measured by moving along a given indifference curve whereas the income effect is measured by moving from one indifference curve to another.

The income and substitution effects provide the formal economic rationale for the downward sloping characteristic of the demand curve of a consumer. Notice that the quantities which are measured along a demand curve are those that maximize the utility of a consumer for various prices of the good and the available budget.

MARKET DEMAND

Thus far we have been concerned with the demand curve of an individual consumer. As we will see shortly, though, the concept of demand is most useful when applied to a market situation—an entire group of consumers. It was necessary to begin our discussion of demand at the level of the individual consumer, however, in order to derive the concept of a demand curve from the closely related concept of consumer indifference curves.

It is a relatively simple step now to develop the idea of a market demand from the demand of individual consumers. First let us suppose that every consumer has a demand for each and every product. For some consumers, of course, the demand will be large at a given price; for others the demand might be zero at the same price. No two consumers need have the same demand for a given product. All we need to do to visualize the idea of market demand is to add up, at each possible price, the quantity demanded by all consumers in the market. In other words, we obtain

FIGURE 3–4.   An illustration of the income
and substitution effects

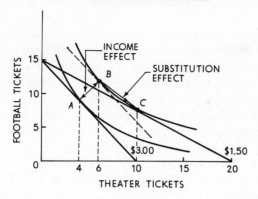

a horizontal summation of the demand curves of individual consumers. Figure 3–5 provides an example of how this might be done.

You might recognize the demand of consumer No. 1 in the first diagram as the same demand as we constructed in Figures 3–3. At $3 per ticket he demands 4 tickets per season, and at $1.50 per ticket he will buy 10 tickets. Consumer No. 2 is less of a theater fan. At $3 per ticket he would not attend the theater at all, and at the $1.50 price he will buy two tickets. Consumer No. 3 is a more ardent theater goer than both one and two. He demands 5 and 11 tickets at the $3 and $1.50 prices respectively.

To keep the example manageable, suppose the market consists of these three demanders. At the $3 price, the market demand is found by the quantity demanded by consumers 1, 2, and 3; 4, 0, and 5 respectively, making a total of 9. At the $1.50 price the quantity demanded by consumers 1, 2, and 3 are 10, 2, and 11 respectively making a total of 23 tickets as shown on the market demand diagram.

Now, of course, it is not realistic to believe that just three consumers will make up a market. If you desire more realism you might visualize a market where there are 1,000 people like consumer No. 1, 1,000 like No. 2,

FIGURE 3–5.   Constructing market demand from individual demand (theater ticket example)

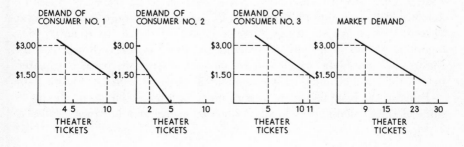

and 1,000 like consumer No. 3. In this case, at the $3 price there would be 9,000 tickets demanded. How many would be demanded at the $1.50 price?

The example we have just gone through represents a theoretical construction of a market demand curve. As we proceed we will find that even a theoretical market demand curve is a useful tool to explain economic phenomena and analyze economic problems. It might be of interest to note as well that economists have estimated the actual market demand curve for many products on the market today. The estimation is done by statistical techniques which are studied in intermediate level statistics courses.

Up to now we have been rather vague about the meaning of a market except to say that it is made up of many consumers. The main reason for this vagueness is that markets themselves are rather vague. The number of consumers and geographic area encompassed by a market varies from product to product. For new automobiles it seems to be nationwide, or even worldwide. For perishable foods, such as fresh milk, the market is much smaller; many times encompassing only a city. The market for the entertainment services provided by a football team will vary from several states for a professional team to only a part of a city for a high school team. The main point is that it is impossible to define the boundaries of what is called a market. These will vary according to the product under consideration, as well as the transportation and communication facilities available.

PRICE ELASTICITY OF DEMAND

Thus far about the only thing said about the shape of the demand curve (individual or market) is that it is downward sloping. It is important, however, that we become more specific than this. For the shape of the demand curve tells us a great deal about how consumers react to a price change. A demand curve that is very steep, for example, implies that consumers do not change their purchases very much in response to a price change, as shown in Figure 3–6. On the other hand a very "flat" curve implies that a price change will cause consumers to change their purchasing habits greatly (Figure 3–7).

In Figure 3–6, a reduction in price from $3 to $2 increases quantity demanded by just one unit (from 12 to 13). But in Figure 3–7, the same $1 reduction in price brings forth a six-unit increase in quantity demanded. A consumer with a demand for theater tickets illustrated by Figure 3–7 would be much responsive to a change in price of theater tickets than a consumer whose demand is characterized by Figure 3–6.

Judging the responsiveness of consumers to a price change by the mere slope of the demand curve involves one major problem, however. Namely,

FIGURE 3–6.   Demand for theater tickets, consumers unrespon-
sive to price

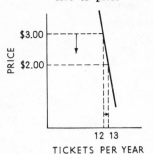

FIGURE 3–7.   Demand for theater tickets, consumers responsive
to price

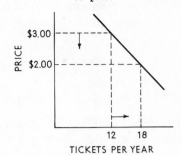

the slope of any curve can be changed simply by changing the units of measure on either the horizontal or vertical axis. For example we could make the curve in Figure 3–7 look very steep simply by changing the unit of measure from tickets per year to tickets per month. The change in the shape of the curve brought on by changing the quantity measure from tickets per year to tickets per month is illustrated in Figures 3–8 and 3–9.

There are of course other ways to change the shape of the curve. We could have changed the physical dimension of the quantity measure, assigning each ticket a larger or smaller distance on the quantity axis. The same manipulations could be performed on the price axis which would also change the shape of the curve. It is always well to keep in mind the possibilities for changing the shape of a curve whenever diagrams are used to describe something. The author can generally make a diagram show what he wants it to show.

One way to avoid the problems encountered by choosing different units of measure is to employ percentage changes. The percent change in a number will not be altered by choosing different units of measure. This

FIGURE 3–8.   Demand for theater tickets (tickets per year)

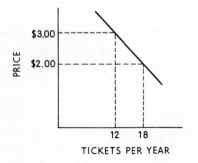

FIGURE 3–9.   Demand for theater tickets (tickets per month)

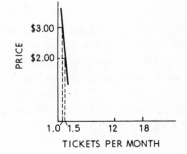

is illustrated below where we calculate the percentage change in quantity of tickets demanded because of the $1 change in price, first on a per year basis and secondly on a per month basis. Both result in the same percentage change even though the absolute changes differ.

1. Percentage change in quantity of tickets per year $= \dfrac{12 - 18}{12} = \dfrac{-6}{12} = -50\%$

2. Percentage change in quantity of tickets per month $= \dfrac{1.0 - 1.5}{1.0} = \dfrac{-0.5}{1} = -50\%$

In order to utilize the advantage of using percentage changes in describing changes in price and quantity, economists have developed the concept of "price elasticity of demand." It is defined as follows:

$$\text{Price elasticity of demand} = \frac{\text{Percentage change in quantity}}{\text{Percentage change in price}}$$

Price elasticity of demand is a number that tells us the percentage change quantity demanded corresponding to a 1 percent change in price. For example a price elasticity of demand of -1.5 tells us that quantity changes 1.5 percent for each 1 percent change in price.

The formula for computing price elasticity of demand is:

$$E_d = \frac{\dfrac{Q_0 - Q_1}{Q_0}}{\dfrac{P_0 - P_1}{P_0}}$$

Where E_d is an abbreviation for price elasticity of demand, Q_0 and P_0 are the beginning quantity and price respectively and Q_1 and P_1 are the ending quantity and price. In order to become somewhat more familiar with the formula let us compute the price elasticity of demand for the change shown in Figure 3–8. In this example the Q_0 is 12, Q_1 is 18, P_0 is $3, and P_1 is $2. Thus we have

$$E_d = \frac{\dfrac{12 - 18}{12}}{\dfrac{3.00 - 2.00}{3.00}} = \frac{\dfrac{-6}{12}}{\dfrac{1.00}{3.00}} = \frac{-0.50}{0.33} = -1.5$$

In this example, then, a 1 percent decrease in price is associated with a 1.5 percent increase in quantity. You will note that the price elasticity of demand is a negative number. This is because moving along a demand curve quantity and price change in opposite directions; when price goes down, quantity goes up and vice versa.

In order to facilitate description, economists have grouped price elasticity of demand into three categories according to the size of the elasticity number, or coefficient as it is often called. The groupings are made by dropping the negative sign on the elasticity coefficient so that we refer to it as an absolute number. These categories are:

Elasticity Coefficient

Less than 1 = Inelastic
Equal to 1 = Unitary elastic
Greater than 1 = Elastic

When the price elasticity of demand for a product is inelastic we can say that consumers are relatively unresponsive to a price change. In this case the percentage change in quantity is always smaller than the corresponding percentage change in price. If demand is elastic, on the other hand, we say that consumers are quite responsive to a price change. Here the percentage change in price is greater than the percentage change in quantity. In the intermediate case of a unitary elastic demand, price and quantity both change in the same proportions.

The smallest possible value of the elasticity coefficient is zero. If E_d is zero, a change in price will not result in any change in quantity whatever. In this case demand is said to be "perfectly" inelastic. Demand that is perfectly inelastic is represented by a demand curve that is perfectly vertical (Figure 3–10). On the other hand, the largest possible value of the elasticity coefficient is infinity. Here a very slight change in price corresponds to an infinitely large change in quantity. In this situation demand is said to be "perfectly" elastic and is characterized by a demand curve that is perfectly horizontal (Figure 3–11).

Economists sometimes illustrate demand that is highly inelastic by a very "steep" demand curve whereas demand that is very elastic will be represented by a relatively "flat" demand curve. However, we should keep in mind that the slope of a demand curve depends on the units on the two axes, except in the two extreme cases of perfectly inelastic or perfectly elastic demand.

There are two characteristics of the elasticity coefficient that ought to be mentioned at this point. Both stem from the fact that elasticity deals with percentage changes. The first characteristic is that the size of the

FIGURE 3–10. Perfectly inelastic demand   FIGURE 3–11. Perfectly elastic demand

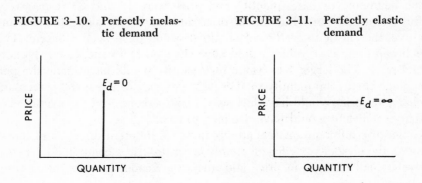

elasticity coefficient will become larger the higher you move up on a downward sloping, straight line, demand curve. The reason for this phenomenon is that the base or beginning values change at different points along the demand curve. At points high on the curve the beginning price will be high. Thus for a given dollar change in price the percentage change will be relatively small. For example, a $1 change in price will only be 10 percent if the beginning price is $10 whereas the same $1 change in price would represent a 100 percent change in price if beginning price is only $1. The same reasoning applies to different points along the quantity axis. Now the beginning or base quantity will be small at points high on the demand curve (small quantity demanded) which in turn results in large percentage changes for a given absolute change in quantity. The effect of a change in base values on E_d is illustrated in the elasticity formulas below. Consider the change in quantity $(Q_0 - Q_1)$ and the change in price $(P_0 - P_1)$ to be the same in each case, so that the only thing changing are the base values.

*Points High on
a Demand Curve*

$$E_d = \dfrac{\dfrac{Q_0 - Q_1}{Q_0} \quad \text{small}}{\dfrac{P_0 - P_1}{P_0} \quad \text{large}} \quad \begin{vmatrix} \text{large} \\ \text{small} \end{vmatrix} \quad \text{large}$$

*Points Low on
a Demand Curve*

$$E_d = \dfrac{\dfrac{Q_0 - Q_1}{Q_0} \quad \text{large}}{\dfrac{P_0 - P_1}{P_0} \quad \text{small}} \quad \begin{vmatrix} \text{small} \\ \text{large} \end{vmatrix} \quad \text{small}$$

A second characteristic of elasticity that occurs because it is measured in percentage terms is that the coefficient will depend upon the direction of a given absolute change in price and quantity. In the example above, the beginning or base quantity and price were 12 and $3 respectively. But if we had started at the $2 price and moved up along the demand curve, the elasticity coefficient obtained would have been different. This is because the base values would have changed to 18 and $2 for quantity and price. The larger base value for quantity would have made the percentage change in quantity smaller (−33 percent), whereas the percentage change in price would have increased to 50 percent. And the overall elasticity coefficient would have declined to 0.66.

Because different answers are obtained for different direction of movement, the elasticity coefficient is only accurate if it is computed over relatively small changes in price and quantity. Economists measuring price elasticity of demand for actual products utilize statistical tools that measure only very small movements in price and quantity.

For teaching purposes economists have modified the elasticity formula slightly, using both beginning and ending values of price and quantity for the base in the numerator and denominator. Here the formula becomes:

$$E_d = \frac{\dfrac{Q_0 - Q_1}{Q_0 + Q_1}}{\dfrac{P_0 - P_1}{P_0 + P_1}}$$

This formula measures the "average" elasticity between two points. And it results in the same answer regardless of the direction of movement. The formula discussed first is sometimes known as the "point elasticity" formula whereas the latter expression has come to be known as the "arc elasticity" formula.

For our purposes here the mechanics of measuring elasticity is not nearly as important as understanding what elasticity means. Keep in mind, that price elasticity of demand measures the responsiveness of consumers to changes in price. An inelastic demand means that consumers are not very responsive to price whereas an elastic demand means that consumers are quite responsive to price changes. The elasticity coefficient tells us the percentage change in quantity demanded for a one percent change in price.

PRICE ELASTICITY AND TOTAL REVENUE

One of the most valuable uses of the price elasticity concept is that it enables us to predict what happens to the total expenditure on a product, by consumers or total revenue going to the seller(s) of the product, when its price changes. To understand how elasticity is related to changes in total expenditure or revenue, it is necessary to first understand that a price change has two offsetting effects on total revenue or expenditure. Consider the case of a price fall. Before the price fall total revenue is given by:

$$TR = P_0 \times Q_0$$

where TR is total revenue and P_0 and Q_0 are beginning price and quantity. After the price fall total revenue is given by:

$$TR = P_1 \times Q_1$$

where P_1 and Q_1 are the new price and quantity respectively.

The reduction in price, of course, has the effect of reducing total expenditure or revenue. On the other hand, if the demand curve is downward sloping the reduction in price will lead to an increase in quantity sold. And the increase in quantity has the effect of pulling total revenue back up. If demand is elastic, quantity increases by a larger percentage than price decreases; in this case total revenue will increase with a price reduction. The opposite occurs when demand is inelastic. Now a price reduction results in a decrease in total revenue because quantity increases by a smaller percent than price decreases.

Figures 3–12 and 3–13 illustrate the relationship between price elasticity and total revenue or expenditure by means of demand curves. The area denoted by a minus sign represents a pulling down of total revenue whereas the plus area represents the augmenting of total revenue because of the price fall. In Figure 3–12, a representation of an inelastic demand, the minus area outweighs the plus area resulting in a reduction in total revenue. The opposite occurs in Figure 3–13 where the plus area outweighs the minus area because of the elastic demand.

FIGURE 3–12. Price reduction with   FIGURE 3–13. Price reduction with
                inelastic demand   elastic demand

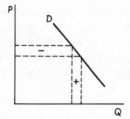
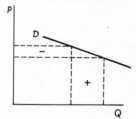

We must realize, of course, that we would observe just the opposite change in total revenue if we consider a price increase. Here an inelastic demand would give rise to an increase in total revenue because price would increase more than quantity would decrease. By the same token, a price rise with elastic demand results in a decrease in total revenue.

In discussing price elasticity of demand, you will recall that elasticity changes as you move along a straight-line, downward sloping demand curve. At points high on the curve price elasticity is a larger absolute number than at points low on the curve. We might expect, therefore, that for most downward sloping, straight-line demand curves, points high on the curve will be elastic whereas points far down the curve will be inelastic. Moreover, there will be a point somewhere in the middle of the curve where the price elasticity will be one.

The relationship between total revenue or expenditure and price elasticity of demand is illustrated in Figure 3–14. Starting at a high price (a point high on the demand curve) and moving down the curve results in an increase in total revenue or expenditure until the point is reached where price elasticity is one. Below this point price elasticity becomes less than one and total revenue declines with a fall in price.

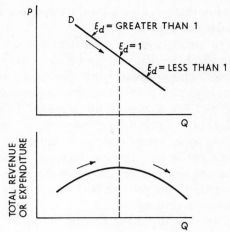

FIGURE 3–14. Relationship between price elasticity of demand and total revenue or expenditure

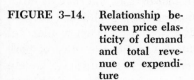

The relationship between price elasticity of demand and total revenue or expenditure is summarized below. This summary applies to both situations mentioned above: (1) the case of a totally elastic or inelastic demand curve and (2) elastic and inelastic segments of a given demand curve.

		Change in *Total Revenue* *or Expenditure*
1.	Elastic demand:	
	a) Price fall...........	...Increase
	b) Price rise..........	...Decrease
2.	Inelastic demand:	
	a) Price fall...........	...Decrease
	b) Price rise..........	...Increase

You might have observed that for an elastic demand price and total revenue or expenditure change in opposite directions whereas for an inelastic demand they change in the same direction.

ECONOMIC FACTORS AFFECTING PRICE ELASTICITY OF DEMAND

We have seen so far that price elasticity is affected by the point we happen to choose along a demand curve. But this is strictly an algebraic phenomenon that occurs because of the way we calculate price elasticity. We now want to explore briefly the economic factors that affect the size of a product's price elasticity of demand. We find the demand for some goods to be elastic and the demand for other goods to be inelastic. Why does this occur?

The first, and perhaps most important, factor influencing the price elasticity of a good is the degree of substitution between the good in question and other substitute goods. The larger the number and the better the substitutes that exist for a good (or service), the more elastic will be the particular good (or service).

To understand the economic rationale of this generalization, consider a product that has many substitutes, pork chops for example. If the price of pork chops should rise, consumers have many other alternative products to choose from—other cuts of pork, all other meat such as beef, poultry, and fish, as well as other protein foods that can be eaten in place of meat such as cheese or the new meat analogs. A rise in the price of pork chops, then, will provide an incentive for consumers to reduce pork chop consumption and increase the use of these alternative products. Pork chop consumption will decline accordingly indicating that consumers are responsive to the price of pork chops and you recall that this is meaning of an elastic demand.

Products that have few or very poor substitutes, on the other hand, tend to have an inelastic demand. Salt is the classic example of such a good. If the price of salt should rise consumers would still have to buy about the same amount of salt since it has no substitute. This means that consumers are not very responsive to a change in price of salt which is just another way of saying that salt has an inelastic demand.

It is important to recognize as well that the definition of a product will influence its elasticity. In general, the more broadly we define a product, the lower will be its price elasticity. This comes about because there are fewer substitutes for a broadly defined product than for one that is narrowly defined. For example, the price elasticity for all pork would be smaller (less elastic or more inelastic) than it is for only pork chops. The substitutes for pork chops include such things as pork loins, pork roast, etc., as well as the pork substitutes whereas the substitutes for all pork includes only the other meats or meat substitutes. Similarly, the demand for a particular brand of salt would be more elastic than all salt because brand X, for example, has substitutes in the form of the other brands of salt on the market.

The second major factor influencing the elasticity of a product is the proportion of the consumer's budget accounted for by the product. Products that take up a very small proportion of the budget tend to be more inelastic than items that are relatively large in the budget. For example, if the price of paper clips doubles the impact on one's budget would be imperceptible, hence there would not be a strong incentive to reduce paper clip use. Yet if something like dormitory room rent rises considerably students are forced to find alternative places to stay such as apartments, private homes, etc., else some are forced out of school. Thus, we would expect that this second factor would tend to make the demand for dormitory rooms more elastic than the demand for paper clips. The following is a summary of the effect of these two factors on the size of the price elasticity of demand.

Factor	Effect on Price Elasticity
1. Many good substitutes	Increase
2. Large item in budget	Increase

It is not unusual to find cases, however, where the two factors each has an opposite influence on the elasticity of a product. That is, a product may have many, good substitutes, making for an elastic demand, but at the same time may be a small item in the budget which makes for an inelastic demand. The resulting price elasticity, therefore, is a summation of these two factors; both must be considered when attempting to assess the elasticity of a product.

You might have noticed that the two factors influencing the price elasticity of a product closely parallel the two effects, discussed previously in this chapter, that account for the downward sloping characteristic of the demand curve; namely the substitution and income effects. This is not just a mere coincidence. The first factor, the degree of substitution possible, assesses the strength of the substitution effect; and the second factor, the importance of the item in the budget, assesses the strength of the income effect. The stronger or more significant these two effects are, the more responsive consumers are to a price change, which in turn implies a more elastic demand.

As a final point, it is sometimes argued that goods or services considered necessities tend to exhibit an inelastic demand whereas the demand for luxuries tends to be elastic. The reasoning here is that people cannot get along without necessities, hence, they will buy about the same amount regardless of price. Of course, we should keep in mind that a so-called necessity need not be viewed as such by everyone. Drugs, for example, might be considered a necessity by someone "hooked" on them but not for someone who abhors their use. In essence, a person tends to view a product as a necessity if to him it has no good substitutes.

MAIN POINTS OF CHAPTER 3

1. Demand is a relationship between price and quantity rather than a fixed amount. Quantity demanded, on the other hand, refers to a fixed amount—a point on the demand curve.

2. Demand reflects wants of consumers, not needs. Also demand reflects what consumers actually do when faced with certain prices rather than what they would like to do.

3. The downward sloping characteristic of a consumer's demand curve for a product is consistent with diminishing marginal utility because with an increase in the price of a product, marginal utility per dollar declines which in turn makes it worthwhile for the consumer to reduce consumption of the product.

4. A downward sloping demand curve is obtained also when a demand curve is derived from an indifference map and alternative budget lines. Each point on a demand curve represents a tangency point between an indifference curve and a budget line.

5. Consumers change their purchases of products with a change in prices because of the income and substitution effects. The income effect occurs because a price change has the effect of changing the purchasing power of our income. The substitution effect reflects the consumer's desire to obtain the most for his money by purchasing the "best buys." These two effects constitute the economic explanation for the downward sloping characteristic of a demand curve.

6. The market demand curve is obtained by adding the demand curves of all the individual consumers in the market. This is done by adding all the quantities demanded by the individuals at each possible price.

7. Price elasticity of demand reflects the responsiveness of consumers to a price change. The elasticity coefficient tells us the percent change in quantity demand resulting from a 1 percent change in price.

8. Demand is elastic if E_d is greater than one; indicating that quantity changes by more than 1 percent when price changes 1 percent.

9. Demand is inelastic if E_d is less than one, indicating that quantity changes by less than 1 percent when price changes 1 percent.

10. The elasticity coefficient can range from zero to minus infinity. Demand is perfectly inelastic if E_d is zero and perfectly elastic if E_d is minus infinity.

11. The elasticity coefficient becomes larger at points high on a downward sloping, straight-line demand curve and smaller at points further down the curve. This is a mathematical phenomenon explained by changes in the base values that are used to calculate percentage changes.

12. Whether or not consumers spend more or less on a product after its price changes depends on the product's price elasticity of demand. If demand is elastic, a price rise reduces total revenue or expenditure whereas total revenue increases with a price rise if demand is inelastic.

13. This relationship between total revenue and elasticity is explained by whether or not quantity changes by a larger or smaller percentage than price. If price rises 1 percent, total revenue or expenditure on the product will decrease if quantity declines more than 1 percent (elastic demand) whereas total revenue increases if quantity declines less than 1 percent (inelastic demand).

14. The two economic factors affecting price elasticity of demand are (1) the number and acceptability of substitute products available and (2) the importance of the product in the budget. A product with many

good substitutes tends to be elastic. Elasticity is increased if it accounts for a sizable portion of consumers' budgets.

QUESTIONS FOR THOUGHT AND DISCUSSION

1. Make a list of some products you would buy more of if their prices declined substantially. What does this imply about your demand curve for these products?

2. The price of a skiing weekend to the mountains is $125. I would like to take at least six such trips per year. This says that $125 and six represent a point on my demand curve for skiing weekends. Comment.

3. In Chapter 2 we learned that a consumer maximizes utility by equalizing as much as possible the marginal utility per dollar for all goods and services he consumes. Explain how this concept is related to the downward sloping demand curve.

4. Think of two goods you consume that are good substitutes for each other. Construct some indifference curves for these two goods that would be realistic for you. Next derive a demand curve for one of these goods from this indifference map plus some budget lines.

5. Explain as you would to a friend or relative who has had no economics what income and substitution effects are as they relate to consumer demand. Also illustrate these two effects on an indifference map.

6. Find in a newspaper or magazine a graph describing a relationship between two items. Indicate how you could change the graph to illustrate a different relationship than was originally described.

7. Explain what is meant by price elasticity of demand.

8. Think of three products that you believe would have a very inelastic market demand. Think of three others that would likely have a very elastic demand. Give economic reasons for your classification.

9. Think of a situation where a college or university could use the concept of price elasticity of demand.

10. Luxuries tend to be elastic in demand whereas necessities tend to be inelastic. Comment.

11. As you move up along a downward sloping, straight-line demand curve, price elasticity of demand increases. This is because consumers are more responsive to price changes when prices are high. Comment.

12. Explain how and why total revenue or expenditure on a product is related to its price elasticity of demand.

CHAPTER

4

PRODUCER CHOICE

THE CONCEPT OF PRODUCTION

Let us now turn our attention from the consumer to the producer and to product supply. This is not to imply, however, that there are two separate groups of people in society: one group producing and the other consuming. Almost everyone is both a producer and a consumer. To appreciate this dual role that most of us play, it is necessary to realize that production is not limited to the factory or farm but rather that it characterizes the daily activity of most people.

For many, the word production conjures up an image of a factory with busy people, machines, smokestacks, and the like turning out some identifiable product. To others, production might be the harnessing of nature's resources to produce food, fiber, lumber, metals, etc. To be sure, all of these activities involve production. But production is more than these. Indeed it is important to be aware that production is any activity that creates present and/or future utility.

If you consider production to be as all inclusive as this, then many activities that you might not have classified as production before now become so. The dentist in filling or pulling a tooth may not create present utility but certainly creates future utility by preventing a future toothache. The artist painting a picture creates present utility for himself and future utility for others who view his work. The symphony orchestra or vocalist creates utility by their production of sound.

By now you probably realize that production is not restricted to traditional business firms. Virtually everyone engages in some form of productive activity. The student takes part in a production process by reading a book or attending classes. The knowledge and experience that is acquired or produced impart both a present and future utility. Present utility is created by the satisfaction of learning something new or by new experiences gained. Future utility stems from an increased awareness and understanding of the world around as well as from widened economic opportunities made possible by an increased earning power.

The activities of housewives in the home also is a form of production. Utility is created or produced by the preparation of meals, the rearing of children, and all the other activities carried out that enhance the lives of themselves and their families. So it is then that production is found in every aspect of our lives. The fruits or output of production may be exchanged in the market or they may be enjoyed by the person performing the production. It may involve the production of tangible items from automobiles and pork chops, to diamond rings, or intangible output ranging from knowledge to all forms of personal services.

In primitive societies of years past or in what we call underdeveloped societies of today, production has consisted largely of the more traditional activities including mainly food, clothing, and shelter. As these basic needs are met, a larger share of available resources are devoted to nontraditional production activities; the production of items that provide diversity for our lives as well as all the services we enjoy and the knowledge we produce and acquire. These latter items satisfy man's wants as much as the basic ones of food, clothing, and shelter.

It would be illogical, therefore, to limit our concept of production to a limited range of products as was done by a group of French economists who lived in the 18th century known as the physiocrats. They believed that all true production came from the soil and that all other activities in society such as teaching, the legal profession, etc., were nonproductive. Occasionally we find some carryover of this thinking today when people refer to management as "nonproductive" personnel, or to some people as the "working class." The agricultural "fundamentalists" who argue that agriculture is the "basic" industry in the economy also still reflect a bit of this old philosophy. It is not correct to limit the concept of production only to items we can package, pile up, or count.

INPUTS IN PRODUCTION

In any production process there must always be one or more inputs that are either transformed or utilized in some way to produce an output. In economic literature inputs will be called by different names. Inputs are also known as resources or factors of production. All three names refer to the same thing.

In a modern, highly developed economy most inputs are themselves the product of some other production activity. For example, the steel input into automobiles is itself an output of the steel industry. Even the human input in virtually all production has been modified or improved by some past training whether it be formal schooling or informal knowledge gained from family, fellow workers, or experience. And, as we know, knowledge also is the output of a production activity.

Most production utilizes several inputs at the same time or in some time sequence. In fact it is rather difficult to think of an example where production is carried on with just one input. One example that comes close would be the production of sound by a vocalist. But even this would not be strictly correct since the singer utilizes energy obtained from food which should be considered an input also.

In reading economic literature, particularly that dealing with production, it is possible to find different ways of classifying or grouping inputs. In years past it was common to see inputs classified into three categories: land, labor, and capital. With the growth of the nonagricultural sector, land has been reduced in importance so that it is now often grouped in with capital. A very aggregative grouping of inputs in an economy now generally includes only labor and capital. Capital can be thought of as inputs which have been produced by man to facilitate production. Buildings, machines, tools, etc., are commonly thought of as capital. Land, of course, is not man-made but is often modified by man in order to be useful in production. Anyone who has ever cleared trees or rocks from land or reclaimed it from the sea will appreciate the role that man has played in making land productive.

It will be useful for our future discussion to group inputs into two other categories: (1) fixed and (2) variable inputs. In most production processes it is possible to identify certain inputs that contribute to production but which for the time period under consideration cannot be increased or decreased in order to change the level of output. These are called fixed inputs. Variable inputs, as the name implies, can be varied according to the desired level of output. For example, in manufacturing the building would be considered a fixed input because it cannot be readily changed to a different size. Variable inputs in this case would include such things as labor, materials, fuel, etc. Now, of course, if we allow a long enough time to elapse, the building can be changed in size, or a new one constructed, so eventually a fixed input can become variable. We will emphasize the distinction between fixed and variable inputs as well as the importance of the time dimension to this classification a great deal in the discussion that follows, particularly in Chapters 6 and 7.

PRODUCTION: ONE VARIABLE INPUT

Let us now look more closely at the production process itself. Obviously each product or output has its own unique inputs and process. Moreover it is easy to find the same output produced by various different methods or inputs. At the same time there are some general principles of production that hold true for all types of production. It is these general principles that will be of interest to us here.

The best way to begin the study of production is to first consider the simplest possible case. In production this is the case of one variable input. As we noted, however, it is quite difficult to imagine a realistic example of carrying on production with just one input. But it is not as difficult to visualize production where one or more fixed inputs such as land or some other physical facility is combined with one variable input such as labor. In this second case simplicity is maintained without sacrificing realism.

We will find it helpful, also, to consider a specific example in developing the general principles of production, much as we did in our study of consumption. Suppose, for example, that there happens to be a ready market in your community for fresh tomatoes. Suppose as well that there is a plot of land in your neighborhood, say one-quarter acre, that is available.

So you decide that an opportunity exists to earn some extra money during the summer by producing and selling tomatoes. For the present we will assume that only two major inputs are used in your tomato production: land, the fixed input, and your labor, the variable input. Of course you will need some seed and a spade or hoe at the very minimum as additional inputs but these are relatively minor, or if you like they can be considered as fixed inputs along with land. The input we will be mainly concerned with is your labor. Specifically we will be interested in the relationship between the amount of effort you devote to your tomato plants and the resulting output of tomatoes.

A PRODUCTION FUNCTION

As you begin your tomato-growing endeavor, one of the first decisions you will have to make is how much time will you spend on this activity. Without having any previous experience in tomato culture it would be difficult for anyone to predict how many tomatoes could be produced and harvested with a given input of labor. To obtain some reasonable estimates of what you might expect from your labor, suppose you consult with an experienced tomato grower. You tell him some possible amounts of time you might spend in your tomato patch and he tells you how many bushels of tomatoes you could reasonably expect, as shown in columns (1) and (2) of Table 4–1. (You might consider each day as equivalent to eight hours. Each eight-hour day doesn't have to be applied at one time.) We realize, of course, that these numbers would only be estimates, but even in actual situations production decisions must generally be made on estimates no more accurate than these. The more experience or knowledge a producer has, of course, the more accurate his estimates will be.

In a production process the relationship between input and output is

TABLE 4-1.   Hours of labor input and resulting output of tomatoes

(1) Labor Input (Days)	(2) Tomato Output (Bushels)	(3) Marginal Physical Product of Labor (Bushels per Day)	(4) Average Physical Product of Labor (Bushels per Day)
0	0	—	—
1	1	1	1.0
2	8	7	4.0
3	20	12	6.7
4	29	9	7.3
5	36	7	7.2
6	42	6	7.0
7	46	4	6.6
8	48	2	6.0
9	48	0	5.3
10	45	−3	4.5

often referred to by economists as a production function. In the example here, the output of tomatoes depends upon, or is a function of, the quantity of labor used. By knowing the production function, I can tell you how many tomatoes to expect if you tell me how much labor is put in. With zero labor, for example, we would expect zero output. And as labor input increases, output increases. For example, additional labor input enables you to plant and harvest a larger portion of the tomato patch as well as to do a better job of controlling the weeds, etc.

MARGINAL PHYSICAL PRODUCT

Let us examine this relationship or production function between labor input and tomato output in more detail. We noted that each additional day of labor brings forth additional bushels of tomatoes. The first day (eight hours) brings forth one bushel. The second day adds seven bushels (eight minus the one produced by the first day's labor). The third day adds 12 bushels over the second, and so on.

The numbers we have been deriving here represent the *additional* output brought forth by an *additional* unit of input. Economists refer to this additional output as the marginal physical product (*MPP*) of the particular input that is being increased, labor in our example. You recall from the discussion in Chapter 2 that the marginal unit is the additional or last unit either added or subtracted off of something. Hence, the marginal product of labor is the additional product obtained by adding one more unit of labor. Or it can be the loss of product by reducing labor by one unit.

In our tomato example it was a fairly easy matter to calculate marginal physical product because the labor input increased by only one unit at a time. In many kinds of production, however, it is not always possible to add or subtract just one unit of an input. Consider General Motors just adding one man to its labor force; the growth in output would be too small to measure.

It is useful therefore to have a formula that will enable us to calculate the *MPP* of an input even if it is not added one unit at a time. The formula is:

$$MPP = \frac{\text{Change in output}}{\text{Change in input}}$$

This formula will give us the *MPP* of any input regardless of whether or not it is changed (increased or decreased) by one unit or by several units at a time. In the preceding example, increasing labor by one unit, from 1 to 2, results in an increase in output from 1 to 8 (a 7-unit change). Thus the denominator in the formula is 1 and the numerator is 7. In writing the *MPP* column you will often see the *MPP* figures written opposite the input that has been added, for example the 7 is written opposite the second unit of input in Table 4–1.

You might try calculating the *MPP* of labor when it is increased from 1 to 3 units at one time (the answer is 9.5). Just as in the case of price elasticity of demand, it is more important to know what *MPP* is than to be able to calculate it by memorizing a formula. Economists have estimated the *MPP* of the inputs employed in producing many products by the same statistical technique used to estimate price elasticity of demand.

THE LAW OF DIMINISHING RETURNS

By now you've probably noticed the change in size of *MPP* of labor (column 3, Table 4–1) as you move down the column. At first, it increases from 1 to 7 to 12 and then begins to decline, eventually becoming zero and negative. Even though this is just a simple example, it depicts fairly well what one might expect in any production process.

At very low levels of use of the variable input its efficiency is low because it is spread too thinly across the fixed input. For example, an input of eight hours (one day) might only enable you to inadequately prepare the soil, plant, and harvest a portion of the quarter acre of land. But an input of two or three days would make it possible to weed and care for the tomatoes such that output increases rapidly.

The region where *MPP* is increasing is known as the region of increasing returns. It extends up to and includes the third unit of the variable input in this example. Increasing returns need not be present in every production process but at very low levels of variable input use it is reasonable to expect such a region.

The region that is of most interest to us, however, begins at the fourth level of labor input. In this region you will note that *MPP* of labor declines at each successive increment of labor. This region is commonly known as the region of diminishing returns. Or the declining characteristic of *MPP* is referred to as the law of diminishing returns. This principle or law states that beyond some point the output resulting from each additional unit of a variable input begins to decline.

The economic logic underlying the idea of diminishing returns is fairly simple and reasonable. As more and more of the variable input is added to the fixed input the productivity of the variable input begins to decline because of crowding and inefficient use of the variable input. Applying more and more labor to the tomato patch, for example, may increase production because of better preparation of the soil, more careful weeding, etc., but there is only so much you can do in a tomato patch. Eventually the added output from more labor becomes negligible. And it is not unreasonable to believe that after some point additional labor may have a detrimental effect and actually reduce output. For example, you may just tramp down plants by adding the 10th day of labor.

The law of diminishing returns is also known by two other names: (1) diminishing marginal physical product and (2) the law of variable proportions. The first term is rather self-explanatory. The second stems from the fact that the proportion of total inputs that are variable changes as more and more of the variable input is added.

AVERAGE PHYSICAL PRODUCT

A second concept stemming from the production function is average physical product (APP). The average physical product of labor, for example, is calculated at each level of labor input by dividing total output by the units of labor employed.

$$APP = \frac{\text{Output}}{\text{Input}}$$

Notice that this formula is similar to the one used to calculate MPP except that the absolute amount of output and input is used rather than changes in output and input.

The APP of labor in our tomato production example is shown by column 4 in Table 4–1. We see that APP increases for a time and then begins to decline just as we observed for MPP. One difference between the two measures, however, is that APP never becomes negative. It may approach a very small number, but as long as output is positive APP must be positive. It will be helpful to employ a diagram in understanding the relationship between MPP and APP.

STAGES OF PRODUCTION

In Figure 4–1 we have plotted the numbers in columns 3 and 4 of Table 4–1. You will notice that we have separated the diagram into three areas or stages. Economists refer to these areas as stages of production. We see that stage I includes the area of increasing returns and extends up to the point where *APP* reaches a maximum. This stage does include, however, a portion of the *MPP* curve that declines. The distinguishing characteristic of stage I is that *MPP* is greater than *APP*. As long as the marginal unit is greater than the overall average, the average will always increase.

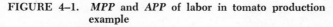

FIGURE 4–1.   *MPP* and *APP* of labor in tomato production example

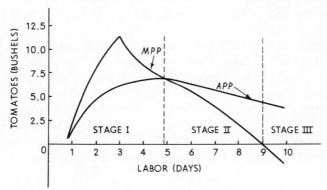

It is easiest to understand the relationship between the average and marginal unit by looking at a simple example. Suppose your overall grade point average in college is 3.0 (out of a possible 4.0). Now suppose during the current quarter you work extremely hard and earn a 3.5. When your overall grade point average is recalculated with the current quarter included, you will of course observe an increase in your overall average. The current or marginal quarter has pulled it up. Or, if you had earned only a 2.5, say, for the current quarter, your overall average would have declined.

By now you've probably noticed that the distinguishing characteristic of stage II is that *MPP* is everywhere less than *APP*. This results in the continual decline of *APP*. Stage II ends at the point where *MPP* becomes negative. Stage III begins where the *MPP* curve crosses the horizontal axis and extends to the right indefinitely as the negative *MPP* continues to pull *APP* down lower and lower, approaching zero but never reaching it.

The significance of the three stages of production will become more clear when we relate them to the concept of supply in the next chapter. For now we will have to settle for just an intuitive explanation of their importance. We can readily see that no producer would ever want to be in stage III. This is evident from our example. By adding the 10th day of labor, total tomato output actually declines. We would be better off to go fishing or stay in bed than to put in a day of work that brings negative results.

It is also true that no producer would ever want to operate in stage I, although the reason why is less clear than for stage III. Consider the region of increasing returns. If it paid to produce any quantity at all, it would always pay to increase the level of the variable input until you were past the level of increasing returns. As long as you are in the region of increasing returns, each additional unit of input adds more and more output. Thus the more input you add the more efficient you become, hence the cheaper you produce the added output. Consequently it would be foolish to stop adding the variable input when in the region of increasing returns.

We have now established that a rational, profit maximizing, producer would add enough of the variable input to go past the region of increasing returns but would stop adding before he entered stage III, the region of negative marginal physical product. Thus a producer will always produce in the region of diminishing returns. Moreover, if he produces at all, he will always avoid stage I even though this stage may contain a small region of diminishing returns as shown in Figure 4-1. For the moment we will just assert this and wait until Chapter 5 to show why it is true.

PRODUCTION: TWO VARIABLE INPUTS

Most production processes, of course, utilize a number of variable inputs along with one or more fixed inputs. Let us, therefore, add a bit more realism to the discussion by considering the case of production with two variable inputs. We can retain our tomato production example by assuming that labor is combined with another variable input. It would be reasonable to assume that even in this small-scale production of tomatoes, the use of some kind of equipment such as a garden tractor and its various attachments would be feasible. Suppose we measure the use of a specific sized garden tractor and its attachments by machine days.

We will assume as well that it is possible to employ various alternative combinations of labor and machine-hours. For example, if little or no machine-hours are utilized, a relatively large amount of labor would have to be employed to produce a given amount of output. Whereas with more and more machine inputs the same output could be obtained with less and less labor.

Thus with two or more variable inputs the producer has to decide not only how much to produce but which combination of inputs will be best for him. The remaining part of this chapter will deal with the second question, the optimum combination of inputs, while Chapter 5 will deal with the optimum level of output.

ISO-QUANTS

Economists have found it useful to devise a technique similar to in-difference curves that will enable us to summarize the relationship be-tween various combinations of the variable inputs. Visualize, if you will, a given amount of tomato output, say 40 bushels. We are assuming now that this level of output can be produced by many different methods using different combinations of labor and machines. We can summarize these combinations by a diagram similar to the indifference curve diagram in Chapter 3.

In Figure 4–2 we present what might be some reasonable inputs of la-bor and machines required to obtain a given level of output. The curves that are drawn in Figure 4–2 are known as iso-quants. Since iso means equal, a more literal translation of these curves is "equal quantity." All the points along a given curve represent the same level of output. The lowest curve, for example, represents 40 bushels, the second 60 bushels, etc. Ac-tually we could draw in almost an infinite number of such iso-quants, but three will adequately serve as an example.

FIGURE 4–2. Iso-quants

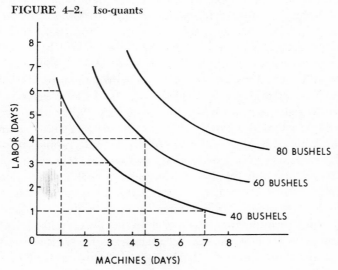

In the above example, we have specified three alternative combinations of labor and machines required to produce 40 bushels of tomatoes. The six days of labor and one day of machines illustrates a labor intensive method of producing tomatoes. That is a large part of the work, such as preparing the soil, weeding, etc., is done by hand.

Of course, it is also possible to utilize machines more fully and reduce the amount of hand labor required. This is illustrated by the one labor and seven machines combination. (Keep in mind here that we are measuring machines by a certain size, say 5 horsepower.) Something of a middle ground is represented by the three labor, three machines arrangement. If we wanted to divide the labor and machine measures into fine enough units, we could obtain an infinite number of labor-machine combinations, although no producer would ever consider quite that many.

As we would expect, higher levels of output, such as 60 or 80 bushels, can be obtained only by increased use of one or both inputs. In Figure 4–2, we see that one possible method of obtaining 60 bushels is by utilizing 4 days of labor and roughly 4½ days of machines. We see also that it is possible to actually increase output when one of the two inputs is decreased. For example, we could have decreased labor from 6 to 4 days and increased machines from 1 to 4½ days and obtained 20 additional bushels. Keep in mind, though, that this involves moving from one iso-quant to another.

You probably have noticed by now that iso-quants are very similar to indifference curves. Both denote a given quantity of something. An indifference curve denotes a given level of satisfaction obtained by alternative combinations of products whereas an iso-quant denotes a given level of output from alternative combinations of inputs. Moreover the shape of indifference curves and iso-quants are similar. Both tend to be convex to the origin. As we explained in Chapter 2, the convex shape of the indifference curve means that the less you have of a good, the more you will have to receive of a substitute good in order to remain on the same level of satisfaction when giving up successive units of the scarce good.

The convex shape of an iso-quant has a very similar meaning. Essentially it implies that the closer you come to using a zero amount of an input, say labor, the more and more of a substitute input, say machines, you will have to use in order to remain on the same level of output. From an intuitive standpoint this is a fairly reasonable thing to expect. There are certain jobs in the production process that can best be done by labor, for example, and other jobs best done by machines.

In the tomato production example it would be very inefficient to substitute machines for labor in, say, harvesting the fruit. Notice as well that the iso-quants do not extend all the way to the two axes. If they did, it would imply that one input be reduced to zero. And it would be difficult to imagine production being carried out with just labor or just machines.

Keep in mind, also, that the concepts of *MPP*, *APP*, diminishing returns, and stages of production apply to each of these two variable inputs just as they did to the single variable input discussed in the previous sections. We will not derive *MPP* and *APP*, etc., for each input again, but we could easily do so simply by varying one of the inputs at a time, holding the other constant.

SUBSTITUTION POSSIBILITIES

The shape of the iso-quants also tells us how easy it is to substitute one input for another and still remain on the same level of output. It is possible to think of some inputs where it is very easy to substitute one for the other; your own labor and hired labor might be one example. Or, we might think of other examples where it becomes extremely difficult to substitute one input for another—seeds and land, for example.

The iso-quant drawn in Figure 4–2 illustrates a situation where the inputs are imperfect substitutes for each other. It is possible to substitute but when you increase one in exchange for the other, it takes more and more of the abundant input to substitute for the input that is becoming relatively scarce. We can also visualize the two extreme situations and illustrate these with iso-quants.

In Figure 4–3 we illustrate a situation where two inputs are perfect substitutes for each other. The iso-quant in this case is a straight, downward sloping line indicating that possibility for substitution remains the same no matter what combination you consider. For example, one day of your own labor might substitute for 1¼ days of hired labor at any combination of the two. At the other extreme we have the case of zero substitution possibility, as illustrated by Figure 4–4. In this case the inputs must be used in fixed proportions. Once the "correct" proportion is reached, additional units of one input without more of the other is wasted since output remains the same. Economists sometimes refer to these as perfect complements because they must be used together.

FIGURE 4–3. Iso-quants illustrating perfect substitutes

FIGURE 4–4. Iso-quants illustrating perfect complements

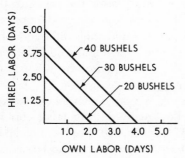

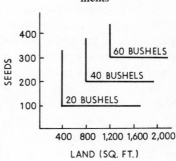

These two extreme cases bring out another similarity between iso-quants and indifference curves. As we saw in Chapter 2 the extreme cases of indifference curves also are perfect substitutes and perfect complements. A straight downward sloping indifference curve illustrates two goods that are perfect substitutes for one another, whereas an iso-quant of the same shape indicates that the two inputs under consideration are perfect substitutes also. The same comparison holds true for perfect complements.

In general, economists have been most interested in the middle case of imperfect substitutes, although the extreme case of perfect complements has received considerable attention through the technique known as "linear programming." This technique is taken up in more advanced, specialized courses in economics.

ISO-COSTS

We are now aware that in many, and possibly most, production processes there is some chance to substitute one input for another. As long as this possibility exists, the production manager must decide the best combination to use at any given level of output. How shall he decide?

It is reasonable to believe that any manager would prefer to produce a given level of quantity and quality of output at the lowest possible cost. This is true whether we produce for the market or for our own use. By minimizing cost we attain a greater profit if we produce for the market or attain more output for a given input if we produce something for ourselves.

It is also reasonable to believe that we will minimize costs if we utilize as much as possible inputs that are relatively inexpensive. We will be able to organize our thinking in this area a bit easier if we develop what economists call "iso-cost" lines. We will see that iso-cost lines are very similar to the idea of budget lines that we developed in conjunction with indifference curves.

In order to conceive of an iso-cost line we must know the prices of the various inputs we consider using. To continue our tomato production example, suppose the price of labor is $20 per day and the rental cost of a given size machine (garden tractor) is $30 a day. It will make no difference if you provide your own labor or hire. We will explain why this is true very shortly at the beginning of Chapter 5.

Now that we have the prices of our inputs we can construct an iso-cost line. The easiest way to begin is to ask, how many days of labor could I obtain for a given expenditure, say $100? Thus at $20, five days of labor could be hired. Therefore, the $100 iso-cost line intersects the labor axis of the iso-quant diagram at five days. Secondly we might ask, how many machine days could be obtain for $100. In this case the iso-cost line would intersect the machine axis at $3\frac{1}{3}$ days.

If we connect these two points with a straight line we have constructed what is known as an iso-cost line. Recall that iso means equal, so all points along this line represent the same total cost. Figure 4–5 illustrates several iso-cost lines along with a 40 bushel iso-quant. The higher the iso-cost, the more inputs that are represented for a given price, hence the higher the total cost.

FIGURE 4–5.   Iso-costs and iso-quant illustrating an optimum input combina-
tion

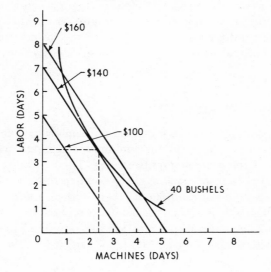

OPTIMUM INPUT COMBINATION

We now have the tools to determine the optimum (least expensive) combination of inputs for a given level of output. You will observe in Figure 4–5 that $100 iso-cost line does not intersect or touch at any point of the 40 bushel iso-quant. This means that there is no way you could produce 40 bushels of tomatoes for $100. On the other hand the $160 iso-cost line intersects the iso-quant at two places; at about 7 days of labor and slightly less than 1 machine day, or at about 4½ machine days and just over 1 day of labor. Thus 40 bushels of tomatoes could be produced by either of these combinations or any point between them that is on the iso-cost line.

Of course it would be wasteful to choose one of the combinations on the $160 iso-cost line because there exists a lower iso-cost line that also touches the 40 bushel iso-quant, namely the $140 line. This line is just tangent to the iso-quant. And the combination of inputs that corresponds to the point of tangency in this example is about 3½ days of labor and 2⅓ machine days, which costs $140. As a general rule, therefore, the optimum or least-cost combination of inputs is the one that corresponds to the tangency point between the lowest possible iso-cost line and the iso-quant.

Again, notice the similarity between the indifference curve–budget line technique and the iso-quant–iso-cost approach just developed. In both cases the tangency point tells you where you get the most for your money. The former tells you how to maximize satisfaction for a given budget or how to minimize the cost of achieving a given level of satisfaction. On the production side the iso-quant–iso-cost technique tells you how to maximize output for a given cost or how to minimize cost for a given output. Both ways of looking at these decisions mean the same thing.

CHANGING INPUT PRICES

One of the most important uses of the iso-quant–iso-cost technique is to show what happens to the optimum combination of inputs when the price of one or more of the variable inputs change. The first thing to recognize is that the slope of the iso-cost line changes when the price of one of the inputs changes. In the last example, if labor becomes more expensive, the same iso-cost line will intersect the labor axis closer to the origin. For instance, if labor increases in price to $25 per day, the $100 iso-cost line will become "flatter" and intersect the labor axis at four days rather than five.

It soon becomes apparent that a change in an input price, and consequently the slope of an iso-cost, has the effect of changing the tangency

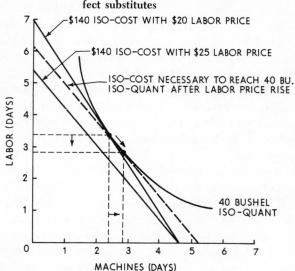

FIGURE 4–6.   Effect of an input price change on imperfect substitutes

point between the lowest possible iso-cost for a given iso-quant. This is illustrated in Figure 4–6. The increased price of labor has the effect of moving the tangency point down, along the iso-quant, away from the labor axis. All this means is that the producer avoids using as much of the higher priced input (labor) in favor of the relatively cheaper one (machines, in this example).

You might notice as well that it is no longer possible to reach the 40 bushel iso-quant with the $140 iso-cost line. The counter clockwise movement of this line due to the labor price increase has moved it away from the iso-quant. Now in order to reach the new tangency point it is necessary to increase total cost as illustrated by the new iso-cost (the dotted line) that runs parallel with the changed $140 line. Even though we conserve on the higher priced input, it is not possible to avoid a rise in total production costs for a given output.

We will be able to illustrate another important point by looking briefly at the affect of an input price change on each of the two extreme iso-quant shapes; the cases of perfect substitutes and perfect complements. The iso-quants representing perfect substitutes, you recall, are straight downward sloping lines. If we impose some iso-cost lines on this kind of iso-quant, as shown in Figure 4–7, the least-cost point can change drastically.

If initially hired labor and one's own labor are both worth $20 per day, no hired labor will be utilized. This happens because the lowest possible iso-cost line touches the 40 bushel iso-quant at a corner which corresponds to 4 days of own labor and zero hired labor. Now if the price put on one's own labor increases to say $40 per day, the iso-cost line changes slope such that after the price rise, the point of least cost intersects the iso-quant on the hired labor axis, corresponding to five days of hired labor and zero own labor. Also notice that the total cost of reaching the 40 bushel iso-quant increases.

An interesting special case occurs with perfect substitutes when the iso-cost line is exactly the same slope as the iso-quant and coincides with it.

FIGURE 4–7. Effect of input price change on perfect substitutes

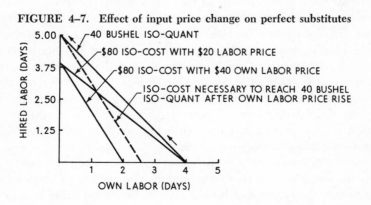

When such is the case it makes no difference what combination of the two inputs are used. All combinations are equally efficient. Also, in this case, an increase in the price of one of the inputs will not increase total cost for a given output. Although when the price of one input increases it now becomes necessary to again shift to employing all of the relatively cheaper input and none of the other.

At the other extreme, the case of perfect complements, a change in the price of either input, seeds or land in our example, has no effect on the combination of these two inputs employed. A change in slope of the iso-cost lines continues to touch the iso-quant at the corner of the rectangle, as shown in Figure 4–8. This is, of course, reasonable because no matter what the price of the inputs are, it is technically feasible only to use them in a certain fixed proportion. Although in this case, as in the others the total cost of obtaining a given output will increase if one or both of the input prices rise.

FIGURE 4–8. Effect of input price change on perfect complements

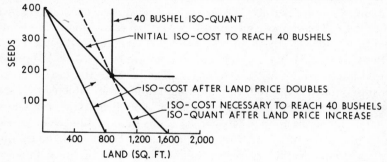

The most important point to be drawn from these examples is that the greater the possibility to substitute one input for another, the greater the effect of an input price change on the combination of inputs used. In the extreme case of perfect substitutes, there was a complete switch from all of one to all of the other. In the middle case of imperfect substitutes, there was some shift away from the more expensive input but not a complete flight. You might want to convince yourself, too, that the more gentle the curvature of the iso-quant, the greater change you will have from the more expensive to the less expensive input for a given input price change. Lastly, in the extreme case of perfect complements or rectangular iso-quants, a change in relative input prices has no effect on the combination of inputs employed to obtain a given level of output.

It is true, of course, that no producer can ever take the time to know exactly the shape and position of iso-quants that pertain to his production. Nevertheless, the concept of iso-quants and iso-costs enable him to organize his thoughts about production and as a consequence they are a valuable tool in making decisions about alternative input combinations in the world of ever-changing input prices.

MAIN POINTS OF CHAPTER 4

1. To be consistent it is necessary to view production in an all-inclusive context as an activity that creates present and/or future utility.
2. Most kinds of production utilize several inputs either at once or in some time sequence. Many inputs are themselves the product of some former production activity.
3. A useful way of grouping or classifying inputs is by dividing them into two categories: (1) fixed and (2) variable. Fixed inputs cannot be varied with the level of production whereas variable inputs can be varied according to the desired level of output.
4. A production function is a relationship between inputs and output. The quantity of output depends upon, or is a function of, the amount of inputs employed.
5. Marginal physical product (*MPP*) of an input is the additional output obtained by adding one more unit of a variable input.
6. According to the law of diminishing returns the marginal physical product of a variable input will at some point begin to decline as more and more of the variable input is added to one or more fixed inputs.
7. The level of average physical product (*APP*) of an input will increase as long as *MPP* is greater than *APP*. The level of *APP* declines when *MPP* is less than *APP*.
8. Economists have divided production into three stages. During stage I, *MPP* is greater than *APP*. In stage II *MPP* is less than *APP* but *MPP* is positive. In stage III *MPP* is a negative quantity.
9. Production should always be carried on somewhere within stage II, which includes the region of diminishing returns.
10. The use of two variable inputs is illustrated by iso-quants. An iso-quant, meaning equal quantity, denotes various combinations of the two variable inputs that will result in the same level of output. Iso-quants are analogous to indifference curves on the consumption side.
11. The shape of an iso-quant tells us the extent that one variable input can be substituted for the other. An iso-quant that is convex means that the two inputs are imperfect substitutes. The case of perfect substitution between inputs is illustrated by a straight downward sloping line whereas perfect complements are represented by rectangular shaped iso-quants.

12. An iso-cost line, meaning equal cost, denotes the various combinations of two variable inputs that cost a certain amount. Iso-cost lines are analogous to budget lines on the consumption side.

13. The point where an iso-quant just barely touches its lowest possible iso-cost line represents the combination of the variable inputs that minimize the production cost of that level of output.

14. A change in input prices generally leads to a change in the least-cost combination of inputs. The extent of this change depends upon the the substitution possibility between inputs which ranges from perfect substitutes (complete substitution) to perfect complements (no substitution). In the middle case of imperfect substitutes, the more gentle the curvature of the iso-quant the larger the change in the optimum combination of inputs that will occur for a given input price change.

QUESTIONS FOR THOUGHT AND DISCUSSION

1. In each of the following activities identify what is being produced (the output) and the major inputs employed.

   a) Preparing a meal.   e) Cleaning the house.
   b) Giving a haircut.   f) Going to college.
   c) Taking a plane ride.   g) Reading a book.
   d) Printing a newspaper.   h) Cutting the grass.

2. Identify as best you can the marginal physical product of your activities today.

3. Think of a specific activity you have been involved in where you experienced a diminishing marginal physical product of your own effort. Try to think of a case where your *MPP* has been negative.

4. For each of the following pairs of inputs and their respective production activity, draw an iso-quant that describes the kind of substitution possibility that you believe exists between the inputs.

   a) Your labor and mowing equipment to cut a lawn.
   b) Gasoline and your time in traveling 100 miles by automobile.
   c) Cotton and buttons in producing mens' shirts.
   d) Brown-shelled eggs and white-shelled eggs in producing an omelet.
   e) Your labor and equipment in clearing trees from a plot of land.

5. In most underdeveloped countries road construction is carried on by very labor intensive means, whereas in the United States this same activity utilizes giant earth movers, etc., with relatively little labor. From what you know about iso-quants and iso-costs can you offer an explanation for this difference in construction techniques? Make use of a diagram.

6. In the United States there has been a trend towards more factory-type construction of components of homes such as pre-cutting of materials, pre-assembling cabinets, etc. From the discussion of iso-quants and iso-costs would you expect this trend to continue? Explain.

7. Can you make a connection between the law of diminishing returns and the convex shape of iso-quants?

8. Explain why the tangency point between an iso-quant and the iso-cost line represents the least-cost combination of inputs.

9. Make a comparison between indifference curves and budget lines and iso-quants and iso-costs.

10. Explain the difference between *MPP* and *APP*. In what kind of units are they measured?

CHAPTER
5
PRODUCT SUPPLY

THE CONCEPT OF COSTS

As we proceed we will find that product supply is solely derived from or based upon production costs. It is important, therefore to thoroughly understand the concept of production costs before we can hope to understand product supply.

It will be useful to group production costs into two categories: (1) explicit or cash costs and (2) implicit costs. The first group, no doubt, is well known to all. Some examples of explicit costs are wages paid to hired labor, interest paid on borrowed money, rent on buildings, cost of supplies and raw materials purchased, etc. These are the costs that are paid for purchased inputs, whether they be fixed or variable.

Implicit costs, however, tend not to be so obvious or noticeable. These are the costs that should be charged to inputs that are provided by the firm or whomever is carrying out the production. A good example of implicit costs can be taken from the tomato-growing endeavor of the previous chapter. In this small-scale enterprise it is reasonable to believe that much of the labor would be provided by yourself. In calculating the total cost of growing a certain output of tomatoes it is necessary to include a charge for your own labor otherwise you will grossly underestimate the cost of your production. By not including the value of your own labor you could easily make the wrong decision when deciding whether or not to grow tomatoes in the first place or what is the most profitable quantity to produce.

A simple example will help make this clear. Suppose you anticipate that your cash or explicit cost of growing 20 bushels of tomatoes is $20 and that you will be able to sell the tomatoes for $2 per bushel. Thus you anticipate spending $20 and taking in $40. Will it pay you to grow tomatoes? On the surface it seems to be a profitable venture, you are left with $20 after paying your bills. But, you still haven't paid yourself. How much is your own labor worth?

The best way to determine the value of your own labor in a self-employed production activity is to determine the wage you could have earned in the best alternative open to you. For example, you might have been able to work part-time at a checkout counter in a grocery store for $2 per hour. If you put in three 8-hour days of labor to grow these 20 bushels of tomatoes, the implicit cost of your labor is $48. We can now summarize your total income and expense from growing 20 bushels of tomatoes:

Total income (20 bushels @ $2)...		$40
Explicit costs	$20	
Implicit costs	48	
Total costs		68
Net Income		−$28

Including the implicit cost of your own labor reduces the attractiveness of this tomato-growing venture considerably from what it first appeared. One way of looking at the outcome is that you paid $28 for the privilege of growing tomatoes. Or, looking at it from another viewpoint you were able to sell your labor for only $6.67 per day ($20/3) as a tomato grower whereas you could have sold your labor for $16 per day in the grocery store. Of course, this is only an example and is not meant to convey the idea that tomato growing is a losing proposition. The main point is that it is necessary to consider all costs, not just explicit costs, when deciding to produce or not to produce.

Quite possibly you have realized by now that the total cost (explicit plus implicit) of producing something depends very much on your alternative employment opportunities. If your only alternative to tomato growing is doing nothing then the implicit cost of your labor would be zero. In this case, the tomato venture reaps a $20 net income over costs. In this situation you would have to decide if $20 is enough to compensate you for the 3 days (24 hours) of leisure you forego.

Even if the grocery store employment, or any other job, is open to you, it is still necessary to decide whether the additional income of this job is sufficient to compensate you for any disadvantages it may have compared to tomator growing. For example, you may be the type of person who puts a high value on independence; you like to be your own boss. In this case, you might be willing to pay $9.33 a day for the privilege of doing what you like best. There is nothing irrational or wrong with choosing work that does not maximize your salary. It is important, though, that you realize how much it will cost you to work in more agreeable surroundings.

THE CONCEPT OF PROFITS

So far in the discussion we have avoided using the word profits. This is not because of any objection to the word but because it is another term in economics that can be given different meanings. Economists have divided profits into two categories: (1) normal profits and (2) pure profits.

Normal profits can be defined as the minimum return to inputs (capital or labor) owned by the firm or individual that is necessary to keep them in a given production activity. If all production activities were equally agreeable or disagreeable to people, normal profits would be the same thing as implicit costs. In this case, inputs or resources would tend to move to their best paying alternatives. In the tomato example just discussed, the normal profit would have been $48. As it was however, less than normal profits were earned. If tomato growing and working in the grocery store were equally attractive, it would be foolish to grow tomatoes and forego the extra $28.

As we pointed out, however, there may well be considerations other than earnings that influence the allocation of resources. These considerations probably are not very important for capital since machines or buildings do not experience psychic pleasure or pain. But people take non-monetary factors into consideration. Thus in the tomato example, normal profits might be either less than or greater than $48. They will be less if you like growing tomatoes and were willing to forego earnings to do so; or they may be more if you dislike this activity so much that you would be willing to work for less elsewhere.

Pure profits, on the other hand, is the return to a production activity over and above all costs (explicit and implicit). These profits would not have to be earned in order to hold resources in a given activity. This is not to say, of course, that producers do not care whether they earn pure profits. In fact it is the possibility of these profits that intice people to take risks and initiate the production of new products or services that just might turn out to be a bonanza and make them rich.

MARGINAL COST

We are now ready to derive the concept of product supply. It will be useful to continue using the tomato production example of the previous chapter. And it will be simplest to begin with the case of one variable input—your labor.

The foundation of product supply is marginal cost. Marginal cost is the additional cost of producing and selling one more unit of output. Or it is the reduction in total cost of reducing output by one unit. As the name marginal implies, it is concerned with the cost of the marginal or last unit of output.

In order to determine costs it is first necessary to assign prices to the inputs employed in the production process. You recall that two kinds or categories of inputs were employed: (1) fixed inputs and (2) variable inputs. If we assign prices to these inputs we have essentially two kinds of costs: (1) fixed costs and (2) variable costs that apply to these two categories of inputs respectively. Do not confuse this grouping with explicit and implicit costs. A fixed cost can be either implicit, explicit, or both. The same is true for a variable cost. It is important to recognize also that a fixed cost is one that does not vary with different levels of output. Variable costs, as the name implies, vary with the levels of output.

Assume that the fixed cost of the tomato production endeavor is $20. Consider this to be mostly land rent although it could well include a charge for seeds as well as some small garden tools. Assume also that the implicit cost of your own labor is $2 per hour or $16 per day. We now have the necessary data to calculate marginal cost (MC) for alternative levels of output.

The first two columns in Table 5–1 showing tomato output and labor inputs respectively are taken from Table 4–1 of the preceding chapter. Total variable cost (TVC) of the labor input obtained by multiplying days of labor times $16 is shown in column three. Total cost (TC) obtained by adding the $20 fixed cost to each level of variable cost is shown in column 4.

TABLE 5–1.   Illustrating total and marginal cost

Tomato Output (Bushels)	Labor Input (Days)	Total Variable Cost	Total Cost	Marginal Cost
0	0	$ 0	$ 20	——
1	1	16	36	$16.00
8	2	32	52	2.29
20	3	48	68	1.33
29	4	64	84	1.78
36	5	80	100	2.29
42	6	96	116	2.67
46	7	112	132	4.00
48	8	128	148	8.00

Marginal cost (MC), shown in the last column, is our main interest at the present. Recall that MC is the additional cost of obtaining one more unit of output. Note that even at zero units of output total cost is $20. Increasing output to one bushel, increases total cost to $36. Thus the marginal cost of this bushel is $16 (36 − 20).

As is so often the case in actual production situations it may not be possible to increase output by just one unit. In this illustration, for example, the second day of labor results in eight bushels of output or an increase in seven bushels over the output at one day of labor. All we can do in this case is to estimate the "average" marginal cost of the output in the range of one to eight bushels. This is obtained by employing a formula very similar to the one used to calculate *MPP*. The formula for *MC* is (the Δ symbol is an abreviation for "change in"):

$$MC = \frac{\Delta \text{ total cost}}{\Delta \text{ output}}$$

Employing this formula, we see that the change in total cost from 1 to 8 bushels is $16 (52 − 36) and the change in output is 7 (8 − 1), so the "average" marginal cost of an extra bushel in this range of output is $2.29 (16 ÷ 7) per bushel. You might try to calculate *MC* at the other levels of output to acquaint yourself with the calculation procedure.

It is interesting to notice that it is possible to calculate *MC* using either the total cost or total variable cost figures. Using the total variable cost figure we see that the *MC* of the first bushel is $16 − 0, or $16, just as it was using the total cost figure. Comparable answers are obtained at the other levels of output also. Thus an alternative formula for *MC* is

$$MC = \frac{\Delta \text{ total variable cost}}{\Delta \text{ output}}$$

It is not difficult to understand why the use of either *TC* or *TVC* results in the same *MC* when we recall that fixed cost remains the same at all levels of output. Thus changing output does not change fixed cost. In other words, the only cost that changes when output changes is total variable cost. As a consequence, fixed cost does not enter into the *MC* calculation.

MARGINAL COST AND MARGINAL PHYSICAL PRODUCT

As we see from Table 5–1, *MC* varies considerably over the range of output shown. It begins at a relatively high figure, $16, declines as output, increases, and reaches a minimum at 20 bushels of output or 3 days of labor. After that *MC* increases with larger levels of output. The behavior of the *MC* figures reminds us somewhat of the *MPP* figures in Chapter 4 (Table 4–1). Although with *MPP* the direction of movement is just opposite; *MPP* begins as a relatively small number, increases to a maximum and then declines.

The relationship between *MPP* and *MC* is shown more clearly in Figure 5–1. The line representing *MPP* is the same as shown in Figure 4–1 of the last chapter. *MPP* is graphed against the figures (bushels of tomatoes) on the left-hand vertical axis and the top set of figures (labor inputs) on the horizontal axis. *MC* is graphed against the cost figures on the right-hand vertical axis and the lower set of numbers (bushels of output) on the horizontal axis. The levels of output shown correspond to their respective labor inputs as presented in Table 4–1.

The most important characteristic of Figure 5–1 is that *MPP* reaches its peak just at the exact level of input, or output, where *MC* reaches its lowest value. This correspondence between *MC* and *MPP* is not a mere coincidence. Both are derived from the variable input—labor in this example. It is reasonable to expect, therefore, that the more productive labor is, the higher is its *MPP*, and the less costly it will be to obtain an additional unit of output.

FIGURE 5–1.   Relationship between *MPP* and *MC*

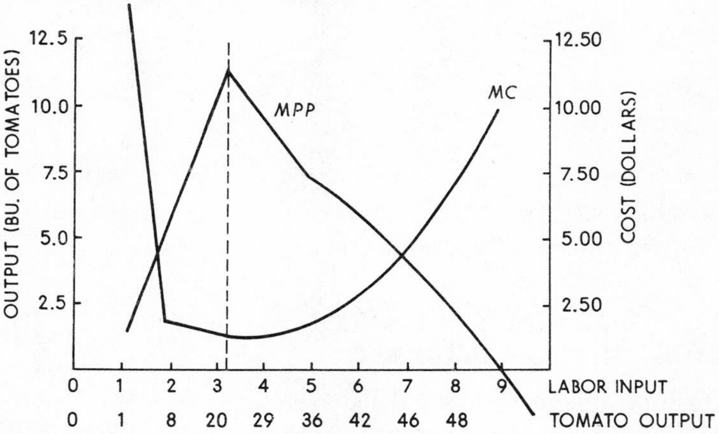

AVERAGE COSTS

In order to derive the concept of product supply it is necessary also to be familiar with the idea of average costs. We shall consider three types of average costs: (1) average fixed costs (*AFC*), (2) average variable costs (*AVC*), and (3) average total costs (*ATC*). As their names imply, each of these average costs are calculated by dividing their corresponding total cost figure by output. Specifically, average fixed cost is found by dividing total fixed cost by the level of output and average variable cost is obtained by dividing total variable cost by output. Average total cost can be calculated two ways: (1) dividing total cost by output or (2) by summing *AFC* and *AVC*.

Again it is easier to understand these measures of cost by looking at a specific example. Let us continue to use our tomato example. Recall that total fixed cost (land rent mainly) was $20 and that labor costs (variable cost) were $16 per day of labor input. The resulting average cost figures for this example is presented in Table 5–2.

Looking briefly at these average costs we see first that *AFC* becomes smaller at larger levels of output. We might expect this since fixed cost is spread across more units at larger output levels so each unit bears a smaller share of the cost. Perhaps most interesting is the behavior of *AVC* and *ATC*. Note first that *AVC* declines over a range of output, or inputs, reaches a minimum point and then begins to increase. The same pattern

TABLE 5–2.   Average fixed variable, and cost obtained from tomato production example

Tomato Output (Bushels)	Labor Input (Days)	AFC	AVC	ATC
1	1	$20.00	$16.00	$36.00
8	2	2.50	4.00	6.50
20	3	1.00	2.40	3.40
29	4	0.69	2.21	2.90
36	5	0.56	2.22	2.78
42	6	0.48	2.29	2.77
46	7	0.44	2.44	2.88
48	8	0.42	2.67	3.09

is observed for *ATC* only these figures continue to decline until a slightly larger output is reached before they begin to increase.

AVERAGE VARIABLE COST AND
AVERAGE PHYSICAL PRODUCT

We will be able to understand the average variable cost figures more thoroughly if we compare them with average physical product (*APP*) that we developed in Chapter 4. Recall that *APP* is total output (tomatoes in our example) divided by the variable input (labor). The relationship between *AVC* and *APP* is most easily seen in a diagram.

In Figure 5–2, the line representing *APP* is the same as shown in Figure 4–1. *APP* is graphed against the figures on the left-hand vertical axis (bushels of tomatoes) and the top set of numbers (labor input) on the horizontal axis. Also *AVC* is graphed against the cost figures on the right-hand vertical axis and the lower set of numbers (tomato output) on the horizontal axis. The levels of output shown correspond to their respective labor inputs as shown in Table 4–1.

The most important characteristic of Figure 5–2 is that *APP* reaches its peak at the exact level of inputs, or output, where *AVC* reaches its lowest value. Just as we noted about *MC* and *MPP*, the correspondence between *APP* and *AVC* is not a coincidence either. Both are derived from the variable input—labor. And the more productive the average unit of labor, the higher its *APP*, the lower will be the variable cost of an average unit of output.

Glancing back to Figure 4–1 again you will be reminded that stage II of the production process begins at the point where *APP* starts to decline. From Figure 5–2 we see that this also corresponds to the point where *AVC* begins to rise. Thus stage II begins at the minimum point of *AVC*.

FIGURE 5-2. Relationship between *APP* and *AVC*

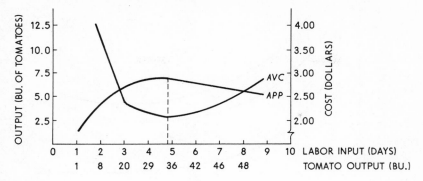

Keep this in mind because it will provide in part the reason why a rational profit maximizing producer will choose only to produce somewhere in stage II. It is best to defer the explanation, however, until after we have derived product supply.

MARGINAL AND AVERAGE COSTS

To fully understand the concept of product supply it is also necessary to understand the relationship between marginal and average costs. As in the previous relationships examined, they are easiest to see when represented by a diagram. In Figure 5-3, the three average costs and marginal cost are superimposed on the same diagram.

Perhaps the most important characteristic to note is that *MC* intersects both *AVC* and *ATC* at their minimum points. The explanation of this characteristic is essentially the same as we set forth for *MPP* intersecting *APP* at its maximum point. Namely, if the marginal unit is below the average, it will pull the average down, or if above the average, the average will be pulled up. The effect of this quarter's or semester's grade point average on your overall grade average was used as an example. If this quarter's grade average (the marginal quarter) is above the overall average, the overall average will improve, and vice versa.

Exactly the same reasoning applies to marginal and average costs. Marginal costs will continue to pull *AVC* and *ATC* lower and lower as long as *MC* is below the averages. Notice that *MC* can be increasing during this time as it is just left of the intersections with *AVC* and *ATC*. To the right of the intersections, *MC* is above the averages and henceforth pulls them up. It follows also from this reasoning that *MC* must intersect *AVC* and *ATC* at their minimum points.

Perhaps the most important thing to note about the average fixed cost curve is that it is not very important. When it is necessary to consider fixed costs they can be found in the average total cost figure. Recall that

FIGURE 5–3.   Relationship between marginal and average costs

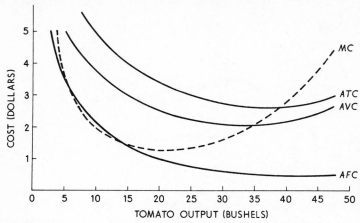

AFC equals ATC minus AVC. Or AFC at any given output is equal to the vertical distance between ATC and AVC at that level of output.

MARGINAL COST AND PRICE

We now come to one of the most important ideas in economics. Marginal cost, we know, is the additional cost of producing and selling one more unit of output. For a small, individual producer, such as we would be in our tomato production example, price of the output is equal to the additional income we receive when selling one more unit of output. In deciding whether or not to produce an extra or marginal unit both marginal cost and price must be considered.

If price is greater than marginal cost, the additional income obtained from the marginal unit will be greater than the additional expense incurred to produce and sell this unit. Whenever you can produce something where your income is greater than your expense, do it. This is the key to success in any production activity. On the other hand, if price is less than marginal cost, the additional income will be less than the additional expense. Your decision in this case should be not to produce this marginal unit.

Subject to some qualifications that will come up later we can formulate a rule: the profit maximizing level of output occurs exactly at the point where marginal cost is equal to price. This rule can be applied, however, only if marginal cost is increasing with increasing levels of output. (The reason will become clear shortly.) Thus if price is greater than MC and MC is increasing, you continue to increase output until you come to the point where price and MC are equal. If you go beyond this point so that price is less than MC you will lose money on each additional unit of output produced. So you will want to cut back until you reach the point where price equals marginal cost. In formulating this price equals marginal cost rule, we will discover shortly that we have essentially derived product supply.

PRODUCT SUPPLY: ONE VARIABLE INPUT

Product supply is defined as a relationship between price and quantity. Intuitively we would expect an individual producer to increase his level of output in response to higher and higher prices. Thus supply, like demand, is not a fixed quantity but rather a relationship between price and quantity.

It is not possible, therefore, to stipulate what level of output will be forthcoming until price is brought into the picture. Given the fact that you decide to produce tomatoes, for example, the number of bushels you produce would likely be different if you could sell each bushel for $10 than if a $2 price prevailed. Quite likely, at the $10 price you would treat your tomato plot with a great deal more tender loving care than at the lower $2 price. But the question remains, how much tender loving care?

The derivation of product supply is easily accomplished with a familiar diagram. Figure 5–4 is essentially the same as Figure 5–3 except that ATC has been deleted and some alternative prices, illustrated by the horizontal dotted lines, have been added. All we have to do is apply the price equal marginal cost rule to find out how much output will be forthcoming at various prices.

At the relatively high $4 price we see that the dotted line intersects the MC at 46 bushels of tomato output. Thus, at $4 quantity supplied is 46 bushels. At a lower price, say $3, the intersection of the line representing this price and MC corresponds to a smaller level of output—approximately 43 bushels. As we continue to lower price, the intersection between the price line and MC continues to move downwards and to the left, corresponding to smaller and smaller levels of output. We see, therefore, that our intuitive idea of supply, larger quantities at higher prices, is consistent with the more rigorous concepts of economics.

As we continue to move down along the MC curve with lower prices we soon reach the intersection of MC and ATC. Recall that this intersection corresponds to the lowest point of the ATC curve. As the name implies, average total cost is the average cost per unit of output of all output produced up to that point. For example, at 42 bushels of output the total cost per bushel averages $2.77 for these 42 bushels. Thus if price falls below $2.77 the total income received from total output will be less than the total cost of producing it. Hence a loss is incurred.

It is reasonable to believe, therefore, than in planning future output, no production will take place if price is expected to be below the minimum

FIGURE 5-4. Deriving product supply

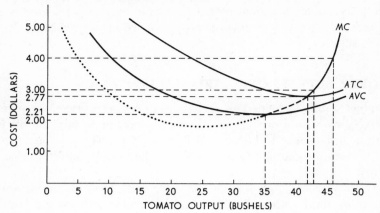

point on the average total cost curve. In the tomato production example we would decide not to rent the land and in so doing avoid the fixed costs.

Taking note of what we have done so far, we see that in planning future output the most profitable level of output at any given price corresponds to that output where price equals *MC*. In other words, the marginal cost curve above the *ATC* curve is really the product supply curve for an individual producer. All we have to do is label the vertical axis price instead of cost and we have the supply curve.

It is not unusual, however, to find situations where the producer either underestimates cost or overestimates price in planning future output. And in committing himself to anticipated future production he might have to incur a fixed cost that must be paid regardless of how much is produced. For example, the land rent for the tomato plot might have to be paid well in advance of the planting date. If anticipated price falls below the minimum point on the *ATC* curve after the fixed cost is incurred, will it pay to still produce and take a loss? The answer might well be yes. For in producing it might be possible to lose less than to not produce at all, paying the fixed costs.

If fixed costs are incurred that cannot be avoided, sometimes called "sunk" costs, it will pay to produce and take a loss as long as price is at least equal to or above the minimum point of the average variable cost curve. If this is the case then we are at least making back all of our variable costs plus some of the fixed costs depending on how much price is above this minimum point. Keep in mind that average fixed cost at any given output level is equal to the vertical distance between *ATC* and *AVC*. Thus if price is higher than *AVC* at the optimum level of output (prices equals *MC*) some of these fixed costs are being made back.

In view of the preceding discussion regarding fixed or "sunk" costs, it is necessary to revise slightly the definition of product supply. If it is impossible to avoid the fixed costs then product supply will consist of the MC curve down to the minimum point on the AVC curve. In Figure 5–4, this is represented by the continuous portion of MC above ATC as well as the broken line portion of MC that lies between AVC and ATC.

In no case will the supply curve extend below AVC. If price is below AVC then all the fixed costs are being lost as well as some of the variable costs. If it is not possible to make the variable costs back you will lose less by doing nothing.

STAGES OF PRODUCTION AND SUPPLY

Recall in Chapter 4 we defined three stages of production and also said that production would take place only in stage II. At that time we gave fairly convincing reasons why it would not be rational to produce in the area of increasing returns (the beginning of stage I) and the area of negative MPP (stage III). But it was not possible to adequately explain then why the last part of stage I (MPP decreasing but APP still increasing) was not a rational production area. The reason can now be easily seen.

Notice in Figure 5–4 that the MC curve turns upward some distance to the left of the point where it intersects AVC. Remember also that the MC curve is a mirror image of the MPP curve so that MPP turns down at the same point where MC turns up (Figure 5–1). But it is irrational to produce if price is less than AVC; thus production only takes place somewhere along the upward sloping portion of AVC, which you recall is comparable to the downward sloping portion of APP. Thus production is rational only in stage II. Figure 5–5 delineates the three stages of production as they correspond to the average and marginal cost curves.

Product supply, therefore, is also meaningful only in stage II. Here price intersects MC above the AVC curve. Moreover, unless there are fixed costs that cannot be avoided, production will be forthcoming only above the ATC curve which in turn means that we are well into the region of diminishing returns before it becomes profitable to produce.

PRODUCT SUPPLY: TWO VARIABLE INPUTS

In the preceding section we have derived product supply for one variable input. However, as we said in the latter part of Chapter 4, most production utilizes two or more inputs. And in Chapter 4, we illustrated how relative prices of these inputs would affect the combination used at any given level of output. Recall that the optimum (least-cost) combination of inputs for a given output level corresponded to the tangency point between the iso-quant and its lowest possible iso-cost.

FIGURE 5–5. Relationship: Stages of production and
cost curves

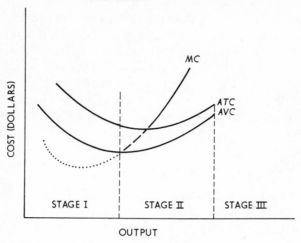

The iso-quant–iso-cost diagram illustrating the least-cost input combination (Figure 4–5 for example) is not particularly well suited, however, for deriving product supply. This is because the diagram contains no information on output price and marginal cost. And, product supply, you recall, is derived from these two items.

However, we might illustrate, schematically at least, how product supply relates to the iso-quant–iso-cost diagram. Moving upwards and to the right on this diagram represents a movement to higher iso-quants, or in other words to higher levels of output. To produce higher levels of output, of course, it is necessary to employ larger quantities of inputs or, in other words, move to higher iso-cost lines. Bearing in mind that marginal cost is the additional cost of one more unit of output, the iso-quant–iso-cost diagram provides sufficient information to compute MC.

In Figure 5–6 a few alternative levels of output, as represented by iso-quants, together with their corresponding iso-cost lines, are shown. At 20 bushels the lowest possible iso-cost line that is tangent to the 20 bushel iso-quant is $60. At 30 bushels, total cost increases to $75. In this range of output marginal cost is equal to:

$$MC = \frac{\Delta TC}{\Delta Q} = \frac{15}{10} = \$1.50$$

Similarly we could calculate MC for other changes in total cost and output. From 30 to 40 bushels, total cost increases to $92, resulting in a MC of $1.70, etc. If we calculate MC for many such changes we could trace out a MC curve such as shown in Figure 5–7. We also could calculate the average costs that correspond to each level of output and plot

FIGURE 5–6.   Deriving *MC* from iso-quants and iso-cost lines

FIGURE 5–7.   Illustrating marginal and average costs from Figure 5–6

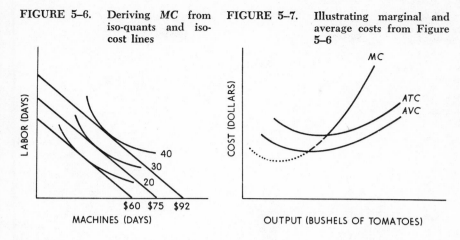

these as we did with *MC*. Thus product supply (*MC* above *AVC*) can be derived from the two variable input case just as for the simple case of one variable input.

Keep in mind, though, that we have not yet determined which of various possible levels of output will actually be produced. In order to know this we must first know the price that will prevail in the market. We will consider this topic very shortly in Chapter 6.

There is one fairly important characteristic of *MC*, or the supply curve if you like, that should be noted at this time. Notice in Figure 5–6 that the total cost figure associated with each level of output presumes that the most efficient combination of resources are used to produce that output. For example, other combinations of inputs could have produced 20 bushels of tomatoes, but they would have all costed more than $60. Thus at all points along a *MC* or supply curve we assume that the most efficient combination of inputs is used.

MARKET SUPPLY

As was true for demand, supply is most useful when considered in the context of the market. We can visualize the market supply curve as the sum of the supply curves of all individual producers. To obtain the market supply, therefore, we add at each price, the supply of all individual producers.

Taking a very simple example, suppose there are three producers in a market. The market supply in this case is just the sum of the three quantities supplied at each possible price. Figure 5–8 illustrates this example. Remember that the supply curve of each producer is also his *MC* curve so that the market supply is the sum of all individual *MC* curves.

FIGURE 5–8. Deriving market supply

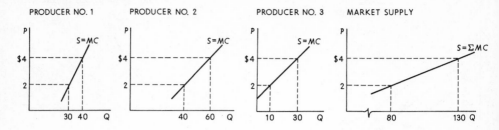

ELASTICITY OF SUPPLY

Thus far we have indicated only that product supply is an upward sloping line, meaning that producers are willing to produce larger amounts when they expect higher prices. But we have not considered how responsive producers are to a price change. Economists employ a concept known as elasticity of supply to measure the responsiveness of producers to a price change. We will see that this concept is very similar to price elasticity of demand, studied in Chapter 3.

Elasticity of supply (E_s) is defined as the percentage change in quantity supplied resulting from a 1 percent change in price. The formula for computing E_s is exactly the same as the price elasticity of demand formula, namely:

$$E_s = \frac{\dfrac{Q_0 - Q_1}{Q_0}}{\dfrac{P_0 - P_1}{P_0}}$$

Only in computing E_s, the quantities, Q_0 and Q_1, refer to beginning and ending quantity supplied rather than quantity demanded.

We might work out a simple example inserting the numbers in Figure 5–9 into the E_s formula. Let \$2 be the initial price, P_0, \$2.50 the new price, P_1, 100 the initial quantity, Q_0, and 150 the new quantity, Q_1. Carrying out the calculation we obtain:

$$E_s = \frac{\dfrac{100 - 150}{100}}{\dfrac{2.00 - 2.50}{2.00}} = \frac{\dfrac{-50}{100}}{\dfrac{-0.50}{2.00}} = \frac{-0.5}{-0.25} = 2$$

The elasticity coefficient of 2 in this example means that quantity changes by 2 percent for each 1 percent change in price.

Since the formula for computing E_s is the same as the price elasticity of demand formula, it suffers from some of the same problems. First, it is

FIGURE 5–9. Example for elasticity of supply
computation

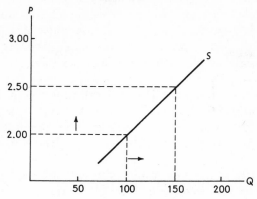

a "point" elasticity formula so it should be applied to only very small changes in price and quantity. In measuring E_s for actual products, economists use a statistical technique that measures very small changes. This technique is studied in intermediate level statistics courses and also in a specialized area of economics known as "econometrics."

Also, E_s varies in size along the supply curve again because the base values change. Although in the case of supply both price and quantity base values (P_0 and Q_0) change in the same direction. As you move up and out along the supply curve, the value of E_s approaches one. And at points low on the supply curve E_s approaches zero if the curve intersects the quantity axis and approaches infinity if it intersects the price axis. You may want to convince yourself of this by working out a few examples.

Economists also classify E_s similar to E_d. If E_s is less than one it is considered inelastic, whereas a supply elasticity coefficient greater than one is said to be elastic. And as E_s approaches zero, a vertical supply curve, E_s is described as highly inelastic. Similarly when it approaches infinity, a horizontal supply curve, E_s is described as highly elastic.

Unlike E_d, however, the size of E_s, whether it be elastic or inelastic, does not influence the direction of movement of total income ($P \times Q$) when price increases or decreases. That is, when price increases both P and Q increase so total income must go up. Similarly, total income declines when price declines because quantity also declines.

FACTORS INFLUENCING ELASTICITY OF SUPPLY

Not all products or production exhibit the same elasticity of supply. Some products exhibit a highly elastic supply; a slight change in price brings for a relatively large change in quantity. For others supply is highly inelastic; a price change has relatively little effect on quantity supplied. Why do we observe these differences in the size of E_s?

There are two major factors influencing the size of the elasticity of supply of a product: (1) the availability of substitute inputs that can be drawn away from other uses and (2) the time allowed for adjustment to take place. Regarding the first factor, if production of a product utilizes inputs that are commonly used to produce other products, it will tend to have a more elastic supply than one which uses specialized inputs suited only for its production.

For example, the supply of all agricultural products in the aggregate is found to be relatively inelastic. This is reasonable to expect since there is only so much agricultural land. If all agricultural prices increase, farmers can increase output somewhat only by using land substitutes such as fertilizer together with more intensive care. But the increase in output will not be nearly as large as would be true if additional land could be drawn from other uses into agricultural production.

Now for an individual agricultural product such as wheat, supply tends to be much more elastic because land and other inputs can be drawn away from other types of agricultural production. In fact, for most individual products or services, it is very hard to imagine examples of any input employed that does not exist in some form in another line of work.

Even the number of people with highly specialized training, such as economists or heart surgeons, could be increased substantially if prices of their services increased and there was freedom of entry into the field. This has, of course, happened in the case of economists; although the number of heart surgeons has not exhibited as large an increase because of restricted entry into the medical profession. Surely it is a serious mistake to underestimate the latent talents of people or the adaptability of resources to many different uses. Our experience during national emergencies such as World War II bears this out.

The second factor, time for adjustment, is important because most production activities cannot be changed in scale over night. Once a producer is committed to a certain level of output, relatively large changes in output level cannot be achieved until the level of fixed inputs can be changed. This may take from a few months in the case of retail trade to several years for heavy industry. Thus the longer time that is allowed for adjustment to a price change, the greater the change in output, hence the more elastic the supply.

There is a second dimension to the time for adjustment factor that is also very important: the length of time that the producer expects the price change to remain in effect. If a price change is expected to be only temporary, there is little incentive for a rational producer to change his level of output substantially. For changes in output often involve additional expense. To increase output he must purchase new equipment, buildings, etc., or to decrease production he might have to let fixed inputs remain idle but still bearing the fixed cost.

Thus month-to-month fluctuations in price would be expected to have only a minor effect on output. Since most producers do not have a crystal ball, any price change must stay in effect for some time before they began to expect price to remain at the new level. As an analogy, you generally do not bother to put on a heavy coat to pick up the morning paper on your door step on a cold day; but when you expect to stay out for an hour the bother of putting on the heavy coat is worth it.

MAIN POINTS OF CHAPTER 5

1. In measuring the cost of producing an item, both explicit and implicit costs should be included. Explicit costs are the normal cash expenses incurred in production whereas the implicit cost of an input is the wage that this input could have earned in the best alternative employment available.

2. A rational person may willingly choose not to work at a job that maximizes his salary. But it is important to know how much income is sacrificed to work in more agreeable surroundings.

3. Normal profits are defined as the minimum return to inputs owned by the firm necessary to keep them in a given production activity. If all jobs were equally agreeable or disagreeable, implicit costs would equal normal profits.

4. The possibility of pure profits provides the incentive for people to innovate and take risks and thus provide new products or services.

5. Marginal cost is the additional cost (explicit plus implicit) of producing and selling one more unit of output.

6. Variable costs vary with different levels of output, but fixed costs, as the name implies, remain the same regardless of the level of output.

7. Marginal costs are derived exclusively from variable costs.

8. Marginal cost and marginal physical product are mirror images of each other. In other words when MPP reaches its peak, MC bottoms out.

9. Average variable and average total cost exhibit the same U-shaped pattern as marginal costs. Both decline if MC is below them and both increase if MC is above. MC intersects AVC and ATC at their minimum points.

10. The same relationship exists between AVC and APP as between MC and MPP. AVC reaches a minimum point at the exact location where APP is at a maximum. Thus stage II begins at the minimum point of AVC.

11. For a small, individual producer the additional income derived from selling one more unit of output is equal to the price of the unit. Thus

if *MC* is less than price, there is an incentive to produce more because the additional income exceeds the additional cost. On the other hand, if *MC* exceeds price, there is an incentive to reduce output because the additional expense exceeds the additional income. Thus a producer maximizes profits (the difference between income and expense) at the point where *MC* equals price.

12. If a producer is not committed to any fixed costs, the supply curve of a firm is the same as the *MC* curve above the point where it intersects *ATC*. If there is a commitment to pay fixed costs, however, the supply curve is the same as the *MC* curve above the point where it intersects *AVC*.

13. Comparing supply with the stages of production, we see that the supply curve lies entirely in stage II, which is characterized at all points by diminishing returns.

14. The supply curve can also be derived from the iso-quant–iso-cost diagram for two variable inputs. All points along a supply curve represents tangency points between iso-costs and iso-quants.

15. Market supply is the summation of the supply of all individual producers at given prices.

16. Elasticity of supply is a measure of how responsive producers are to a price change. Its coefficient indicates the percentage change in quantity supplied for each 1 percent change in price.

17. The two major factors influencing elasticity of product supply are: (1) the availability of substitute inputs that can be drawn away from other production and (2) time for adjustment. The more substitute inputs that are available and the longer the time for adjustment, the more elastic the supply. There are two dimensions of the time factor. First, it is necessary for the price change to stay in effect long enough so that it is profitable to change the level of output and second there must be sufficient time to change physical facilities which will allow a change in scale of output.

QUESTIONS FOR THOUGHT AND DISCUSSION

1. "In the United States most food is produced on family owned and operated farms. This is a more efficient organization of production than plantation or corporation farms because family farms do not have to pay for most of the labor input." Comment.

2. Estimate your total cost of attending college this quarter or semester. Be sure to include implicit cost. Dividing total cost equally between all your courses, how much is this economics course costing you? How much per lecture? Is it worth it?

3. Occasionally we hear of high-salaried executives giving up lucrative careers in business to become ministers, teachers, politicians, etc. Is there any way that these people could justify their action on economic grounds or is it irrational from an economic point of view?

4. It is sometimes argued that a period of low prices and profits is good for an industry because it forces out the low-paid, unproductive, and inefficient people or firms. Comment on this argument keeping in mind what you know about implicit costs.

5. "Normal profits and implicit costs are the same thing." Comment.

6. "Since pure profits are not required to hold inputs or resources in a given production activity the government should pass a law that requires all pure profits to be taxed at a 100 percent rate." Comment.

7. In textbooks and classrooms marginal cost is traditionally represented as a U-shaped curve. Is it reasonable to expect MC to behave in this manner? Why or why not?

8. "Marginal cost has no relevance for large firms such as General Motors or U.S. Steel because it is impossible to conceive of just one extra unit of output for firms of this size." Comment.

9. If you were production manager for a company that produces ball point pens how would you go about determining your marginal cost? Would it be necessary to know what MC is? Why?

10. Is there any relationship between the law of diminishing returns and marginal cost? Explain.

11. "Sometimes it pays to produce even making a net loss." Comment.

12. Explain why the supply curve of a firm is the same thing as its marginal cost curve. Does the supply curve correspond to the entire MC curve? Explain.

13. Economists have said that the elasticity of supply of all food, taken in the aggregate, is very inelastic. What do they mean by this statement? Would you reasonably expect this to be true? Explain.

14. For many products the price fluctuates up and down from month to month. However producers do not vary their level of output very much in response to these price changes. From these observations we can conclude that the supply of these products is very inelastic and a significant and prolonged rise in price would not result in much change in quantity supplied. Comment.

CHAPTER
6

DEMAND AND SUPPLY
IN THE PRODUCT MARKET

Thus far we have been concerned with developing the concepts of demand and supply. Taken alone, however, these concepts have only limited usefulness. Granted of course, each of these concepts helps us to understand the motivations and actions of people in their roles as consumers and producers. But demand and supply become even more useful when used in conjunction with each other to explain past behavior of markets and predict future behavior.

EQUILIBRIUM IN THE MARKET

Our first task, then, is to combine demand and supply and develop the concept of equilibrium in the market. As you recall from Chapters 2 and 3 the demand of an individual consumer for a good or service is represented by a downward sloping line—the lower the price, the higher the quantity demanded. And market demand, the summation of the demand of individual consumers, also is represented by a downward sloping line. Essentially the same procedure was followed in Chapters 4 and 5 to derive product supply both for the individual producer and for the market. And product supply, you recall, is represented by an upward sloping line—the higher the price the larger the quantity supplied.

Let us now superimpose both demand and supply on the same diagram, as in Figure 6–1. The concepts of demand and supply are undoubtedly the most important and most used concepts in economics, which explains why diagrams resembling Figure 6–1 are so prevalent in economic literature. This will become apparent throughout the remainder of the book.

To understand what constitutes a market equilibrium, it is helpful to first consider a market that is not in equilibrium. Consider, first, the price P_0 in Figure 6–1. What would happen in a market for a good or service if this price prevailed? At this relatively high price you will note that a relatively small amount is demanded, Q_0^d in the diagram. On the other hand, a relatively large amount is supplied, Q_0^s in the diagram. Thus at price P_0, the quantity supplied is greater than the quantity demanded. Hence there will be a surplus in the market; more goods or services are offered for sale than are brought. Inventories pile up or people offering services remain underutilized. The inevitable result of this situation is a downward pressure on price. Sellers, in an attempt to dispose of this surplus, are forced to take a lower price.

Equilibrium is defined as a state of stability. Either there is a perfect offsetting of opposing forces or there are no forces present that can cause movement. It is evident, therefore, that the situation just described is not one of equilibrium. The surplus in the market sets up forces that exert a downward pressure on price.

Let us consider a second situation where the price is relatively low, say P_1 in Figure 6–1. Now we see that at price P_1 the quantity demanded, Q_1^d, is greater than the quantity supplied, Q_1^s. At such a low price there is an incentive for people to buy more of the good but at the same time there is relatively little incentive for producers to supply it. As a consequence there is a shortage; the product disappears from shelves, inventories are drawn down, or people providing services are swamped with customers. The inevitable result of this situation is an upward pressure on price.

**FIGURE 6–1. Demand and supply showing equilib-
rium price and quantity**

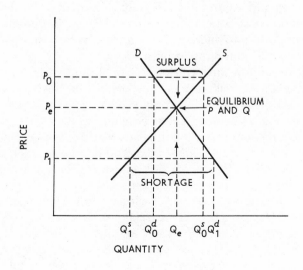

After all why sell your product at a low price when you can dispose of all you have at a higher price.

By now it is probably clear to you that there is only one price that will result in neither a surplus nor a shortage—P_e in Figure 6–1. At this price producers are willing to put quantity Q_e on the market and consumers or buyers are willing to buy this exact quantity at price P_e. Once the price finds this equilibrium point there is no pressure, either from a surplus or a shortage, to pull price down or push it up. For this reason the price and quantity corresponding to the intersection of the demand and supply curves are known as equilibrium price and quantity.

When using the concepts of supply and demand it is necessary to keep in mind that a market may not be in equilibrium at all times. In fact, in a dynamic, ever-changing economy such as the United States or any other free market country, equilibrium situations probably are the exception rather than the rule. The reason is that the equilibrium price is rarely known with certainty by both buyers and sellers. As a result there has to be a continual searching by both buyers and sellers for the price that entices buyers to take off the market the exact quantity that sellers offer.

If, for example, there is an accumulation of unsold goods or services, buyers or sellers, or both parties, know that price is too high and it must come down. Or if shortages are the rule then one or both parties know that price is too low and upward pressure on price will prevail. Thus there is a continual process of adjustment in most markets which results in small price movements towards the equilibrium. Or in some cases there may be an overshooting of the equilibrium. If price is above equilibrium and moving down it may come down too far and result in a shortage. In such cases there will be upward pressure on price which in turn might result in yet another overshooting of the equilibrium. At any rate it is this continual process of adjustment to equilibrium that is the distinguishing characteristic of most free markets rather than an instantaneous change from one equilibrium to another. We will discuss very shortly the factors that change equilibrium positions in markets.

The rapidity of adjustment towards equilibrium varies to some extent between different markets. In a market such as the stock exchange where both buyers and sellers are well informed about price and factors affecting the market, the adjustment to a new equilibrium may take only a matter of minutes. On the other hand, with goods that are seldom purchased and the exact price for a given quality difficult to determine, such as the retail market for eye glasses, the process of adjustment is slower and the time to reach equilibrium may run into years.

In spite of the time it takes to reach an equilibrium in a market, we might reasonably expect that the markets for all goods or services would if given enough time eventually reach equilibrium. If this happened then all prices would settle at their equilibrium values and never move again. But we know this does not happen; prices of most goods and services are generally on the move, rarely if ever settling at their equilibrium points. Why? The basic reason is that the equilibrium points are continually changing because of changes, or shifts, in the demand and/or supply curves. Let us now turn to a discussion of the meaning of a demand or supply shift and the factors that cause these shifts to take place.

A CHANGE OR SHIFT IN DEMAND

In Chapter 3 we saw that demand was a relationship between price and quantity. It was convenient to express this relationship by a demand curve —a downward sloping line. If the line moves to a different location on the diagram, we have what is termed a change or shift in demand, as shown in Figure 6–2.

FIGURE 6–2. Shifts in demand

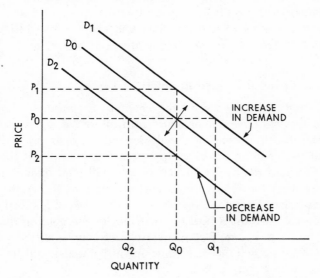

Think of D_0 in Figure 6–2 as a demand curve that exists for a good or service during some time period. Then suppose for some reason, which we will explain shortly, the demand changes position, say to D_1. This would represent an increase or an upward shift in demand. One way of interpreting this shift is that buyers will take more off the market at any given price. For example, with the original demand, D_0, quantity Q_0 is demanded at price P_0. Now with D_1 demanders will buy a larger quantity, Q_1, at price P_0. A second way of looking at an increase in demand is that demanders are willing to pay a higher price for a given quantity. With the increase in demand buyers will pay price P_1 for quantity Q_0. At the original demand buyers would only pay P_0 for this quantity.

The meaning of a decrease in demand, as illustrated by D_2, is strictly parallel to an increase. At a given price, say P_0, the quantity demanded declines from Q_0 to Q_2. Or, looking at it the second way, the price buyers will pay for quantity Q_0 declines from P_0 to P_2.

FACTORS SHIFTING PRODUCT DEMAND

Whenever you draw a demand curve for a product or conceive of such a curve, it is important to remember that everything that might possibly influence this relationship between price and quantity is held constant. We are forced to make this restriction because we are dealing with only a two-dimensional diagram. In other words we can consider only two items at a time. With demand these two items are price and quantity.

The world, of course, is never so kind as to hold everything constant other than the two items we are interested in. Things can and do change that influence the relationship between price and quantity. It is these outside influences that shift the demand, either increasing or decreasing it. There are a number of major factors that economists consider as important product demand shifters. These are:

1. Change in Prices of Related Products

A. Substitutes. As we saw in the chapter on consumer choice, most products or services have one or more substitutes. We know also that the quantity of substitutes consumed will depend on their price relative to the price of the good or service in question. For example, if the price of margarine declines relative to butter, people will tend to shift their purchases away from the relatively expensive butter to the relatively inexpensive margarine. Therefore a decrease in the price of a substitute good will decrease or shift downward the demand for the good in question, as illustrated by D_2 in Figure 6–2. Conversely, of course, an increase in the price of a substitute will increase (shift upward) the demand for the good in question, D_1 in Figure 6–2.

B. Complements. Not all pairs of goods are substitutes for each other. There are certain pairs of products, which we call complementary goods, that are consumed together. Bacon and eggs would be an example. If the price of eggs increases, people tend to have eggs for breakfast less frequently and as a consequence the quantity of bacon sold decreases. Thus the demand for bacon would decrease, D_2 in Figure 6–2, because of the increase in price of eggs, a complementary product.

2. Change in Consumer Incomes

For many products an increase in incomes of consumers results in an increase in the demand for these products. Some of the increase can come from using the product more frequently, such as having eggs more times per week, or from additional consumers coming into the market. For example, people tend to enter the Cadillac market as their incomes approach the 25 to 30 thousand dollars per year bracket. The more people there are in this income bracket, the greater the demand for Cadillacs. Economists refer to goods that increase in demand with higher incomes as superior goods. This name does not necessarily imply that such goods are made better or last longer than other goods. It is just a name for a category of goods or services.

There are examples of other goods or services that decrease in demand as incomes increase. For example, people tend to buy less of the starchy, high calorie foods as their incomes grow. With higher incomes they buy more steak, fruit, and fresh vegetables. Thus the demand for starchy foods declines, shifts to the left, as incomes increase. Economists refer to these goods or services as "inferior" goods, again without any intention to describe the durability or quality of the good.

It is possible to find, as well, goods whose demand does not change at all with an increase in consumer incomes. One example, is the aggregate demand for all food in the United States. Because of the relatively high incomes enjoyed by a large part of the U.S. population, food consumption for most people is already at a maximum. For some, food consumption is even too high, causing weight problems. Thus with continued increase in incomes people tend to buy about the same quantity of food while increasing their purchases of other amenities of life.

In order to measure the response of consumers to a change in income, economists have developed a measure, similar to price elasticity of demand, known as income elasticity of demand. Income elasticity measures the percent change in quantity demanded resulting from 1 percent change in income, holding price constant. This measure can be illustrated by Figure 6–2. Suppose demand shifts to D_1 because of an increase in family income, say from \$6,000 to \$7,000 per year. Because of this shift, there is an increase in quantity at any given price. For example, at P_0 quantity increases from Q_0 to Q_1. The formula for calculating income elasticity of demand (E_i) is given below. I_0 and I_1 refer to per capita or per family income at the beginning and end of the time period respectively. Q_0 and Q_1 refer to beginning and ending quantities demanded.

$$E_i = \frac{\dfrac{Q_0 - Q_1}{Q_0}}{\dfrac{I_0 - I_1}{I_0}}$$

Because demand can either increase, decrease, or remain the same with changes in income, income elasticity can be a positive number, a negative number, or zero. If demand increases, shifts to the right, with an increase in income, income elasticity is positive. Thus a superior good has a positive income elasticity. The opposite is true for an inferior good, where demand shifts left with an increase in income and the resulting income elasticity is negative. If there is no change in quantity with a change in income, E_i is zero.

3. Change in Consumer Expectations
regarding Future Prices and Incomes

Since no one knows the future with certainty, our actions at the present are influenced a great deal by what we expect the future to bring. This is quite important in the case of product demand. If, for example, you expect a product to be scarce and high priced in the future, you will likely increase your purchases (demand) at the present in order to avoid the higher future price. Thus an expected higher price will likely result in a shift to the right in demand, as illustrated by D_1 in Figure 6–2. Expecting a lower price in the future will, of course, have the opposite effect; present demand will decrease such as D_2 in Figure 6–2 as buyers wait for more favorable prices.

Anticipated changes in income also tend to affect present demand. If you expected a rich uncle to leave you a million dollars in one or two years, you would likely be a little more liberal in your spending habits even now well in advance of the date you actually receive the money. Thus your demand for many products or services would shift to the right as is shown by D_1 in Figure 6–2. Or if you expect your present source of income to dry up, you no doubt would become more frugal, meaning that your demand for some items shifts left.

It is important to realize that current demand depends very heavily on your long-run expected income. College students illustrate this idea very well. They tend to enjoy a considerably higher standard of living while going to college than people with similar incomes but without much hope of substantial raises in the future.

4. Changes in Tastes and Preferences

There are a few products or services whose demand is influenced by the changing whims or fancies of consumers. Mainly these are the fads or items that often change in fashion or style. For example, there is not much demand nowadays for dresses that extend to the ankle. Nor is the demand for high-button shoes very large. On the other hand, there seems to be a resurgence in demand for wide neckties and double-breasted suits. In economic terms, the demand for goods that are no longer "in" shifts to the left, as in D_2, whereas the demand for items that "are in" shift to the right, D_1 in Figure 6–2.

5. Changes in Population

As we said in Chapter 3, the market demand for a good or service is made up of the sum of all individual demands. Thus the greater number of individuals in the market, the greater is market demand. Population growth, therefore, is an important factor shifting the demand to the right, such as, D_1 in Figure 6–2. For example, population growth is about the only factor shifting the demand for all food to the right. In fact the demand for most goods and services is being shifted steadily to the right because of growth in the size of the population.

A CHANGE OR SHIFT IN PRODUCT SUPPLY

In Chapter 5 we saw that supply is derived from marginal cost and, similar to demand, is defined as a relationship between price and quantity. Supply is conveniently represented by an upward sloping line, indicating a larger quantity supplied at higher prices. Just as is true for demand, representing a supply curve by a two-dimensional diagram makes it necessary to hold constant the other factors that can affect supply. If these factors do not remain constant, which is usually the case, there will be a shift in the supply curve from one position to another. Both an increase and a decrease in supply are illustrated in Figure 6–3.

FIGURE 6–3.   Shifts in supply

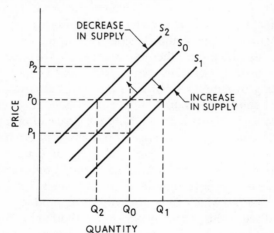

An increase in supply, illustrated by a shift from S_0 to S_1 in Figure 6–3, has two meanings. First, at a given price, say P_0, producers will offer a larger quantity on the market: Q_1 instead of Q_0. A second way of interpreting an increase in supply is that producers will supply the same quantity, say Q_0, at a lower price. Both ways of looking at an increase in supply have the same meaning.

The meaning of a decrease in supply, as illustrated by S_2 in Figure 6–3, is strictly parallel to an increase. At a given price, say P_0, the quantity supplied declines from Q_0 to Q_2. Or, looking at it the second way, the price suppliers will require for quantity Q_0 increases from P_0 to P_2.

FACTORS SHIFTING PRODUCT SUPPLY

Let us now consider the major factors that shift product supply. These are:

1. Change in Prices of Inputs

As we saw in Chapter 5, product supply is really the same thing as marginal cost. Thus anything that changes production costs should eventually change supply. If, for example, there is an increase in the price of labor, total variable cost of a given output will increase, which in turn will have the effect of increasing marginal cost—the cost of an extra unit of output. Thus an increase in input prices or cost has the effect of decreasing supply, shifting it upwards and to the left as shown by S_2 in Figure 6–3. Conversely a decrease in input prices will increase supply or shift it to the right, S_1 in Figure 6–3.

Keep in mind, as well, that marginal cost includes implicit as well as explicit costs. Thus any change in employment opportunities in other lines of work will affect the supply of a given product. For example, the supply of tomatoes in our example would decline with an increase in supermarket wages. We must be aware, therefore, of the interdependence that exists between industries regarding wages, costs, and supply.

It is interesting to note also that a change in fixed costs will not shift marginal cost or short-run product supply. This is because marginal cost reflects only *changes* in costs between different levels of output, and fixed cost, by definition, does not change as output changes. A change in fixed cost, however, does shift the average total cost curve upward and as a result the minimum price that will insure a normal profit rises. Thus after producers are able to relieve themselves of any sunk cost commitments, the minimum price at which they are willing to produce anything will rise. We will discuss this phenomenon more thoroughly in Chapter 7 when we take up long-run adjustment by a competitive industry.

2. Change in Price of Other Products

Most inputs, including labor, can be employed in any one of a number of production activities. If the price of an alternative product that can be produced increases, there is an incentive for producers to shift out of former lines of production into the production of the good that has risen in price. Not to do so would mean that producers deliberately forego higher incomes. For example, in our tomato-growing endeavor, the decision to grow tomatoes would depend upon the price of sweet corn, strawberries, beans, etc. If we could sell our labor for $3 per hour growing sweet corn, why should we grow tomatoes if this activity only returns $2 per hour? Thus an increase in prices of other products tends to decrease, shift to the left, the supply of the product in question. Of course, the converse is also true.

3. Change in Producer Expectations of Future Prices

Since producers are human beings and therefore cannot know the future with certainty, many of their present production decisions are based upon what they believe will happen in the future. If producers have a reason to expect changes in future prices, either in the prices of the product they presently produce and prices of products they could produce, they will likely begin to adjust their production capacity. But it is not possible to generalize across all situations the effect of, say, an expected increase in price. Each situation must be analyzed separately. For example, if the product can be stored, an expectation of higher future prices, either for this product or alternative products, will lead to a reduction in the present supply. Of course, the expected price increase must at least compensate for storage costs.

For products that cannot be stored, such as tomatoes, the expectation of higher future prices will most likely lead to an increase in present supply as producers begin to expand capacity for the future.

A very important item to keep in mind, also, is the expected duration of a price change. If producers expect only a temporary rise in future prices they will be less willing to make extensive changes in productive capacity than if they expect higher prices to prevail for many years. Thus the magnitude of the supply shift will depend upon the length of time the expected price change is expected to stay in effect. If the expected duration is short, the supply shift will be small and vice versa.

4. Change in Technology

In general new technology has the effect of making presently used inputs more productive or creating new inputs that are more productive than the old. Either or both of these effects results in higher productivity. Proceeding one step further, we can define higher productivity as decreasing the cost of a given level of output, say Q_0 in Figure 6–3; or increasing the level of output for a given cost such as P_0 in Figure 6–3. And you will recognize that either of these changes describe an increase in product supply. Thus new technology has the effect of always increasing supply. We will go into more detail on technology in Chapter 12 where we discuss the economics of research and new technology.

5. Change in Number of Producers

As we stated in Chapter 5, the market supply of a good or service is just the summation of the supplies of all individual producers. Thus the more producers there are of a given size the greater will be supply. Thus as the population and the economy grows the growth in number of firms shifts product supply for many goods and services to the right. Of course, if the average size of firm increases substantially there can be an increase in supply even with a reduction in number of firms. United States agriculture is a good example of this phenomenon.

RISING MARKET PRICE

After considering the many factors that can shift demand and supply, five for each, it is not surprising to observe a great deal of price change taking place in product markets. Everytime there is a shift in either demand or supply a new equilibrium price is established which set in motion forces that tend to either push price up or pull it down towards a new equilibrium. And as price moves, so do the quantities demanded and supplied. Let us now explore in some detail the factors or combination of factors that can lead to a rising market price for a good or service.

In a nutshell, any factor that increases demand, decreases supply, or some combination of the two, can result in a price increase. The simplest cases, an increase in demand or a decrease in supply, are illustrated in Figures 6–4 (A) and (B) respectively. The increase in demand can be caused by any one or all of the five factors that shift demand such as rising consumer incomes, expectation of increased incomes or prices in

FIGURE 6–4.   Illustrating a rising market price

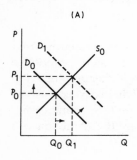
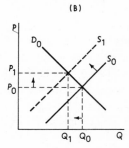
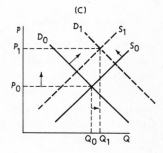

the future, higher prices of substitutes goods, a larger population, or some unexplained preference shift toward this product. We must remember that in many situations two or more of these demand shifters can be operating at the same time. Moreover, some of these demand shifters might serve to decrease demand, and in so doing nullify or at least mitigate the upward shift of the other factors.

A decrease, or leftward shift in supply, as shown in Figure 6–4 (B) above, can also cause a rise in market price. Again, any one of the supply shifters mentioned earlier, with the exception of technological change, can decrease supply and in so doing create a new, higher equilibrium price. Factors including higher input prices, higher prices of other products that can be produced, expected higher future prices of storable goods, or an exodus of suppliers, all can result in a higher market price of a good or service.

There is no reason, of course, to believe that demand and supply shifters must operate separately from each other. Although a demand shift, per se does not cause a supply shift, and vice versa, both sets of shifters can and do operate at the same time in the same market. If the demand shifters increase demand and the supply shifters decrease supply, as shown in diagram (C) of Figure 6–4, then both sets of circumstances will lead to an increase in market price. In situations such as these, the price rise is usually substantial.

You might have noticed by now that a rising market price can be associated with either an increase, a decrease, or little if any change in quantity. These situations are illustrated in diagrams (A), (B), and (C) above. If there is only an increase in demand, equilibrium quantity will increase; with only a supply decrease, equilibrium quantity will decrease. If both an increase in demand and a decrease in supply take place at the same time, it is impossible to predict what will happen to equilibrium quantity. If the demand increase dominates, quantity will increase, whereas if the supply decrease is most important, quantity will decrease. It is certainly possible that both factors could cancel each other out so equilibrium quantity remains the same.

The existence of simultaneous shifts in both demand and supply has caused many people to draw erroneous conclusions about the responsiveness of consumers or producers to a price change. We can observe a price increase, for example, with little or no change in quantity exchanged as in diagram (C) of Figure 6–4. As a result some have argued that demand in many markets is almost perfectly inelastic (price has little or no effect on quantity demanded) while others have said that supply is close to perfectly inelastic (price has little no no effect on quantity supplied). In reality both are wrong if the situation resembles the one depicted in diagram (C) of Figure 6–4. In working with demand and supply it is fully as important to know of the shifts that can take place as it is to know about the elasticity of demand and supply.

FALLING MARKET PRICE

We need not go through the same detail in explaining a falling market price. The same demand and supply shifters causing demand to decrease, supply to increase, or some combination of the two can lead to a lower price of a good or service. Moreover we can observe a decrease, an increase, or no change in quantity with these shifts just as we saw in the previous section. You might want to prove this to yourself by drawing these demand and supply diagrams on a scratch paper.

Of these 10 demand and supply shifters, there is one, a change in technology, which shifts supply only one way—to the right. The reason, as we explained earlier, is because increasing productivity reduces costs and allows suppliers to sell a given quantity for a lower price. Thus technological change has the effect of reducing market price, or at least making price lower than it would otherwise have been.

The effect of technological change, or the lack of it, is quite noticeable in the U.S. economy in the present. A few products, such as poultry meat, actually sell for a lower price today than 30 years ago, in spite of the inflation that has taken place. The primary reason is the decrease in production costs, hence increase in supply, brought about by new technology.

On the other hand, in some industries, particularly the service industries, technological change has been slower. This is an important reason for the rapidly increasing costs of schooling. As yet educators have not been very successful in increasing teaching productivity in schools and colleges, while improving or even maintaining quality of instruction.

GOVERNMENT IN THE MARKET

Society has seen fit to intervene in most markets through the vehicle of direct government action or laws. There is a great deal of disagreement between people about the desirability of government in the market. People with a fairly conservative political outlook in general argue that markets are capable of running themselves, or at least there is little need for more intervention. Those of a more liberal political attitude will in general defend the role of government in the market.

We will not attempt here to argue one point of view over the other. Instead we will attempt to identify and briefly evaluate the effects of some of the major governmental action that has affected markets so that you will be better able to formulate your own opinions on the proper role of government in the market.

ESTABLISHING THE "RULES OF THE GAME"

Although we will not dwell at length on the legal aspects of product markets, we should be aware that in order for any market to function properly both buyers and sellers must obey certain rules. An important function of the government in any market is to establish basic rules of behavior and enforce them.

Perhaps most basic is the law requiring buyers to pay sellers for goods purchased or services rendered. For many people this rule would not be necessary; payment of one's debts for many is a matter of personal integrity. But for others payment would not be forthcoming unless the threat of legal action and punishment existed. A few people of course still attempt to gain ownership without payment; we call these people thieves.

Without reasonable assurance of payment for goods or services, sellers of course would find it virtually impossible to remain in business. Those that did remain would be required to charge higher prices so that the people who paid would cover the loss of those who did not. Needless to say, a market characterized by gross nonpayment by buyers would soon break down. The honest people would quickly grow tired of paying for the goods and services consumed by their dishonest neighbors.

A second important role of government regarding the operation of the market is to provide information to buyers about products or to require that this information be available to prospective buyers. As we saw in Chapter 2, a consumer maximizes utility by equating marginal utility per dollar for each good purchased. If information about the product or its price is lacking or wrong, it is not possible to compare the MU per dollar of the product against possible alternatives. Most all of us have purchased goods or services that we would not have bought had we known its true characteristics or price.

The recent truth in packaging and truth in lending legislation are attempts to improve buyer information in the market. As a rule it is much easier and more successful to provide buyers with correct information and let competition take its course than to attempt to closely regulate sellers.

Government also is active in setting standards and testing products before they are put on the market. This is particularly important for potentially harmful items such as drugs and food. Granted harmful products would eventually come to the attention of buyers and be forced off the market. But needless injury or death is avoided if these products can be identified beforehand.

CEILING PRICES

There are times, generally during war, when society believes that the prices of certain goods or services are too high. This belief probably stems from the idea that excessive pure profits are being earned in the production or supply of these items. As a consequence the government may enact legislation that establishes maximum prices of certain goods or services, making it illegal for suppliers to sell any of the regulated items for a higher price.

The prices that are established are known as "ceiling prices" because the selling price is not supposed to rise above this maximum. The ceiling price is of course below the market equilibrium otherwise it would not be a ceiling or have any effect in the market. What are the consequences of a ceiling price?

This question can be most easily answered by the use of the traditional demand-supply diagram, as in Figure 6–5. Let P_c represent the ceiling price which is below the market equilibrium, P_e. You will note at P_c that quantity demanded, Q_d, is greater than quantity supplied, Q_s. At price P_c, people want to buy more than is being offered for sale. Thus some buyers will have to settle for less than they would like. How should the available supply be allocated?

FIGURE 6–5. Ceiling price in a market

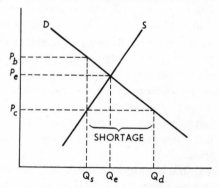

One option open to the government is to allocate the available quantity on a first-come, first-served basis. The problem with this approach is that it is very wasteful. Countless hours of time are spent by people standing in line as they are forced to do in order to obtain a portion of the scarce item. The total output of goods and services to society could be increased if people devoted their energies to production rather than to standing in line, or attempting to bribe the distributors of the product.

An alternative and more efficient method of allocating the available output is to issue ration stamps more or less equally among the population. Although many people cannot buy as much as they like under this scheme, at least there is a little for everyone and also it eliminates a large part of wasted effort mentioned earlier. At any rate, it is important to recognize that a ceiling price inevitably creates a shortage in the market and as a consequence makes it necessary to impose some sort of rationing scheme.

A second important side effect of a ceiling price is that it reduces the quantity produced of the already scarce commodity. As you can see in

Figure 6–5, before the ceiling price output is at Q_e whereas after the ceiling is imposed output declines to Q_s. This happens because the lower price provides an incentive for suppliers to reduce their production of the good or service in question, perhaps increasing their output of nonregulated items.

Because of food shortages and subsequent high food prices the governments of numerous developing nations have used ceiling prices on food as a device to hold down inflation. However, from our analysis of the effect of ceiling prices it is quite evident that such policy only makes the problem worse by reducing even more their meager output of food. Low food prices also reduce the incentive for public and private research agencies to provide new technology for agriculture and as a result there is relatively little increase (shift) in the supply curve of food.

A third effect of a government imposed ceiling price is the creation of a so-called "black-market" where some people desiring a larger amount than their quota are willing to pay a very high price in order to obtain it. The exact "black-market" price can be determined from Figure 6–5. At quantity Q_s the demand curve tells us that people are willing to pay P_b. However this price is illegal because it is above the ceiling which probably explains why it is called the "black-market" price. You might notice, as well, that the black-market price is substantially above market equilibrium price, P_e. Thus the black-market price is not a valid indicator of the price that would prevail without the price ceiling.

SUPPORT PRICES

In other situations society has decided that prices of certain items are too low and as a result government action is undertaken to keep prices above the market equilibrium. The motivation for this action generally stems from a belief that producers of the supported products suffer from low incomes and that raising the price of the products they sell will in turn raise their incomes.

The effect of a support price in the market can be seen by use of a demand-supply diagram, Figure 6–6. At the support price, P_s, you will note that the quantity supplied, Q_s, exceeds the quantity demanded, Q_d. As a result there is a surplus in the market which amounts to the difference between Q_s and Q_d. The only way the government can maintain the support price, therefore, is to buy up this surplus and keep it off the market. Otherwise the excess output will exert a downward pressure on price and drive it down towards the equilibrium.

The best example of support prices and their effects can be seen in U.S. agriculture as well as the agriculture of many other developed nations. The clusters of large round grain bins that we used to observe along the highways of the country are evidence of this surplus. In recent years

FIGURE 6–6.   Support price in the market

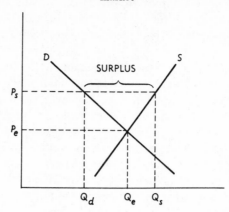

the surplus has become less noticeable as the government began paying farmers to store the surplus production on their farms.

You will note also that the existence of a support price provides an incentive for producers to produce even more of the already over-abundant product; at the equilibrium price Q_e is supplied whereas at the higher support price Q_s is offered for sale. In an attempt to reduce this surplus the government has restricted the use of land by those producers who wish to sell at the higher support price. Unfortunately restricting land has not been a very successful means of restricting output because producers have been able to increase output by increasing the use of inputs that substitute for land, particularly fertilizer and improved varieties of crops.

The ability of support price programs to substantially increase the income of producers who really need help is increasingly being questioned. Support price programs in general have not been effective as an income supporting scheme because the low income producers tend to be the small producers. Doubling the price of wheat from one to two dollars per bushel only adds $500 per year to the income of a 500 bushel per year producer but adds $20,000 per year to a 20,000 bushel producer. Thus price support programs have a tendency to help higher income producers relatively more than their low income counterparts.

SALES AND EXCISE TAXES

A common method of obtaining revenue by governments, both state and federal, is through sales and excise taxes. By in large these taxes are levied as a percentage of the selling price of the goods or services they cover. Some items, particularly things that society regards as luxuries or nonessentials may be covered by more than one such tax; new automobiles, for example, are covered by a federal excise tax plus in many states a state sales tax. Other items such as food and clothing may be taxed at a lower rate or not at all.

The effect of sales and excise taxes can also be evaluated by the simple demand-supply diagram. A convenient way of thinking about a sales or excise tax is that it increases the price of a given quantity of the item taxed. In other words, we can think of a sales or excise tax as decreasing supply or shifting the market supply curve upwards and to the left. Because of the tax a given quantity will cost more to buy. The imposition of such a tax is illustrated in Figure 6–7 where the supply curve after the tax is represented by S_1.

Notice, first, that the market equilibrium price increases from P_e to P_d after the tax is imposed. But it is also important to recognize that with a downward sloping demand and an upward sloping supply, the price rise to consumers is less than the amount of the tax. From Figure 6–7 we see that the amount of the tax at quantity Q_t is equal to the distance from P_s to P_d on the vertical axis. This is the amount that the supply curve has been shifted up because of the tax.

However we see also that the price producers obtain after the tax, P_s, is less than the initial equilibrium price, P_e. Thus consumers pay more after the tax and producers receive less. The amount of the tax borne by consumers therefore is equal to the distance between P_e and P_d, while the amount borne by producers is equal to the distance between P_e and P_s.

FIGURE 6–7. Effect of a sales or excise tax

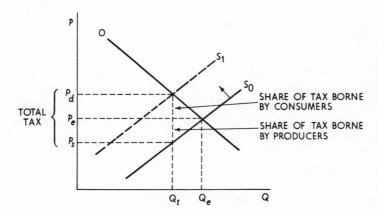

Notice as well that the quantity produced after the tax declines to Q_t. This is reasonable to expect because if producers receive a lower price there is an incentive to reduce output of this item and produce more of something else. We will see in the following two chapters that any distortion in the market, such as a sales or excise tax, causes a reduction in the value of output to society from a given amount of resources employed.

An intuitive explanation for this outcome is that resources are pushed into lines of production whose products are valued by society less highly than the taxed item. But let us postpone a more thorough explanation of this until the end of Chapter 7.

ILLEGAL GOODS OR SERVICES

Most societies enact laws that forbid the use of certain goods or services. Laws of this kind generally stem from the belief that consumption of the illegal items either harms the individual that consumes them or people he comes in contact with. Examples of illegal goods and services in the United States at the present time include such things as the mind-distorting drugs, pornographic literature, prostitution, and abortion. Unfortunately passing a law against the use of a good or service does not eliminate the demand for it. Indeed, there would be no need for such a law in the first place if the demand for the good or service did not exist.

Just as for any other good or service, we can visualize both a supply and demand for the illegal item. We have no reason to believe that its demand curve will not slope downwards and to the right as any other market demand curve. There probably will not be as many demanders in such a market because most people do not buy illegal items. Moreover, as the equilibrium price increases we expect the number of people who buy in these markets to decline; also we expect the quantity demanded per person to decline.

Regarding market supply, there is no reason to believe that higher prices will not bring forth additional quantities. As long as there is a demand for the illegal item there will always be willing enterprenuers ready to supply it for a profit. And as prices increase so do profits which provides even more incentive for the illicit suppliers to do their thing.

Although the market demand and supply of illegal goods and services can be represented by the traditional downward sloping and upward sloping lines respectively, there is one important consideration that is not present for legal goods and services—the penalty for getting caught. We can think of the penalty as a demand shifter if it applies only to the person consuming the good or service. If the penalty only applies to the supplier, it will primarily be a supply shifter. And if it applies to both parties we would expect the penalty to shift both demand and supply.

In general, the imposition of a penalty or an increase in the harshness of the penalty will decrease (shift to the left) the demand, supply, or both. For example, imposing a "slap on the wrist" or a suspended sentence will not decrease the demand for marijuana nearly as much as a certain five-year prison term. Thus we can expect that increasing the harshness of the penalty on buyers will shift demand to the left, reducing market price and quantity exchanged, as illustrated in Figure 6-8 (A).

On the other hand, if there is a increase in the penalty on suppliers we can expect a decrease in supply. For example, many "ladies of the evening" likely would find alternative ways of making a living if the penalty of the trade consisted of a $1,000 fine compared to a $100 fine. The effect of a penalty on suppliers is illustrated in Figure 6–8 (B).

FIGURE 6–8. **The effects of penalties in the market for illegal goods and services**

(A) PENALTY ON THE CONSUMER

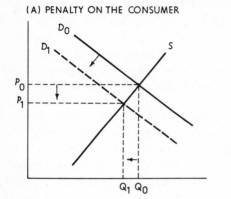

(B) PENALTY ON THE SUPPLIER

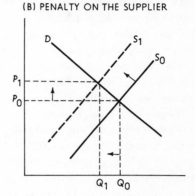

Although a penalty on either the demander or supplier will decrease the quantity of an illegal good or service, we can see that the price change will depend on who is penalized. Goods or services where only the supplier is penalized will tend to have a higher price than would exist in a free market. Most illegal goods or services fit this description. Imposing a penalty on consumers will tend to lower the market price from what it would be in a free market, or from what it would be if only suppliers are penalized.

THE RATIONING FUNCTION OF PRICE

At the very beginning of this book we stated that scarcity is the major reason for economics to exist. There is rarely enough of anything to bring everyone to a state of complete contentment. Thus there has to be a scheme for rationing the available output between all who "want a piece of the action."

The most successful scheme for rationing output yet devised by man is price. No doubt the key to the success of price as a rationing device is that each individual imposes rationing upon himself rather than having his consumption restricted by a person or agency with power to dole out the available output. Each of us, being mortals, has a limited capacity to produce and hence we must limit our intake of the goods and services produced in society. Since our income measured either in money or in terms of real output is limited, we must spend it wisely, trying to get the most for what we have to exchange.

As you recall from the discussion on consumer choice in Chapter 2 each of us maximizes our utility or satisfaction if we allocate our purchases such that the marginal utility per dollar is equalized among all things we purchase. Now if a good or service becomes scarce, its price will rise. Since marginal utility per dollar is equal to marginal utility divided by price a rise in price decreases MU per dollar which in turn gives us an incentive to reduce its use and look for other things that will give us more MU per dollar. No one has to tell us or order us to do so; we do it of our own accord. Moreover, there is no incentive for us to cheat by attempting to consume more. Even though we are free to consume a relatively large quantity of a scarce item, it is irrational to do so because it would just reduce our overall satisfaction.

Thus market price is an ideal rationing device. It rations available output efficiently and automatically. Scarce resources do not have to be devoted to rationing the available output. This is a serious mistake made by some developing nations. They have decided to use too many of their meager resources to ration what little they have. Letting market prices accomplish the rationing task and freeing resources to produce goods and services has proven to be a wiser policy. Also if governmental agencies do the rationing it can be very profitable for those obtaining the goods to spend a great deal of time and resources attempting to obtain a larger slice of the pie. Market price, being impersonal, does not respond to favor or bribe.

The fact that price rations the available output automatically and efficiently does not imply, however, that everyone is happy or satisfied with the prevailing price or resulting allocation. Indeed it is likely that most sellers would like price to be higher and most buyers would like it to be lower. When there is extreme dissatisfaction with price, either by buyers or sellers, the government may step in and establish a ceiling or support price as we pointed out a few pages back. It is important to remember, though, that establishing a ceiling price takes away the rationing function of price generally leaving it in the hands of governmental agencies.

THE ALLOCATING FUNCTION OF PRICE

Market price, in addition to rationing the available output, also serves to allocate available resources to their most valuable use. For example, if buyers reduce their demand for a product we know there is a tendency for price to fall as demand shifts left and intersects supply at a lower level. The lower price serves as a signal for producers, telling them that consumers no longer desire as much of this product. Producers, in turn, seeing their profits decline as price falls begin to search for other things to produce that consumers desire more. This action on the part of producers does not have to be motivated by any love or empathy for consumers but rather by a desire to improve their own incomes and purchasing power.

Some nations, in particular the communist countries, have attempted to allocate resources by govenmental agencies. These agencies decide what and how much is to be produced and then they establish quotas for producers to meet. The problem, however, is that the wishes or desires of the government officials may not coincide with the desires of consumers. As a result we hear of cases where warehouses of unwanted merchandise pile up before a change is made in the production schedule. At the same time, we hear of instances where production of other items is set too low resulting in long lines of people standing in front of stores as they attempt to obtain a share of the scarce goods.

The problems encountered when allocation is done by hand, so to speak, is not restricted to communistic or centralized decision-making societies. Indeed in a relatively free market economy such as the United States there are many goods and services, we call them public goods, which are allocated by a public agency or institution. In allocating public goods the objective is to obtain the quantity and type that will maximize the welfare of society. However in a society where change is the rule rather than the exception, the amount and type of public goods that once maximized welfare will not likely continue to do so for long.

The problem then is to transmit the changing demands of society to the agencies or institutions that provide these goods. The process of adjusting the mix and amount of public goods is generally slow and often painful. In recent years people have used the demonstration, and sometimes riots, as a means of transmitting their wishes to public institutions. If enough people make enough noise there will likely be some change; if no one complains, there is little incentive to change. It has been said somewhat jokingly that if the Edsel were produced by a public institution it would still be coming off the assembly lines.

But providing signals for change through riots or demonstrations tend to be very disruptive and inefficient. Can you imagine people picketing the Ford Motor Company in an attempt to coerce the company to produce something other than black cars, or cars with a square, box-like shape? If Ford Motor Company were a public institution this might be about the only pressure for change that could be directly brought against it by consumers. And if the government forbid demonstrations, such as many repressive governments do, about all the public could do then is "grin and bear it" until the state of affairs deteriorates to the point of mass disruption or revolution.

It is important, therefore, that public institutions keep responsive to the wishes of the public. Unless this flexibility is assured, the eventual outcome might be forceable overthrow of the government or public institutions such as schools and colleges. History is quite clear on this matter; the downfall of the Roman empire, the French, Russian, and American revolutions all coincide with the existence of unresponsive public institutions that turned to serving a small minority made up of the rich and powerful, or themselves, rather than the general public.

TIME FOR ADJUSTMENT

When dealing with prices and markets it is important to realize that change is seldom instantaneous. On the demand side of the market we know from experience that a change in price may not precipitate an immediate response. For example, if the price of our favorite tooth paste increases it may take us a certain amount of time to even find out about the price increase. The first time we buy another tube the price may seem a bit high but not having considered another brand we go ahead and buy it. By the time we are ready for the next tube, however, we might well compare prices of the various brands; if our favorite brand is "out of line" with the others, we might try a lower priced alternative.

The same process can go on in the event of a price decline of a good or service. If we are not already buying it, the lower price will not likely come to our immediate attention. Again after we have time to find out about the price decrease and find out something about the good itself we may give it a try. It is reasonable to believe, therefore, that the longer time consumers have to adjust to a price change, the more responsive they will be.

This idea can be represented by demand curves with differing slopes or elasticities. If only a short time is taken for adjustment to a price change the demand curve will be relatively steep, or less elastic, than if a long period of time is considered. This is illustrated in Figure 6–9, where D_s represents a demand with only a short time to adjust, whereas D_L represents a demand where adjustment by consumers takes place over a longer period. If supply shifts from S_0 to S_1 (a decrease) and price increases, some consumers begin to decrease their purchases and quantity sold begins to decline and approaches Q_{s1} rather quickly. However, as more and more consumers adjust to this price increase quantity decreases further, eventually reaching Q_{L1}.

The same diagram can be used to represent a price decline that might take place by an increase in supply as illustrated by supply shifting from S_0 to S_2 in Figure 6–9. Here a few consumers increase their purchases soon after the price fall so that quantity increases to Q_{s2}. Then as more consumers adjust, quantity continues to increase, eventually approaching Q_{L2}.

It is interesting to note, as well, the pattern of price changes that take place. With a decrease in supply price moves upward rather rapidly, then

FIGURE 6–9.   The effect of time for adjustment on product demand

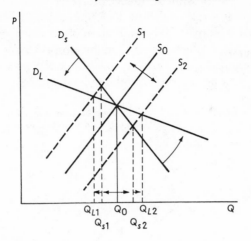

as consumers are able to adjust their purchases toward other products, price levels off and even decreases somewhat. With an increase in supply price falls rather abruptly but as consumers take note of this and adjust their purchases toward this product, price reaches a minimum and begins to ease upwards slightly.

Time for adjustment is perhaps even more important for supply than demand. There are two reasons why producers do not adjust immediately to a price change. First, from a technical standpoint, it generally is not physically possible to either acquire fixed inputs rapidly or, because of contractual commitments, to dispose of them quickly. Secondly, from an economic standpoint, changing the level of production to a sizable extent generally requires additional expense. To increase output, new facilities and equipment will have to be bought and additional personnel hired. Thus a producer wants to be sure that a price increase will stay in effect for a fairly long period of time before he undertakes this expense. Similarly a producer who disposes of a machine or structure before it has been substantially depreciated may have to bear a substantial loss. Thus he may try to "ride out" a period of low prices hoping for higher prices in the future.

Because of these factors the elasticity of supply allowing a long period of time to adjust is higher (more elastic) than its elasticity allowing little time to adjust. This is illustrated in Figure 6–10 where price is assumed to change because of shifts in demand. If demand declines, say to D_1, quantity produced will at first decline relatively little to Q_{s1}. But if price remains low for a time, more adjustment will take place, reducing quantity supplied even more to Q_{L1}. The same rationale applies to an increase in demand where quantity supplied increases at first Q_{s2} and later to Q_{L2}.

You will notice also, as we did with demand, that the process of moving to a longer time for adjustment affects the price of the good or service. For example there is a rather abrupt decline in price as demand decreases but after producers adjust their production downward price eases back up slightly. The same phenomenon can be observed for an increase in demand. Only here price rises rather abruptly and then eases back down a little as producers adjust their production upward.

FIGURE 6–10. The effect of time for adjustment on product supply

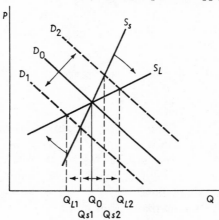

One very important point that should always be kept in mind when thinking about this process of adjustment either by producers or consumers is that not every producer or consumer need change the quantity produced or consumed when price changes. All that is required to obtain a market response to a price change is that a few "marginal" people change their quantities bought or sold. The fact that not everyone changes quantity demanded or supplied with a price change has led many to the erroneous conclusion that price has little effect in the market. Indeed if everyone reacted to a price change, there would be drastic changes in quantities exchanged in markets to just a minor change in price.

MAIN POINTS OF CHAPTER 6

1. Equalibrium price and quantity in a market occurs when the quantity demanded exactly equals quantity supplied. This corresponds to the point where the demand and supply curves intersect.

2. At any point in time there is no reason to expect that a market will be in equilibrium. But if not in equilibrium, forces exist which will push or pull price towards the equilibrium.

3. Equilibrium points in markets change because of shifts in demand and supply.

4. A change or shift in demand can be interpreted to mean that buyers change the amount they will buy at a given price, or will buy a given amount at a changed price.

5. The major factors shifting demand include (*a*) change in prices of related products (substitutes and complements), (*b*) change in consumer incomes, (*c*) change in consumer expectations regarding future prices and income, (*d*) change in tastes and preferences, and (*e*) change in population.

6. A change or shift in supply can be interpreted to mean that sellers change the amount they will sell at a given price or will sell a given amount at a changed price.

7. The major factors shifting supply include (*a*) change in price of inputs, (*b*) change in price of other products that can be produced, (*c*) change in producer expectations of future prices, (*d*) change in technology, and (*e*) change in number of firms.

8. A rising market price can be caused by an increase (shift) in demand, a decrease (shift) in supply, or some combination of the two. In the event of an increase in demand and a decrease in supply it is not possible to predict whether equilibrium quantity will increase, decrease, or remain unchanged without knowing the extent of the two shifts.

9. A declining market price can be the result of a decrease in demand, an increase in supply, or some combination of the two.

10. Ceiling prices create a shortage in the market which makes it necessary for the government to impose some kind of rationing scheme. Black-market activities also are an inevitable result of ceiling prices and rationing.

11. Support prices create surpluses in a market making it necessary for the government to buy up the surplus and keep it off the market in order to hold price up.

12. Sales and excise taxes on products increases the price paid by the consumer and decreases the price received by the producer.

13. Penalties on buyers of illegal goods or services tend to decrease the demand for these items and lower their price. Penalties on sellers tend to decrease supply and increase market price.

14. Price is the most efficient rationing device yet devised by man. Individual consumers voluntarily reduce their purchases of a scarce item as its price rises in order to maximize their utility for a given budget.

15. Price also allocates resources to the goods or services most desired by consumers since a rising price tends to increase profits for producers

and thus provides them with an incentive to produce more of the most wanted items. By the same token a decrease in the desirability of a good or service leads to a fall in its price which tends to lower profits of producers and provides them with an incentive to produce things more appealing to buyers.

16. The process of adjusting to a price change is not instantaneous. Both buyers and sellers require time to adjust their purchases or production after a price change. Thus demand and supply curves that allow for adequate time to adjust are more elastic than those which do not allow sufficient adjustment time.

17. Only a relatively small proportion of buyers or sellers need respond to a price change to obtain a change in the quantity bought and sold in a market.

QUESTIONS FOR THOUGHT AND DISCUSSION

1. Explain why the equilibrium price in a market is the price where quantity supplied equals quantity demanded.

2. Think of some goods or services where the market price seems to be in equilibrium. Think of some other products where the equilibrium price recently changed.

3. Think of a good or service that has recently increased in price, perhaps one you mentioned in Question 2, and explain by means of demand or supply shifters, or both, the likely reason for the price rise. Do the same for a good or service whose price has declined recently.

4. The market for many commodities is seasonal in nature. Christmas cards and fresh strawberries are two examples. Christmas cards increase in sales during the last three months of the year, and fresh strawberries are sold mainly during the summer months, at least in the North. However the price movements of these two products are quite different: Christmas cards increase in price during their peak season whereas strawberries decrease in price. Using supply-demand diagrams explain (a) why the price of Christmas cards go up and (b) why the price of strawberries go down.

5. Some time ago the U.S. government tightened the inspection procedure at the entry points between the U.S. and Mexico in an effort to reduce the inflow of marijuana into this country. Using supply-demand diagrams explain the effect of this action on (a) the price and quantity of marijuana sold in the U.S., particularly the west; and (b) the price and quantity sold of other mind-distorting drugs.

6. We observe that the price of Volkswagens has increased substantially in the United States over the past 10 to 15 years even accounting for inflation. However we also observe that the number of Volkswagens sold also has increased during this period. Do these facts indicate that the demand curve for Volkswagens is an upward sloping line, i.e., the higher the price the

larger the quantity demanded? If not, explain using a supply-demand diagram.

7. During periods of rising prices some people suggest that the government impose ceiling prices on certain goods or services. Suppose the government imposes a ceiling price on new automobiles. Using a supply-demand diagram explain what would happen to the quantities demanded and supplied. Also show the resulting black-market price. Do the elasticities of supply and demand have any effect on the consequences of a ceiling price?

8. "Excise taxes are borne solely by consumers because they are added to the retail price of goods or services." Comment.

9. Suppose two of your friends are having an argument about the meaning of an increase in supply. One argues that an increase means that producers are willing to produce more at a given price. The other argues that an increase means that producers are willing to take less for a given quantity. Which of your friends is right? Explain.

10. You are having coffee with a friend who mentions that the price of gasoline at his favorite station has just increased from 32.9 to 36.9 cents per gallon. But, your friend says that he will go on buying his normal amount of gasoline at that station because it is too inconvenient to go out of his way to another station. From this can we conclude that station will continue to sell the same amount of gas as before? Explain.

11. Water, one of the basic necessities of life, is in most places very cheap if not free. Diamonds, on the other hand, a very nonessential item in our lives, are very expensive. Can you explain this rather perverse behavior of price? (Hint: Use supply and demand.)

CHAPTER
7
PERFECT COMPETITION IN THE PRODUCT MARKET

Thus far we have been concerned mainly with the general characteristics of market demand and supply and their interaction in the product market. In this and the next chapter we will be concerned mainly with the individual firms producing and selling goods and services. As we observe firms doing business in the economy we see a great deal of diversity. Some are small, one-person enterprises such as small farms or retail shops. Others are giant corporations employing thousands of people, selling their products throughout the world.

Let us now attempt to create some order out of this diversity by studying the characteristics and behavior of different types of firms. We will begin with the type of market situation that economists have labeled perfect competition. Agricultural production probably provides the closest example of perfect competition that we have today.

THE PERFECTLY COMPETITIVE FIRM—A PRICE TAKER

The distinguishing characteristic of a perfectly competitive firm is that the price charged by the firm is determined solely in the market. The firm itself has no power to alter the price of its product. For this reason the perfectly competitive firm is often called a "price taker." The firm takes the price as determined in the market.

But let us proceed one step further and ask, why does the firm have to charge the price that the market determines? There are two basic reasons: (1) The firm sells a product that is undifferentiated from the product of all the other firms in the market and (2) the firm sells a very small proportion of the total market.

The fact that a perfectly competitive firm sells a product undistinguishable from the other firms in its market means that buyers have no preference for the product of one firm over any other. Thus each and every firm must sell its product at the price all the other firms are obtaining. For example, why should buyers pay $2.25 per bushel for wheat from farmer Jones if 10,000 other farmers are selling exactly the same product for $2 per bushel? In other words, each producer must conform to the market price.

We know also that because of the downward sloping nature of market demand curves, market price can only be changed if the quantity sold is changed; quantity must decrease to obtain a higher price or any increase in quantity demanded must be accompanied by a reduction in price. But because the perfectly competitive firm sells just a minute fraction of the market, each firm cannot alter market price by producing more or less. For example, suppose farmer Jones decides that the market price of wheat is too low. What can he do about it? If he reduces his production by one half (a drastic measure by a firm), the total market supply would remain virtually unchanged because taking a few hundred bushel or even a few thousand bushel from a market where millions of bushels are traded would have an imperceptible effect; something like taking a handful of sand away from a beach. Thus, no matter what quantity the firm decides to produce, within reason, the market price remains the same.

To summarize briefly, the characteristic of an undifferentiated product requires each perfectly competitive firm to sell at the same price as all other firms, i.e., market price, and the characteristic of producing just a small fraction of the market means that each firm has no power to alter market price.

DEMAND FACING A PERFECTLY COMPETITIVE SELLER

We can obtain a better understanding of the relationship between a perfectly competitive firm and the market in which it sells by means of diagrams. The traditional market demand and supply curves are depicted in Figure 7–1 (A). These are the curves that we developed in Chapters 2 through 6. The equilibrium price and quantity that will prevail in this market are denoted by P_e and Q_e. The price that each firm will face, therefore, is P_e, if the market is allowed to reach an equilibrium.

The individual perfectly competitive firm operating in this market is represented by Figure 7–1 (B). Its supply curve, as we know, is simply the marginal cost curve above the point where it intersects the average varible cost curve if it is already committed to its fixed costs. The price that the firm can expect to receive for its product is P_e, as determined by market supply and demand. This price, P_e, can be thought of as the demand facing this firm. The price line, P_e in this example, is a demand curve in the sense that it tells the firm what price it will receive for its product. the fact that the demand curve is a perfectly horizontal line (perfectly elastic) means that the firm can produce and sell any output within reason at this price. In other words, the market stands ready to buy any reasonable quantity from this firm at price P_e. Thus the line showing the price is in reality the demand curve facing this firm.

FIGURE 7–1.   Relationship between the market and the perfectly competitive firm

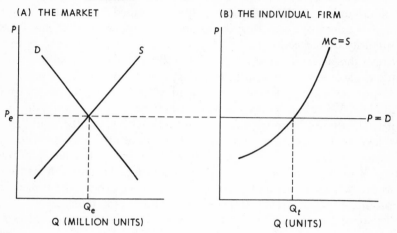

From our discussion relating to product supply we know that a producer of this nature maximizes profits where price equals marginal cost. Since MC is supply and price represents demand, the firm maximizes profits at the point where the firm's supply curve intersects the demand curve that it faces. This quantity is represented by Q_t in Figure 7–1 (B). Notice, of course, that the units of measure on the quantity axis differs greatly between the market and the firm. The market quantity might be measured in terms of millions of units whereas the firm's quantity might just be number of units. The units of measure on the price axes are, of course, the same for the market and the firm.

We might pause briefly at this point to summarize the different kinds of demand curves we have studied. There are three. The first is the demand of an individual consumer. This one is represented by a downward sloping line, indicating that quantity increases as price decreases and vice versa. The second demand curve is market demand—the sum of all the individual demanders in the market. This one as we know is also represented by a downward sloping line, as in Figure 7–1 (A). The third is the demand curve facing an individual seller. For the perfectly competitive seller this demand curve is a perfectly horizontal line indicating that the market will take any reasonable quantity he wishes to produce at the market price.

PRICE, COSTS, AND PROFITS

The perfectly competitive firm, as we know, takes the price as determined in the market and decides whether or not it should produce, and if so, how much. Recall from our discussion on product supply in Chapter 5 that pure profits are earned only if price is greater than average total cost at the quantity the firm chooses to produce. And we also know that the profit maximizing quantity will correspond to the point where marginal cost equals price.

The three diagrams in Figure 7–2 illustrate the three possible profit positions for perfectly competitive firms. The price, P_e, that is shown is determined, of course, by market demand and supply as illustrated in Figure 7–1 (A). Diagram (A) illustrates a firm that is earning pure profits in its business. In other words, the resources (inputs) used in this production activity are earning more than they could in other kinds of work. The total pure profits for the firm are represented by the shaded area. Notice that total profits are maximized at a level of output beyond the point where profit per unit is the largest, i.e., the point where the distance between price and ATC is the greatest. Such an outcome is reasonable because the firm is interested in maximizing total profits rather than profit per unit.

FIGURE 7–2. Illustrating possible profit or loss positions of perfectly competitive firms

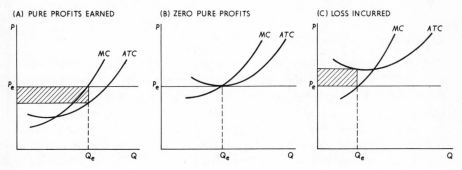

The situation depicted in Figure 7–2 (B), zero pure profits, is one where the resources employed by this firm are just earning what they could earn in some other alternative occupation. This situation is the only one of the three shown where the firm will produce a quantity corresponding to the minimum point on its average total cost curve. The case of a firm that is not covering its costs (implicit plus explicit) is shown in diagram

(C) of Figure 7–2. In this example the resources employed by the firm are not earning what they could in other occupations. This does not necessarily mean, however, that this firm's cash expenses are greater than its total sales. Because, as you recall from Chapter 5, the *ATC* curve includes a charge for the resources owned by the firm as well as its cash expenses.

If we were able to perfectly measure the costs of individual firms at any point in time, we would likely observe all three of the above situations existing in a given market or industry. There would likely be a few, well-managed, low-cost firms, making pure profits, as illustrated in diagram (A) of Figure 7–2. There would be other firms just "breaking even" but doing as well as they could in any other occupation. And there would likely be a few other firms, making less than they could in other occupations, perhaps looking for a chance to sell their assets and begin some other line of production.

We should be aware, however, that diagram (C) of Figure 7–2 need not depict a badly managed, "slipshod" kind of enterprise. The costs for this firm might be high because it has better alternatives than the other firms in the market. For example, the owner of the firm in diagram (C) might be a highly educated wheat farmer who has the opportunity of working in a nearby bank at a salary much higher than his neighbors could obtain in their best alternative occupations. Thus a firm's cost might be high either because the owner is a bad manager or because he has superior talents that are in high demand elsewhere. It is not valid to conclude, therefore, that an industry which is losing firms is losing its least productive people. It may well be losing some of these but at the same time it can be losing its most productive people because of superior opportunities elsewhere.

LONG-RUN ADJUSTMENT

Economists have given rather precise definitions to the terms "short run" and "long run" as they apply to production and supply. The short run is defined as the length of time too short to change the level of fixed inputs employed, or the number of firms in the industry, but long enough to change the level of output by means of changing variable inputs. Essentially the marginal physical product curve, and its mirror image, marginal cost, reflect short-run changes in production.

On the other hand, the long run is defined as a period of time long enough to change either the level of fixed inputs employed by firms or to change the number of firms. Unfortunately it is not possible to designate a period of time that constitutes the long run for all different types of firms or even for different situations. The length of this period differs between types of firms depending on how difficult or costly it is to change fixed inputs. If production requires extensive fixed inputs, say extensive irrigation or drainage facilities, the length of time to reach a long-run adjustment will be much longer than will be the case for firms carrying on production in small rented facilities, say barber shops.

The length of time to reach a long-run adjustment will depend also on how profitable it is to adjust. For example, if it is very profitable for a firm to expand its fixed inputs or for new firms to enter, the adjustment time will generally be shorter than if it just barely pays to change the level of output or to enter or leave the industry. For example, if it is very profitable to expand facilities, a contractor will in most cases be willing to step up the completion date if he is paid to do so. A higher fee will enable him to pay his employees for overtime work, say longer days or weekends in order to finish the job more quickly.

Let us now look at this process of long-run adjustment for a perfectly competitive industry in somewhat more detail. Suppose we start where the market is in equilibrium, i.e., price corresponds to the intersection of supply and demand, as shown in Figure 7–1 (A). Suppose also that the typical firm in the industry is making substantial pure profits, as shown in Figure 7–2 (A) we will assume as well that each firm is maximizing its profits by producing an output that corresponds to the point where price is equal to marginal cost, Q_e in Figure 7–2 (A). These two conditions—(1) market price is at the point where quantity demanded equals quantity supplied and (2) price equals marginal cost for each firm—constitute a short-run equilibrium for an industry. This situation is illustrated in the two diagrams in Figure 7–1.

Now if each firm is making pure profits, however, it is reasonable to expect that existing firms will expand their facilities (increase their fixed inputs) and/or additional firms will enter this industry to "get a piece of the action." We need not assume that all firms are making substantial pure profits for this to happen. In fact, some might be characterized by Figures 7–2 (B) and (C). All we need to assume is that a sizable portion of existing firms are making pure profits.

Recall from the discussion on product supply that an increase in the number of firms or an increase in the size of firms have the effect of shifting the market supply curve to the right as shown in Figure 7–3 (A). The effect of an increase in supply, of course, is a reduction in market price. And as market price falls so does the price that faces each firm. Thus as supply shifts right and market price falls, the pure profits that each firm is making are competed away. This process is illustrated in Figure 7–3, diagrams (A) and (B).

This process of new resources coming into an industry to compete away pure profits probably will be most noticeable at levels of pure profits that are relatively high. Then as price falls closer and closer to the zero profit point (P_2 in Figure 7–3), it is to be expected that entry of additional resources will slow down as the prospects for pure profits diminish. Although it is not uncommon to observe situations where firms have built up optimism over a period of time and continue to expand until price falls below the zero pure profit point. As soon as this happens, of course, some firms find more profitable opportunities elsewhere, move out of this industry, and contribute to a decrease in supply which eventually pulls price back up towards the zero pure profit equilibrium.

FIGURE 7–3.   Long-run adjustment to pure profits by entry of additional resources or firms

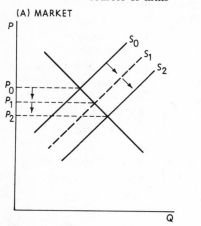

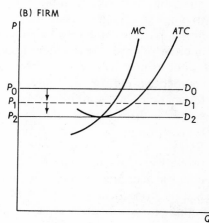

A similar but opposite process of adjustment would take place if a large share of the firms in a market or industry are suffering losses or negative pure profits. Here we would see firms moving out to more profitable opportunities, decreasing market supply, and raising market price. You may want to illustrate this process with diagrams of your own similar to Figure 7–3 (A) and (B).

We have seen so far that the existence of either pure profits or losses results in a long-run adjustment characterized by either the entry or exit of resources or firms. It is also possible to observe adjustments on the cost side. Suppose, for example, in the production of tomatoes there are a few firms that enjoy some special advantage such as very productive soil. The entry of new firms might push price down to the zero profit position for just about every firm in the industry except for these privileged few. They might continue to reap pure profits, however.

Eventually these unusually profitable firms will be sold to new owners. It is reasonable to except that the price paid for these firms will reflect the pure profits that can be expected in the future. In other words, the new owners would be willing to pay more for productive land than for poor land. With an increase in the land price, there will be an increase in the cost of production mainly because of the increase in the interest charge (explicit or implicit) and taxes. If the sellers of these very productive firms are shrewd bargainers, they will obtain a price that pushes ATC just about up to the expected future price, as illustrated in Figure 7–4.

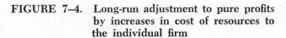

FIGURE 7–4.   Long-run adjustment to pure profits by increases in cost of resources to the individual firm

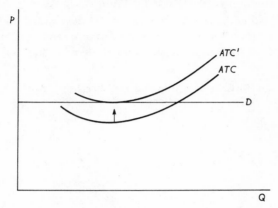

This phenomenon of cost adjusting to price has been particularly important in U.S. agriculture. As we pointed out in Chapter 6, the government has attempted to increase incomes by establishing support prices of various products. In this situation price is fixed, but over the years pure profits have been eroded away because of the bidding up of land prices. So eventually the producers are forced back to the same zero profit position as existed before the support prices came into being.

We should always bear in mind, though, that adjustment is not instantaneous. Pure profits or losses will likely exist for different firms at any point in time. The important thing to realize is that there will be adjustment to a long-run zero profit equilibrium if pure profits or losses exist.

THE CONTINUAL SEARCH FOR LOWER COSTS

We must keep in mind that even though all firms in a perfectly competitive industry face a common market price, there is likely to be substantial differences in costs between firms. As we pointed out, high costs may be due to low productivity resulting from inept management or because of high implicit costs stemming from high-paying opportunities in other lines of work. We know, of course, that a perfectly competitive firm has no control over the price of its product. It is also true that such a firm cannot alter the opportunities that exist elsewhere. In fact, high implicit costs stemming from superior opportunities elsewhere would be welcomed because they represent opportunities to increase income.

Most perfectly competitive firms can, however, do something about the efficiency of their production process. And the more efficient a firm is in transforming inputs into output, the lower will be its production costs, and the higher will be its profits. Thus most firms, at least those managed by alert people, are continually searching for new cost reducing inputs or techniques in order to increase profits. The effect of achieving a cost reduction in production is illustrated by Figure 7–5. Average total costs are shifted downward and marginal cost is shifted downward and to the right. If price is at P_0, then the firm can move from a zero pure profit position to a position of positive pure profits after the cost reduction.

FIGURE 7–5.   Illustrating the effects of a cost reduction

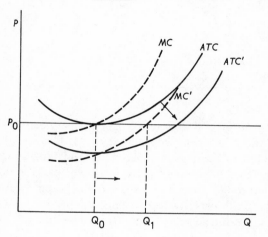

In addition to creating pure profits for the firm (in this example) a second very important effect of a cost reduction to take note of is the shift downward and to the right of the marginal cost curve. Essentially this tells us that the firms now can produce an additional or marginal unit cheaper than before. But we must also keep in mind that the MC curve is also the supply curve of the firm. At the original MC, Q_0 is produced by this firm, whereas at the new, lower MC, Q_1 is produced. Of course, if just one firm finds a way to reduce costs and shift its supply curve there will be no perceptible effect in the market. Increasing production of wheat by 100 bushels, for example, will not be noticed in a market where millions of bushels are traded.

Although the increased production by a single firm has no appreciable effect on the market, similar action by many such firms will have the effect of shifting the market supply curve to the right. And, as we know, this has the effect of reducing market price. Furthermore, the lowering of market price has the effect of squeezing the newly created pure profits out of the firms that have achieved lower costs.

Once a significant proportion of firms adopt a new cost reducing input or technique and market price begins to fall, the firms that have not reduced their costs find their profit positions eroding and consequently they have no choice but to also adopt these inputs or techniques else they must suffer losses or eventually leave the industry. This process of the early adopters reaping pure profits and the subsequent erosion of these profits to these firms and losses to the remaining firms is somewhat like being on a treadmill; each firm must run faster and faster (decrease costs more and more) just to stay even. Although each firm may not appreciate this continuous struggle, consumers and society in general gain from it because more and more output is obtained from our scare resources.

THE PLANNING CURVE

There comes a time in the life of every firm when it must make decisions affecting its long-run future. This time might come when it first starts in business, or at any other point it decides to change the level of its fixed inputs such as land, buildings, or equipment. For a perfectly competitive firm, which by itself cannot affect market price, we might reasonably expect it to be interested in finding the level of fixed inputs which will minimize its average total costs. Because only by achieving a size that will minimize per unit cost can it hope to compete in the long run with other firms who are also searching for the most efficient size.

Ideally a firm would like to utilize experts such as engineers, architects, cost accountants, economists, and the like to estimate the potential average total costs for various levels of output at various levels of fixed inputs. In other words, it would like to know the short-run average total cost curves for various sizes of plants or facilities. One possible configuration of short-run average total cost curves is represented by Figure 7–6.

In this example we see that the level of ATC is relatively high at relatively small levels of fixed inputs and output, as illustrated by ATC_1. Then as the size of fixed inputs is increased the ATC curves shift down and to the right, reaching a minimum at ATC_3. Further increases in size of fixed inputs still shifts the short run ATC's to the right but at the same time shifts them upwards indicating that per unit costs increase at larger firm sizes.

Although only five alternative sizes are illustrated in Figure 7–6, there is no reason why many more could not be estimated and drawn in. The individual firm may not wish to consider an excessive number of alternatives, however, because of the cost of estimating the various ATC's. At any rate, it would be possible with only the number of ATC's shown in Figure 7–6 to estimate what economists call a planning curve or long-run

ATC curve. Such a curve is constructed by tracing out an "envelop" of all the short-run *ATC*'s.

Essentially, the planning curve, or the *LRATC*, shows the lowest possible cost of obtaining a given output. For example, at output Q_1 the level of fixed inputs represented by ATC_5 would be most efficient. Producing Q_1 by a smaller plant, ATC_4 for example, would result in higher unit costs. Also the planning curve shows the level of fixed inputs that would result in the overall lowest possible *ATC*—that level represented by ATC_3. Thus a firm that wanted to minimize *ATC* in the future would utilize this level of fixed inputs and produce output Q_0. Producing Q_0 by any other level of fixed inputs, say ATC_2 or ATC_4, would result in much higher unit costs.

FIGURE 7–6.   The planning curve or long-run average total cost curve

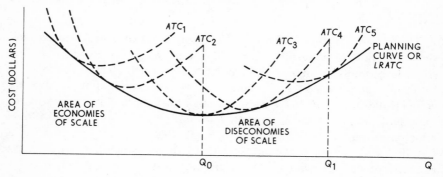

In reality, of course, a firm especially a small firm, may not wish to incur the expense of estimating in detail many possible short-run *ATC*'s. Instead the firm may simply try to estimate the lowest possible point on a few possible *ATC*'s and in so doing attempt to obtain a rough idea of what its planning curve or *LRATC* might look like. At least, rough information of this kind is helpful in deciding on the size that comes close to minimizing *ATC* over the long run.

ECONOMIES AND DISECONOMIES OF SCALE

The planning curve or *LRATC* brings out a concept long used by economists, namely economies and diseconomies of scale. As the name implies, economies of scale means that average total cost declines as the size or scale of the firm increases, as illustrated by the decreasing portion of the planning curve. Perhaps the greatest source of economies of scale is the more efficient utilization of fixed inputs in large compared to small firms. For example, equipment depreciation charge per bushel is likely to be higher on a 100-acre wheat farm than on a 1,000-acre farm. Also the implicit cost of the farmer's own labor would have to be covered by fewer bushels on the small farm, unless he is able to obtain a part-time job or produce something else along with the wheat.

Diseconomies of scale implies the opposite of course, namely that per unit costs increase at larger firm sizes, as illustrated by the increasing portion of the planning curve. Management problems appear to be the major factor causing diseconomies of scale. As a firm increases in size the task of management becomes more and more complex. Managing a firm is something like staging a puppet show. The larger the firm, the greater the number of puppets that must be manipulated at the same time. Some men such as Henry Ford have a genius for this sort of thing. Others of more normal fabric are not capable of staging such grand productions.

Because people differ a great deal in management ability, it is reasonable to expect that diseconomies of scale set in sooner for some firms than for others. This probably explains why some firms grow larger and larger, continuing to prosper, while others stay about the same size for the life of the owner or manager. Indeed, a relatively poor manager might go bankrupt at the level of production that minimizes costs for a good manager. Thus it is important for the owner or manager to assess his management skills in estimating his firm's long-run ATC curve.

PRODUCTION COSTS: THE FIRM VERSUS THE INDUSTRY

In our discussion of economies and diseconomies of scale, we focused our attention exclusively on the individual firm. However, we ought to keep in mind that a firm's production costs can be affected by what the other firms in the industry do.

One way that this can happen is through the price of resources. If just one or a few perfectly competitive firms expand or contract, there is not likely to be any change in the price of resources because they most likely employ a very small part of the industry total. On the other hand, a change in output by all firms in the industry or a substantial change in the number of firms might well change the price of the resources employed in this industry.

A substantial contraction by the industry, for example, releases resources that must find alternative employment. To find this employment they might be required to accept lower prices. On the other hand, in order to attract a substantial quantity of additional resources, their price might be bid up in order to draw them away from other industries.

From our discussion of product supply, we know that an increase in the price of resources shifts the cost curves for the individual firm upwards and to the left. Thus, in the case of industry expansion, there are two offsetting forces operating: the increase in size or number of firms shifts product supply to the right but an increase in resource prices has the opposite effect so that the net shift is smaller than without the resource price rise.

In addition to resource price increases, expansion by the entire industry can affect the individual firm's cost curves through what economists call "technical or nonpecuniary" diseconomies. The most common example here is waste disposal. If the industry is small and its firms scattered, disposing of waste tends to be less costly than if the industry is large and highly concentrated. For example, one or a few small firms may pipe its wastes into a stream or body of water without causing public alarm. But with growth of the industry, each firm may have to construct costly waste disposal facilities which has the effect of increasing the cost curves of all the individual firms.

Economists refer to industries that experience a rise in costs, either through resource price increases or through technical diseconomies, as increasing cost industries. Notice that as this kind of industry expands, the minimum point on each firm's long-run ATC curve increases so that the zero pure profit price rises higher and higher. Thus as the industry grows larger, the long-run equilibrium price for the industry increases. This situation is illustrated in Figure 7–7 (A) where it is assumed that the industry expands by adding additional firms.

Although increasing costs are a reasonable thing to expect in many industries, it is not impossible to visualize one that can expand its output without incurring increasing costs. This could happen if the resources employed by the industry make up a small proportion of the total employment of these resources. Tomato production might be a possible example because this industry employs only a small proportion of the total land, labor, and other resources that can be used to produce tomatoes. Also there must be no technical diseconomies present. Economists refer to such an industry as a constant cost industry because each firm's cost curves and the long-run equilibrium price does not change as the industry expands to large levels of output (Figure 7–7 [B]).

There is a third possibility, known as a decreasing cost industry, in which costs decline as the industry grows. This is less common than the first two cases but still possible. Decreasing costs can occur if the price of the industry's resources decline as the industry grows. This phenomenon would be most likely to occur in new, developing areas. If only a few firms are present, many of the resources it employs will have to be shipped in from distant places or produced locally on a small scale at high costs. Also if the industry is small and insignificant there will not likely be any public effort to establish institutions to serve this industry or train people to work in it if special skills are required.

On the other hand, an industry that becomes a significant part of an area's or nation's economy can expect to enjoy some special advantages. Supporting industries which can supply resources at a minimum cost will emerge, financial institutions will consider it a better risk and loan money at a lower rate of interest, and public schools might offer special training to young people who want to find employment in the industry. Economists refer to these circumstances as "external economies." The coming of additional firms lowers costs for all firms. It is not totally unexpected, therefore, that we often observe industries tending to concentrate in specific areas rather than spreading out excessively. Decreasing costs are illustrated in Figure 7–7 (C).

FIGURE 7–7.   Long-run average total cost curves for a typical firm in increasing, constant, and decreasing cost industries

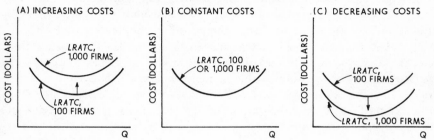

We should bear in mind, however, that an industry might exhibit all three situations at different stages of its development. When an industry is young and becoming established, it might enjoy decreasing costs. Then for a time when it is moderate in size it might expand with constant costs. Finally as it becomes a major industry, using a significant proportion of the resources it employs, it may run into increasing costs.

MAXIMIZING VALUE OF OUTPUT

For a long time economists have used perfect competition as a standard by which to evaluate or judge other industries. This implies, therefore, that perfect competition is something to be desired or strived for. Why? The basic reason why perfect competition is used as a standard is that it results in a maximum value of output to society for a given amount of resources.

To understand why value of output is maximized under perfect competition, it is first necessary to remember that each firm in a perfectly competitive industry attempts to produce up to the point where price of the product is equal to marginal cost. And you recall the firm strives to equate MC and price in order to maximize its profits (Figure 7–2). This equality between price and marginal cost is *the* reason why value of output to society is maximized.

In order to appreciate the importance of the equality between price and MC, it is necessary to understand what price and MC represent. First, the price of a product is the value that society assigns to a marginal unit of this product. For example, if the price of tomatoes is $2 per bushel, we can infer from this that society values an extra bushel of tomatoes at $2 else it would not choose to buy it for this price.

Marginal cost, on the other hand, represents the cost to society in terms of other products given up of obtaining an extra unit of this product. For example, if the marginal cost of tomatoes is $2, then in order to produce an extra bushel of tomatoes, $2 worth of some other good or service must be given up, assuming that these other things are produced in an industry where price and marginal cost also are equal.

It is perhaps easiest to understand why the equality of price and *MC* results in a maximum value of output if we first look at situations where price does not equal marginal cost. Suppose that for some reason price of a bushel of tomatoes is $3 and its marginal cost is $2. This means that society values an extra bushel of tomatoes at $3 and values the goods or services given up to produce this extra bushel at $2. Now if one extra bushel of tomatoes is produced, society gains $3 and gives up $2, leaving a net gain of $1. Thus it behooves society to increase the production of tomatoes under these circumstances because the value of total output is increased using the same amount of resources. In other words, there is a underallocation of resources to the production of a good or service if its price is greater than its marginal cost.

Taking the opposite situation, say price is $1 and marginal cost $2, we see that by decreasing the production of tomatoes by one bushel, society gives up $1 worth of tomatoes but gains $2 worth of other goods and services resulting in a net gain of $1. Thus if price is less than *MC*, there is an overallocation of resources to the production of this product because by reducing its production total value of output is increased with a given amount of resources. Now it is possible to see that value of output is maximized only if price equals marginal cost. Because only when price equals *MC* it is not possible to reallocate resources to increase total value of output. And, as you recall, perfectly competitive firms attempt to produce at the point where price equals *MC*.

A very advantageous characteristic of perfect competition, at least from society's point of view, is that each individual producer in attempting to maximize his own profits by equating price and marginal cost, also maximizes the value of output to society. This idea was first introduced by an early economist and philosopher, Adam Smith, in his book *The Wealth of Nations*. He called this phenomenon the "invisible hand." Each producer in attempting to maximize his own profits also maximizes the value of output to society as though guided by some "invisible hand."

ECONOMICS OF POLLUTION AND OTHER SOCIAL COSTS

Society has become very concerned of late with the problem of pollution. When population was smaller and more dispersed, and industrial output was considerably less, much of our waste material was disposed of by dumping it into water or the atmosphere. Little thought was given to the cost of waste disposal probably because it was relatively cheap to let nature do the disposing and relatively few people at least those with any influence complained about the effects of waste materials in the environment.

Society is now becoming increasingly aware, however, that the cost of disposing of wastes by dumping into the environment is much more than is borne by the one doing the dumping. For example, the cost of piping waste material into a stream far exceeds the cost of the pipe, at least from society's point of view.

Economists have long been aware that certain production costs are not taken account of by the individual firm but nevertheless represent a cost to society. These are called "social costs." Pollution represents a rather significant social cost at the present. Accidental destruction of life and property because of alcohol or drugs also is a social cost that has concerned society for some time.

We can obtain a somewhat clearer picture of the economic effects of social costs, such as pollution, by use of a diagram. Suppose MC in Figure 7–8 represents the traditional implicit and explicit marginal costs of producing a product. Also suppose that the production of this product results in certain waste materials that are disposed of by dumping them into a river. These waste materials, however, represent an additional cost to society either because they must be taken out downstream in order for the water to be re-used, or because people living downstream suffer the cost of viewing unsightly water and are not able to use it for other purposes. For example, if pollution prohibits recreational uses of water, people must bear the cost of traveling to alternative areas where the water is not polluted.

If the firm were required to bear the full cost of disposing of its waste material, then the true or full marginal cost curve would be somewhat higher for a given output, such as MC' in Figure 7–8. If the firm does not

FIGURE 7–8. **Divergence of private and social marginal cost because of pollution**

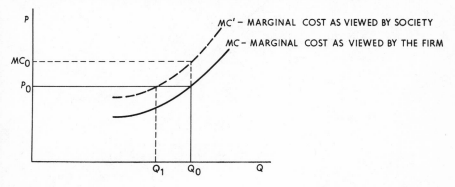

have to pay the full cost of waste disposal it will base its production decisions entirely on MC rather than MC'. In other words, MC is the firm's marginal cost where MC' is society's marginal cost. The latter includes the private marginal cost of the firm plus the social cost of pollution.

Assuming, as is reasonable, that the firm tries to maximize profits it will produce quantity Q_0 if faced by price P_0. However you will note that if all costs are taken into account, the additional cost to society of one more unit of the product is given by MC_0 on the vertical axis. In other words, MC_0 represents the value of goods or services given up to obtain one more unit of this product—say it is tomatoes. Since consumers value an extra bushel of tomatoes at P_0, we see that in terms of value society gives up more to obtain this extra bushel than they get from it.

We must conclude, therefore, that the existence of a social cost such as pollution in the production of a product results in an overallocation of resources to this product, even though production is carried on by perfectly competitive firms. The "correct" amount that will maximize the value of output to society is Q_1, where price is equal to the true or full marginal cost.

In the future we will likely see more and more legislation requiring firms to construct facilities to dispose of waste materials, or to stop using resources such as DDT that create wastes or residue. In other words, firms will be required to bear a greater share of the true costs of producing its product.

As firms bear a larger proportion of the full production costs, MC as viewed by the firm will move up and towards the true marginal cost MC' in Figure 7–8. We know, however, that an upward shift in the marginal cost for each firm also will have the effect of shifting the market supply curve of the product upwards and to the left, as shown in Figure 7–9. And

FIGURE 7–9.   The effect in the product market of pollution control

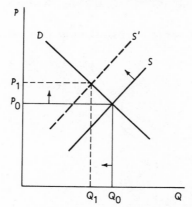

the inevitable consequence of this shift is a rise in the market price of the product.

We should not be surprised, therefore, if our efforts to control pollution results in higher prices for the products affected. This is not to say that pollution control is undesirable because we will be buying cleaner air and water along with these products. The main point is that clean air and water are not free goods in an industrialized society.

THE PERFECTLY COMPETITIVE BUYER

Thus far in this chapter we have considered only the selling side of the market. It is necessary, however, to realize that there are two sides to every market: the selling side and the buying side. In the product market, the buying side is made up mainly of ordinary consumers such as yourself.

There is only one characteristic that we need consider on the buying side, however, and that is the amount that each buyer purchases relative to the total market. If each buyer in a market is small and purchases only a small proportion of the item traded, then economists would classify such a market as perfectly competitive on the buying side.

Because the perfectly competitive buyer buys only a minute proportion of the market, he alone has no influence over the market price. For example, if you decide that the price of a textbook is too high and henceforth refuse to buy it, your decision not to buy will have virtually no effect on the quantity exchange in the market, and hence no effect on market price. On the other hand, if you wish to double, or triple your usual purchases of an item, say football tickets, you could do so without causing an increase in the price of the tickets.

You probably recognize by now that a perfectly competitive buyer faces a situation very similar to a perfectly competitive seller. Neither can influence the price of the product bought or sold. The distinguishing characteristic of a perfectly competitive buyer is that he buys only a minute fraction of the market. The same characteristic is also true for a perfectly competitive seller only here the additional characteristic of selling a homogeneous product is also required.

SUPPLY FACING A PERFECTLY COMPETITIVE BUYER

The fact that a perfectly competitive buyer has no control over market price of a good or service implies that the supply curve facing the individual buyer of this item is represented by a perfectly horizontal line, as in Figure 7–10 (B). The meaning of this supply curve is that the individual buyer can purchase any reasonable amount without having to pay a higher price for large quantities. Essentially this supply curve reflects the price of the item as determined in the market.

The market supply and demand, which determines price, is illustrated by Figure 7–10 (A). If there were no further services involved between the producer and the buyer, Figure 7–10 (A) would be exactly the same as Figure 7–1(A). The market price would be P_e, and the total quantity exchanged would be equal to Q_e (Figure 7–1 [A]). Each producer or firm would supply Q_t (shown in Figure 7–1 [B]), and each consumer would buy Q_b as determined by his own individual demand for the items (Figure 7–10 [B]).

FIGURE 7–10.   Relationship between the market and the perfectly competitive buyer

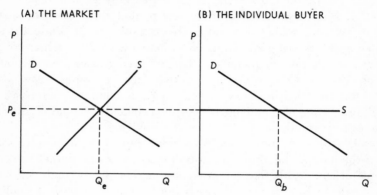

To summarize briefly, we have up to now studied three different kinds of supply curves: (1) the supply of the individual firm (really his MC curve), (2) the market supply which is just a summation of the individual firms' supply curves, and (3) the supply curve facing the individual buyer. You might recognize that these three supply curves are strictly analogous to the three different demand curves that were summarized in the beginning of this chapter. Thus with a total of six different demand and supply curves it is necessary to be careful not to confuse one with another. We should be aware, as well, that a perfectly competitive seller does not have to be a perfectly competitive buyer and vice versa. In fact, most goods and services are purchased by perfectly competitive buyers but produced by imperfectly competitive sellers. In the following chapter we will turn our attention to the imperfectly competitive seller.

MAIN POINTS OF CHAPTER 7

1. The perfectly competitive firm must take the price as determined in the market because it sells a product undistinguishable from other firms in the market and sells a very small proportion of the total market.

2. We have studied three different kinds of demand curves: (1) the demand of an individual consumer, (2) the market demand, and (3) the demand facing an individual producer or seller.

3. The demand facing an individual perfectly competitive firm is perfectly elastic meaning that the firm can sell any reasonable amount at the going market price.

4. A perfectly competitive firm maximizes profits (or minimizes losses) by producing up to the point where price equals marginal cost.

5. At any point in time, there will likely be some perfectly competitive firms that are making pure profits, others making zero pure profits, and still others incurring negative pure profits (or losses).

6. If a substantial share of the firms are making pure profits, existing firms will likely increase in size and/or new firms will enter leading to an increase in market supply, a decrease in price, and a competing away of the pure profits.

7. If a substantial share of the firms are incurring negative pure profits (earning less than they could in other lines of work) there will be a decrease in size and number of firms leading to a decrease in supply, an increase in price, and a restoration of at least zero pure profits.

8. Long-run adjustment to zero pure profits also occurs because of changes in the price of resources owned by the firm, hence changes in the firm's costs.

9. It is in the interest of each firm to search for new cost reducing techniques or resources in order to increase profits. Firms that do not adopt cost-reducing techniques or resources eventually incur losses and/or are forced out of business.

10. The planning curve or long-run average total cost curve ($LRATC$) represents an envelope of all possible short-run average total cost curves. From the planning curve the producer is able to determine the size of fixed inputs that will minimize unit costs of a given output as well as the size that will minimize unit costs overall.

11. The downward sloping portion of the planning curve represents the range of economies of scale. Scale economies generally result from a more efficient utilization of fixed inputs.

12. The upward sloping portion of the planning curve represents the range of diseconomies of scale. This phenomenon generally results from management problems brought on by increasing firm size.

13. An increasing cost industry is one in which the production costs of all firms in the industry increase as the industry expands. This takes place because of an increase in the price of resources and/or because of technical diseconomies which increase production costs for all firms as the industry grows.

14. In a constant cost industry the expansion of the industry does not affect the cost curves of the individual firms.

15. A decreasing cost industry is characterized by a reduction in firm costs as the industry grows. This phenomenon is most likely to occur in newly developing areas.

16. The perfectly competitive industry maximizes value of output to society because each firm attempts to equate output price and marginal cost. Price represents the value to consumers of a marginal unit of this output, and MC represents value of alternative goods or services given up. Thus whenever price does not equal MC it is always possible to reallocate resources to obtain more than is given up, holding constant the quantity of resources employed.

17. The existence of social costs such as pollution results in an underestimation by the firm of the true or full marginal cost of producing a good or service. Since the true MC will be greater than price, there will be an overallocation of resources to goods or services that entail social costs even though production might be carried on in perfect competition.

18. Laws that require polluting firms to bear a greater share of the cost of pollution likely will shift MC and product supply of their goods or services upward, thus increasing their market price. Pure air and water are not free goods in an industrialized society.

19. On the buying side of the market, perfect competition results if each individual buyer purchases only a small fraction of the total market. Most individual consumers are perfectly competitive buyers.

20. We have studied three different kinds of supply curves: (a) the supply of an individual producer, (b) the market supply, and (c) the supply facing an individual buyer.

21. The supply curve facing a perfectly competitive buyer is perfectly elastic meaning that the individual buyer can purchase any reasonable amount at the going market price.

QUESTIONS FOR THOUGHT AND DISCUSSION

1. Christmas tree production in the United States is carried on by many firms each selling a product undifferentiated from all other firms. Explain, using diagrams, how the price of Christmas trees is determined and how this price relates to the individual firm producing Christmas trees.

2. "Products produced by perfectly competitive firms contradict the theory of demand (people buy more at a lower price and vice versa) because the demand curve for these products is horizontal." Comment.

3. Suppose plant breeders developed a new variety of wheat that yields about double the old varieties.

   a) Explain, using a diagram, the effect this new variety would have on costs and profits for the alert, early adopting managers.

   b) Explain, using diagrams, the long-run adjustment of the wheat producing industry to this new development.

   c) Explain, using a diagram, what would happen to producers who do not adopt the new variety.

4. It has been argued that the major beneficiaries of government price support programs for agriculture are landowners. Comment.

5. "Every perfectly competitive firm is doomed to a life of zero pure profits because competition immediately forces price down to the zero profit point for each firm." Comment.

6. A profit squeeze from time to time in a perfectly competitive industry is good for the industry because it forces out the inefficient, high-cost producers. Comment.

7. "Economies of scale contradict the law of diminishing returns because at larger firm sizes unit costs decrease." Comment.

8. Suppose you consider growing tomatoes as a full-time occupation. What major cost factors would you consider and how would you go about constructing a "planning curve" for your proposed firm?

9. Do you think expansion or entry of other tomato producing firms would likely have any effect on the costs in your firm? In view of your conclusions, what would economists call the tomato producing industry?

10. Suppose you accidentally discovered a tomato plant that yielded twice the number of tomatoes as the best variety now on the market. Illustrate with a diagram, your production costs and profits as opposed to other producers. What would happen if other tomato producers found out about your discovery?

11. Adam Smith would say that tomato production would proceed as though guided by some "invisible hand." Explain fully what he would mean by this phrase?

12. Suppose an insecticide that you used in your tomato patch washed down into a lake killing off the fish therein. Explain, using a diagram, what effect this phenomenon would have on the allocation of resources in the economy.

13. Suppose the government passed a law forbidding the use of any insecticides you might employ. Illustrate what would happen to the costs for your firm and other tomato producers, as well as the price of tomatoes in the market.

14. Later suppose the government modified this law allowing the use of this insecticide in areas over 10 miles from a lake. What would happen to the location of tomato production?

15. A student can be referred to as a perfectly competitive buyer of textbooks. What does this statement mean? Illustrate with a diagram.

CHAPTER
8
IMPERFECT COMPETITION
IN THE PRODUCT MARKET

By far the largest proportion of goods and services in the United States is produced or sold in an environment that economists refer to as "imperfect competition." This is not to say, however, that it is unnecessary or unimportant to understand the concept of perfect competition. For we will find it instructive as we go along to point out the similarities and differences of these two types of competition. Only by understanding perfect competition, can we fully understand the idea of imperfect competition.

THE IMPERFECTLY COMPETITIVE
FIRM—A PRICE MAKER

You recall that there are two main characteristics that make a perfectly competitive firm what it is: (1) each firm produces a small share of the market and (2) the product of each firm is undistinguishable from the other firms in the market. Agriculture is a good example.

Imperfect competition results if one or both of these two characteristics are changed. For example, a firm may be very large and produce a significant share of the market, or the firm may be small, producing still a small proportion of the market, but sells a slightly differentiated product from the other firms it competes with. As a third possibility the firm may be both large, selling a significant proportion of the market, and producing a differentiated product.

In summary, then, imperfect competition results when (1) each firm produces a sizable share of the market and/or (2) each firm sells a product distinguishable from its competitors. We will give specific examples shortly as we consider each of the three main categories of imperfect competition.

144

As opposed to the perfectly competitive firm which is known as a "price taker," the imperfectly competitive firm is often referred to as a "price maker." This is because each firm has some control over the price it charges for its product. Unlike the perfectly competitive firm, each firm selling in a market characterized by imperfect competition can raise its price, at least slightly, without being compelled to reduce its sales to zero.

At the same time, we must understand that the phrase "price maker" does not mean that each imperfectly competitive firm has complete control over the price it charges. We will see shortly that the degree of control over price varies considerably between firms but never reaches a point where any one firm can raise the price of its product indefinitely without losing all of its customers.

Demand Facing an Imperfectly Competitive Firm

We will be able to understand the meaning of the phrase "price maker" a bit better if we can gain an understanding of the demand facing each individual firm. Recall in the case of perfect competition that each firm faces a horizontal demand curve, meaning that the firm takes the price as determined in the market and has no control over this price. And if you further recall, the basic reasons for this phenomenon are that the firm produces only a minute proportion of the market and produces a product undifferentiated from the other firms in the market.

Now in the case of imperfect competition where each firm sells a differentiated product, serves a sizable share of the market, or both, the firm has some control over the price of its product(s). If a firm sells a product that is slightly different than its competitors, it can raise the price of its product, at least a little, without having its sales decline to zero. Or if a firm supplies a substantial proportion of the market and it wishes to sell at a higher price, it can do so by cutting back on production. The fact that the firm sells a substantial portion of the market means that the reduction in the firm's output is noticed in the market and as a result market price is increased, assuming that the market demand for the product, or general category of products such as automobiles, is downward sloping. The implication of this behavior is that the firm faces a downward sloping demand curve as shown in Figure 8–1.

If the firm raises its price, say from P_0 to P_1, it is forced to reduce its sales from Q_0 to Q_1. Or if the firm wishes to increase its sales, say from Q_0 to Q_2, it must lower price from P_0 to P_2. Thus a common characteristic of all imperfectly competitive firms is that they face a downward sloping demand curve. We must keep in mind, however, that even though the demand curve facing the individual firm is downward sloping and resembles the market demand curve for the product, it is not the same thing as the market demand. (Pure monopoly is an exception which we will discuss later.) As long as there is more than one firm selling in a market, the demand curve facing each firm will be more elastic than the market demand curve.

FIGURE 8–1.   A demand curve facing an imperfectly competitive firm

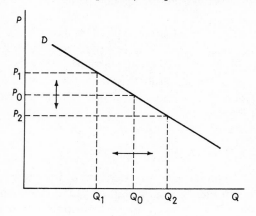

THE CONCEPT OF MARGINAL REVENUE

The phenomenon of an individual firm facing a downward sloping demand curve makes it necessary to introduce a new concept—marginal revenue. Marginal revenue (MR) is defined as the additional revenue obtained by producing and selling one more unit of a good or service. Or conversely it is the reduction in revenue caused by a one unit reduction in sales.

As we pointed out in Chapter 4, it is not realistic to believe that a firm can change its production or sales by just one unit. For this reason economists generally refer to a change in production and sales over a small range of output and compute MR for a unit change of output within this range. The formula for computing marginal revenue is:

$$MR = \frac{\text{Change in total revenue}}{\text{Change in quantity sold}}$$

This formula will be a bit easier to understand if we apply it to a specific example. Suppose Figure 8–1 depicts a demand curve facing a shoe manufacturer. Let us assume that the firm charges $20 per pair for its shoes and sells 1,000 pair per week. (For the moment let us not be concerned with how the firm arrived at this price.) This price and quantity would correspond to P_0 and Q_0, respectively, in Figure 8–1. Multiplying price times quantity results in a total revenue to the firm of $20,000 per week.

Now suppose the firm wishes to expand its sales to 1,500 pair per week. Suppose in order to increase its sales by 500 pair of shoes per week it must lower their price to $19 per pair. With the new lower price and larger quantity, total revenue becomes $28,500 per week. We now have enough information to compute the marginal revenue of an extra pair of shoes sold in this range of output.

$$MR = \frac{\$28,500 - \$20,000}{1,500 - 1,000} = \frac{\$8,500}{500} = \$17$$

In this range of output, an extra pair of shoes sold adds $17 to total revenue.

MARGINAL REVENUE AND PRICE

Recall that because of the downward sloping demand curve, the firm had to lower price from $20 to $19 to sell the additional 500 pair per week. But we might ask a reasonable question at this point. If an extra pair of shoes sells for $19 why doesn't it add $19 to total revenue?

The reason why marginal revenue is less than price is because the lower $19 price applies to all of the weekly sales, not just to the extra or additional sales that result from the lower $19 price. It would not be reasonable to expect the firm to sell the initial 1,000 pair for $20 per pair and the extra 500 pair for $19. No one would want to buy any of the initial 1,000 pair. Thus when price is reduced to sell more of the product, the lower price must apply to all units sold not just to the marginal units. As a result MR is even less than the new lower price because the new lower price reduces the total revenue obtained from the original quantity sold from what it would otherwise be.

We should keep in mind, however, that marginal revenue is less than price only if the firm faces a downward sloping demand curve. If, as we saw in perfect competition, the firm faces a horizontal demand curve, then MR is equal to price. In this situation, the firm does not have to reduce price to sell additional units. So the addition to total revenue (MR) is exactly the same as the price that the marginal unit sells for.

If we were to graph MR at various levels of output, we would obtain for perfect competition a horizontal line that is equal to price, which in turn is equal to the demand curve facing the individual firm (Figure 8–2 [A]). For imperfect competition the MR line would be less than price at any given level of output. Thus the MR line would be lower than its corresponding demand curve and slope down more steeply (Figure 8–2 [B]).

Although imperfectly competitive firms all share one thing in common, they all face downward sloping demand curves for their good or service, there is a great deal of diversity between these firms. Economists have attempted to create some order out of this diversity by classifying imper-

FIGURE 8–2. Marginal revenue and demand facing the individual firm

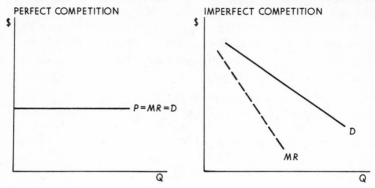

fectly competitive firms into three categories: (1) monopolistic competition, (2) oligopoly, and (3) pure monopoly. Let us now examine each of these three types of firms in some detail.

MONOPOLISTIC COMPETITION

As the name implies, monopolistic competition is similar in some respects to perfect competition. The two distinguishing characteristics of monopolistic competition are (1) there are many firms each selling a small proportion of the market and (2) each firm sells a product slightly different than its competitors.

The characteristic of many firms each selling a small proportion of the market makes monopolistic competition very similar to perfect competition. On the other hand, the fact that each firm sells a product slightly different than its competitors results in a downward sloping demand curve facing each firm. Because its product or service is slightly different than its competitors, the firm has some control over the price it charges.

The multitude of firms engaged in retail trade offer the best examples of monopolistic competition. Service stations, barber shops, department stores, grocery stores, florists, and repair shops of all kinds are some examples of monopolistic competition. In addition most of the relatively small manufacturing firms would fall under this category.

You might reasonably ask at this point how a firm such as a gasoline station can be said to sell a product different than a competitor especially one that sells the same brand. In the case of retail trade we should bear in mind that the location of the firm is in itself a part of the product sold. For example, a Standard Oil Station located on a well-traveled, easily accessible location sells in a sense a different product than another Standard Station in a remote location. Other things equal, the product that is more accessible to us is the more desirable product. And most people are willing to pay a bit more for a more desirable product.

Another factor that distinguishes two seemingly identical products is service. Some people prefer to purchase their clothing in intimate little shops where the clerk is very friendly and instantly available for assistance. Others buy their clothes in large department stores with very little assistance and impersonal check-out counters. Even though the physical characteristics of the items sold in these two types of stores may be identical, the customer who wants to consume more service along with the item will buy from the small intimate shop.

We should realize, however, that providing services involves a cost so we should expect to pay a higher price where more service is provided. You might have noticed that "cut-rate" gasoline stations rarely clean windshields or check oil levels. In "name-brand" stations you generally buy these services along with the gasoline. As an individual consumer we have to decide if the marginal utility per dollar for these services is at least equal to the marginal utility per dollar of other things we buy.

PRICE DETERMINATION IN MONOPOLISTIC COMPETITION

The fact that the goods or services sold by monopolistically competitive firms differ in some respect, either physically or because of location or services, allows this firm some flexibility in the price it can charge. This does not mean, of course, that a service station for example, could charge 40 cents per gallon for regular gas when other stations are charging 32.9 cents. To do so would be foolhardy because it would soon lose most of its customers. But it might be able to charge somewhere in the range of 30.9 to 34.9 cents per gallon, without either causing a price war or losing most of its sales.

If the station manager feels that he can clear more net profit by a narrow margin, high-volume operation, he will probably charge just a bit less than his competitors. If he thinks he can make more with a wider margin, lower volume business, he will probably charge a bit more than the average price of his competitors.

Thus in monopolistic competition, the range of price within which the firm can operate is determined largely by the average price of his closest competitors. The individual firm may diverge slightly from the average market price depending on the kind of business he wishes to operate. It is a mistake, however, to believe that just because a firm selling in monopolistic competition places a price tag on its product that it can charge any price it pleases. Most firms in this kind of market are restricted to a rather narrow range of price. They have a bit more freedom, however, than the perfectly competitive firm which has absolutely no leeway in the price that it can charge.

In the case of perfect competition we were a bit more precise in determining price and output for an individual firm. Recall that a perfectly competitive firm maximizes profits if it produces a quantity that corresponds to the point at which marginal cost is equal to market price. And we were able to illustrate this point with a diagram. We can utilize a similar technique for monopolistic competition, only in this case we must keep in mind that the firm faces a slightly downward sloping demand curve. Moreover, the marginal revenue of an additional unit sold is somewhat less than the price of this unit because the new lower price must apply to all units sold. There is no difference in the way costs are derived, however, between perfect competition and imperfect competition on the selling side, so we can continue to use the average and marginal cost concepts that we used in Chapter 7.

As a general rule, an imperfectly competitive firm maximizes profits if it produces or sells a quantity that corresponds to the point at which marginal cost is equal to marginal revenue. Recall that MC is the cost of producing or selling an additional unit of output. And marginal revenue, you remember, is the additional revenue obtained from this extra or marginal unit sold. For example, if it costs a service station 25 cents to sell an extra gallon of gasoline and the marginal revenue from this extra gallon is 30 cents, the station can increase its profits (or decrease losses) by 5 cents if it sells this extra gallon.

Moreover it is to the firm's advantage to continue to increase output as long as MR is greater than or at least equal to MC. We illustrate why this is the case in Figure 8–3. Suppose we cut in at a quantity of output just short of the point where MC equals MR, call it Q_1. If we increase output by one additional unit past Q_1, our total costs increase by the distance from the horizontal axis up to the MC curve. However, our total revenue increase is shown by the distance between the horizontal axis and MR. The difference between these two distances represent the additional profit that the firm captures by producing this extra unit.

If we continue to increase output we see that the distance between MC and MR continues to grow smaller. But as long as there is any distance between them at all, total profits can be increased by increasing output. Total profits are maximized (or losses minimized) at the quantity where MR equals MC, Q_0 in Figure 8–3. To stop producing short of this point, say at Q_1, means that the firm needlessly foregoes profits (or incurs unnecessary losses) equal in value to the area of the shaded triangle in Figure 8–3.

We can use Figure 8–3 to illustrate also the profit maximizing price that a monopolistically competitive firm would charge. If the firm chooses to maximize profits and produce or sell Q_0, then the demand curve facing this firm indicates that the price its customers are willing to pay is equal to P_0. The firm would not want to charge a lower price because in so doing it would just throw away profits. On the other hand, it could not charge a higher price because its customers will only pay price P_0 for quantity Q_0.

FIGURE 8–3.   Profit maximizing price and quantity for a monopolistically competitive firm

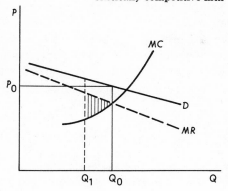

In Figure 8–3 there is no indication, however, whether the firm is making a pure profit or incurring a loss. All we can tell from this diagram is that P_0 and Q_0 are the optimum price and quantity, respectively, meaning either that the firm's losses are minimized or profits maximized. In order to determine the extent of profit or loss we must know average total cost. If ATC is below price at the optimum quantity, the firm reaps a pure profit; if ATC is above price, the firm incurs a loss.

In Figure 8–4 (A), we illustrate a situation where the firm is making a pure profit, meaning that the resources employed by the firm are earning more than they could make in some alternative activity or occupation. The total dollar value of the pure profit is illustrated by the shaded area. A firm can find itself in this enviable position for one or both of two reasons: (1) the firm is managed very well so that the firm's costs are low or (2) the firm sells a desirable product so that the demand curve that it faces is high relative to its competitors.

FIGURE 8–4.   Illustrating profit and loss situations for a monopolistically competitive firm

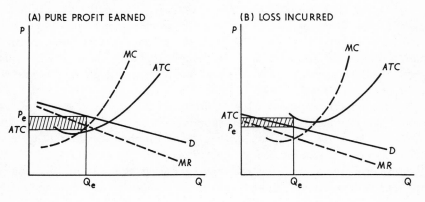

Figure 8–4 (B) depicts a less fortunate firm that is making a loss. In this situation the resources employed by the firm are earning less than they could in alternative employment. The total dollar value of the loss is illustrated by the shaded area. A firm can find itself in this circumstance if its costs are high either because of high-paying alternative employment for its resources or because of poor management. Or the firm can incur losses if the product it sells is not as desirable to consumers as the products sold by its competitors so that the demand it faces for its good is relatively low.

LONG-RUN ADJUSTMENT IN MONOPOLISTIC COMPETITION

Just as we saw in the case of perfect competition the existence of either pure profits or losses for a substantial number of firms in a monopolistically competitive market can be expected to give rise to adjustments by the industry. For example, if a substantial share of the firms are reaping pure profits, this is a signal for existing firms to enlarge their enterprises or for new firms to enter. In either case the demand curve facing each firm begins to decrease, shifting downward to the left. A decrease in demand, you recall, has two meanings: (1) the firm's consumers will now buy a smaller amount at a given price or (2) its consumers will buy a given amount only if price is lower.

This phenomenon is somewhat easier to understand if we visualize ourselves as owners of a service station which is making substantial profits. Seeing a good opportunity, another firm builds a station across the street from ours and begins to take some of our customers, perhaps by selling at a slightly lower price. As our customers leave, the demand curve facing our firm begins to decrease. We lower our price somewhat in order to compete with this new firm, and to adjust to new, lower demand and marginal revenue curves. As we lower price our pure profits decline and we approach a zero pure profit position as illustrated in Figure 8–5 (A).

It is usually possible to find a few firms in every market that have some special advantage, however. It might be situated at a prime location, such as easy access to customers, or it might sell a well-liked, hard to duplicate product. For firms such as these the entry or enlargement of competitors might have a relatively minor effect on the demand that it faces. For example, if we established a new toothpaste factory, our product would probably have a very negligible effect on the demand facing Colgate or some of the other well-known brands.

Even after time is allowed for expansion of the industry, therefore, we would likely find a few firms in every monopolistically competitive market making pure profits, together with a large number of other firms just breaking even or possibly a few incurring losses.

Most firms that are able to reap pure profits in the long run eventually are sold to new owners, however. When this occurs there is a tendency for the price of the firm to reflect the pure profits that can be expected in the future. It is reasonable to expect that buyers of firms are willing to pay more for a firm that is very profitable than one which is just breaking even or running a loss.

The higher price paid for high-profit firms results in turn in higher production costs mainly because of the higher interest (explicit or implicit) and depreciation charges that stem from this higher price. Thus when a high-profit firm changes hands, there is a tendency for ATC to shift upward as in Figure 8–5 (B). The end result is much the same in this case as in the case of demand shifting down and to the left: the pure profits are eventually squeezed out of the industry. The phenomenon of the cost curves shifting probably occurs much more slowly and takes much longer, however, than the entry of new resources.

FIGURE 8–5.   Long-run adjustment by individual firms to pure profits in monopolistic competition

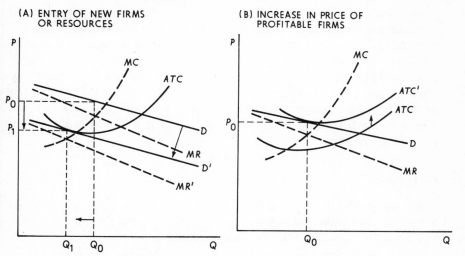

We must keep in mind, of course, that in any industry circumstances are continually changing. Thus it is not likely we could ever observe a situation in which every firm is at a zero profit, long equilibrium. Rather it is more realistic to visualize a situation where there is continued movement towards equilibrium but few instances where it is ever reached. We would expect to observe, therefore, at any point in time a wide variety of profit positions by firms; some might be enjoying substantial pure profits, others just earning what might be earned in other industries, and still others incurring losses.

We could go through the same analysis for a case where a substantial share of the firms in a monopolistically competitive market are running losses. Just the opposite would occur in the case compared to the pure profit situation. Now firms would leave the industry, shifting the demand curve facing the remaining firms upward and to the right. Also firms that had shut down might be repurchased for a lower price which in turn lowers costs and restores at least a normal profit position once again. You might find it useful to draw diagrams corresponding to Figure 8–5 (A) and (B) that illustrate a long-run adjustment to losses.

You might have noticed by now that the process of adjustment, either to pure profits or losses, in monopolistic competition is very similar to perfect competition. In the case of pure profits, the demand curve facing the individual firm shifts down in both perfect competition and monopolistic competition, eventually competing the profits away in the long run. Similarly the presence of losses prompts resources to leave both types of industries resulting in an upward shift of the demand facing each firm.

There is also a long-run adjustment on the cost side for both types of competition. Recall that when a firm changes hands the record of profits or losses will be reflected in the price of the firm and consequently into its production costs. This type of adjustment is probably more frequent in monopolistic competition, however, because a firm can enjoy special advantages (or suffer special disadvantages) because of its product it sells as well as because of the resources it owns.

One additional difference in monopolistic competition is the tangency point between the demand curve facing the firm and its *ATC* curve. In perfect competition this tangency point occurs at the low point of the *ATC* curve whereas in monopolistic competition it occurs a bit to the left of the low point.

OLIGOPOLY

Let us now turn to a market situation that economists have labeled oligopoly. This rather strange sounding word is derived from the Greek word "oligos" meaning few. The meaning of the word "oligos" provides a hint of the kind of industry we are dealing with. Basically an oligopoly is an industry where a few firms, say 3 or 4, produce the major share of the market. Oligopoly is commonly found in heavy industry or in products marketed nationally. Autos, steel, airplanes, drugs, farm equipment, minerals, petroleum, and computers are some examples of products that are produced by oligopolies.

Unlike monopolistic competition, the firms in an oligopoly market do not necessarily produce a differentiated product. In fact, petroleum, steel, and minerals could all be classified as homogeneous products. A ton of steel produced by U.S. Steel is essentially the same product as a ton produced by Bethlehem or Jones and Laughlin. There are, of course, oligopolies that produce differentiated products such as automobiles or appliances. Thus the distinguishing characteristic of an oligopoly is the small number of firms in the market.

OLIGOPOLY PRICE DETERMINATION

The fact that each firm sells a substantial share of the market or sells a differentiated product makes it possible for each firm to influence to some degree the price of its product. For example, if one of the large steel companies reduced its output, there would be a noticeable decline in the amount of steel on the market. This would, in turn, result in an increase in the price of steel. Thus each firm has some control over the price of the product it sells, which is just another way of saying that each firm in an oligopoly faces a downward sloping demand curve.

We should recognize, however, that each firm's ability to influence the price of its product is limited by the substitute products available. Each firm, therefore, must sell its product at a price somewhere in line with prices of its competitors. For example, it is not likely that Ford would sell many cars if their price was several hundred dollars higher than comparable Chevrolet models. For homogeneous products produced in an oligopoly market, there is even less chance for price differentials to exist. Abstracting from transportation changes, no one would want to buy steel from U.S. Steel if they charged just slightly more than the other companies.

We should not be surprised, therefore, when we observe all firms in an oligopoly market changing their prices at about the same time. This is just an indication that consumers regard the products of the major firms in a oligopoly market as close substitutes for each other. If a firm's price rises out of line with the prices of other firms, its customers soon discover substitute products that give them more for their money.

If the products of firms in an oligopoly market are close substitutes for each other, steel for example, there will be virtually no difference in price between the products. For products such as luxury automobiles which consumers regard as less perfect substitutes, wider differences in price between firms can be observed.

In dealing with prices of oligopoly products, we ought to distinguish between the list price, the price on the window sticker for automobiles, and the actual price that consumers pay. The difference between these two prices can be substantial for highly differentiated products. The list price of two products might be very similar but the actual price widely divergent, as is shown below for Cadillacs and Chryslers (see Table 8–1).

Although Chryslers' list price is close to the Cadillac list, its actual price is much lower. This implies that consumers do not regard these two automobiles as close substitutes. On the other hand, the difference between list price and actual price is about the same for Fords and Chevrolets, implying that these two makes are very close substitutes in the minds of consumers.

The figures in Table 8–1 also help make it clear that oligopolies are not able to charge any price they would like. No doubt all of these firms would like to charge the list price but none of them can. If these firms did hold to the list price, they would find themselves with a substantial stock of unsold automobiles at the end of the model year. The actual price is the price that makes consumers willing to purchase all the cars that are manufactured, i.e., the equilibrium price that clears the market.

TABLE 8–1. List price versus actual price for selected makes of automobiles*

	List Price	Actual Price
Cadillac	$5,884	$5,400
Chrysler	5,956	5,059
Chevrolet	3,038	2,496
Ford	3,043	2,473

*Source: 1970 Consumer Guide, published by Buyer's Guide.

Following our procedure with monopolistic competition, oligopoly price determination can be illustrated also with a diagram. As a matter of fact, the exact same diagram we used for illustrating optimum price and quantity for a monopolistically competitive firm might be used also for an oligopoly. About the only difference is that an oligopoly faces a slightly less elastic demand curve than a firm in monopolistic competition, as shown in Figure 8–6. This occurs because an oligopoly by definition sells a substantial portion of the market. Otherwise the two types of firms are similar in that the oligopoly attempts also to equate MC with MR to determine the most profitable output. The price charged by the firm is determined by the demand that faces the firm at this output. The profit maximizing price shown in Figure 8–6 is actual price, not list price.

In this particular example, price is greater than average total costs so the firm would be earning a pure profit. Of course, this is only an example. If the ATC curve was everywhere above the firm's demand curve, the firm would have no choice but to take a loss or shut down. You might illustrate this situation with a similar diagram of your own.

INTERDEPENDENCE OF FIRMS

An inevitable result of the few number of firms in an oligopoly market is that the action of any one of the major firms will have a significant affect on the sales and/or price of the other firms in the market. For example, suppose General Motors grants a wage increase to its employees which in turn leads to an increase in the cost of production as shown in Figure 8–7 (A). We can see from Figure 8–7 (A) that it would be in GM's interest to raise the price of its cars from P_0 to P_1 and reduce quantity sold from Q_0 to Q_1 in order to again equate MC and MR. For if they continued to charge P_0 and sell Q_0, MC would be greater than MR so they would be losing money on the marginal units produced.

FIGURE 8–6.   Profit maximizing price and quantity for an oligopoly

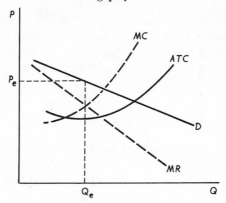

Recall from our discussion of consumer demand that when the price of a good increases there is an increase in demand for substitute goods. We can predict, therefore, that an increase in the price of GM cars will lead to an increase in demand for the other makes, as shown in Figure 8–7 (B). In other words, consumers will try to avoid the higher prices of GM cars by purchasing more of other makes. But an increase in the demand for other makes will in turn lead to an increase in both price and quantity of these cars as the other firms attempt to equate *MC* with *MR* also (Figure 8–7 [B]).

We see, therefore, that an increase in costs and price of just one of the major firms in an oligopoly market leads to an increase in price of the other firms as well. You might also want to prove to yourself that a decrease in costs and price by one firm will also lead to a decrease in price of other firms by constructing diagrams of your own.

FIGURE 8–7.   Illustrating the effects of an increase in manufacturing costs of General Motors automobiles

(A) GENERAL MOTORS

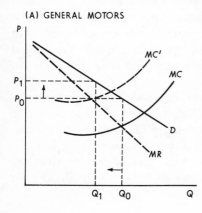

(B) OTHER AUTO MANUFACTURERS

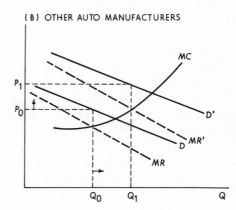

We ought to point out as well, that the increase in demand and price shown in Figure 8–7 (B) will in turn lead to a slight increase in demand for GM cars, resulting in a slightly greater increase in price for these cars than we originally specified in Figure 8–7 (A). In fact we could trace this process of cause and effect back and forth indefinitely. But as a rule the largest and most interesting changes come on the first round so economists have not been greatly concerned with the second or third order effects.

THE KINKED DEMAND CURVE

Compared to the products sold by firms in perfect or monopolistic competition, the products sold by firms in an oligopoly market tend to exhibit relatively small price changes. In an attempt to explain this phenomenon, economists have devised a theory of the "kinked" demand curve.

The basic assumption of this theory is that each firm attempts to retain its present customers or attract new ones. Let us see how the kinked demand curve is derived. Suppose General Motors raises its price. It is assumed in this case that the other auto manufacturers will hold to their original price in order to take GM's customers. Thus GM experiences a substantial reduction in sales, as shown in Figure 8–8 where price increases from P_0 to P_1 and quantity declines from Q_0 to Q_1. On the other hand, if GM reduces prices from P_0 to P_2, it is assumed that other firms also reduce their prices so GM is able to obtain only a modest increase in sales, say from Q_0 to Q_2. Thus we have a kink in the demand curve facing the individual firm.

You will notice also that the kinked demand curve results in a discontinuous MR curve. The elastic portion of the MR curve is derived from the elastic segment of the demand curve and the inelastic portion from the inelastic part of demand. You will notice also that the two segments of the MR curve are joined by a vertical line. Now if MC should intersect MR at some point within this vertical section, a shift in MC, as shown in Figure 8–8, would not change the optimum price and quantity for the firm. That is, the profit maximizing price and quantity would remain at P_0 and Q_0, respectively, for either MC or MC'. As a result, the kinked demand curve is sometimes used to explain why oligopoly prices do not exhibit a large amount of fluctuation.

The theory of the kinked demand curve has been criticized by some economists. For one thing, it is argued that it is not possible to derive from the kinked demand curve how the going price and quantity come to be what they are. These magnitudes have to be assumed as given.

Secondly, doubt has been expressed as to whether oligopoly prices are as inflexible as generally assumed. Even though list prices might remain

FIGURE 8–8. The kinked demand curve

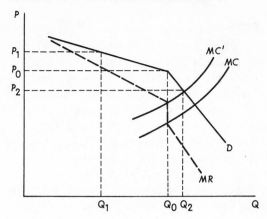

unchanged over a long period, actual prices may vary considerably. For example, the actual price of a new car tends to fall from the beginning to the end of the model year even though list price stays the same. The same is true for appliances. Or if an oligopoly firm mistakenly produces more of an item than it thought would sell at the list price, price cuts are in evidence.

PURE MONOPOLY

We now turn to the other end of the spectrum of industry types: pure monopoly. Pure monopoly exists where there is just one firm providing a good or service in a market. This kind of market tends to exist only when the government has the exclusive right to supply a good or service, such as the post office, or where the government has given exclusive right for a firm to operate, such as your local light and power company.

The existence of a pure monopoly depends also upon how broadly we define a good or service. For example, the post office has a monopoly on mail service but not upon all communications. Or the local light and power company has a monopoly on centrally generated electricity but not on factory or home-generated electricity, or other sources of light and power such as gas or oil. It is not correct to assume, therefore, that consumers are forced to buy from a monopoly or else go without. Rather there are substitutes for goods produced by a monopoly, albeit imperfect substitutes. And as the price of the monopoly's good or service rises higher and higher, these imperfect substitutes come into greater demand.

A monopoly is able to persist for any length of time only if entry into the industry is blocked. The most effective means of blocking entry into an industry is for the government to reserve exclusive right of production to itself, or to firms that it designates by means of a license. Sometimes a firm can gain a temporary monopoly by discovering a new product or input and patenting it. Monopolies such as this, however, tend to be short-lived, or at least very narrowly defined because patents can usually be circumvented by producing something just slightly different.

The reason usually given for the government creating and nurturing a monopoly is to avoid excessive duplication. For example, if there were several telephone companies in your area, there would have to be as many sets of lines and switchboards. Moreover there would tend to be excessive inconvenience when people on one company's lines attempted to call people buying telephone service from a different company, unless there was some sort of central clearinghouse for calls.

As time goes on, however, it is becoming less clear that the benefits of avoiding all duplication exceed its costs. For as long as a firm or institution enjoys exclusive right to operate free from competitors there is little incentive to search for cost reducing techniques or to provide better goods or services. There is nothing like a little competition, even one competitor, to keep the supplier of a good or service "on his toes." Complaints of bad service, protests, and the like tend not to be nearly as effective as the possibility of losing one's job to a competitor.

Even in the field of education there is probably too much monopoly and too little competition. At the elementary and secondary level of education, and partly at the college level, everyone must pay for public schools regardless of whether their children attend private or parochial schools. This tends to place the private and parochial schools at a competitive disadvantage in providing an educational service. Under the present system, public schools can become very bad before it pays to send children to private schools. It is argued that a system of providing educational vouchers to students which they could "spend" at the school of their choice is one means of promoting more competition in the education "industry."

It has been argued as well that the general public would gain if public schools also were allowed to compete with each other. Under the present setup a child is forced to attend a designated public school or no public school at all. Hence it is argued that improvement would take place in the poorer public schools if the children attending these schools were allowed to take their business elsewhere.

Even within a school, particularly at the college level, it is possible that there is too much monopoly and too little competition. Almost every student experiences at one time or another a course that is badly taught but impossible to avoid because it is required for graduation. This kind of problem is less likely to come up if students are given a choice of instructors or courses that satisfy a given requirement. Competition would tend to encourage poor instructors to improve their performance or find another line of work just as it does for inefficient firms. Of course most people like competition to exist for others but not for themselves. Consequently, people who now enjoy monopoly privileges generally have an ample supply of reasons for keeping things as they are.

MONOPOLY PRICE DETERMINATION

Since government has created or at least sanctioned most present-day monopolies and therefore controls their prices, there is relatively little chance for a private monopoly to set a profit maximizing price. We might, however, first determine what this price might be and then determine the "socially optimum" price of a monopoly supplied good or service.

The diagram for illustrating monopoly price and output is essentially the same as the diagrams employed to illustrate price and output for monopolistic competition and oligopoly. The only difference for a monopoly is that the demand curve facing the firm is the same thing as the market demand curve for the good or service sold by the monopoly. Thus for a given good or service the demand facing a monopoly is somewhat steeper or more inelastic than the demand facing an oligopoly firm.

As shown in Figure 8–9, the profit maximizing price and quantity are P_m and Q_m, respectively. We should not take this to mean, however, that a monopoly is always assured of a pure profit. If the average total cost curve is everywhere above the demand curve, the monopoly either takes a loss or shuts down. In fact, cases of monopoly losses are not uncommon in the public utilities. You might illustrate a monopoly loss situation with a diagram of your own.

As we mentioned, present-day monopoly is generally regulated by the government. Since the government is supposed to represent the general

FIGURE 8–9. Monopoly price and quantity

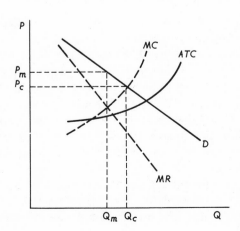

public, at least in a democracy, we would expect it to set a price and quantity that would somehow maximize the general welfare of the people, i.e., consumers. To understand what this price and quantity might be, we must go back to what we said about perfect competition.

Recall, that the value of output to society is maximized if each firm produces up to the point where the price of the marginal unit produced is equal to its marginal cost. Recall also that the price of the marginal unit is its measure of value to society and its MC is the value of goods given up to produce this extra unit. You will note in Figure 8–9, however, that price is greater than MC at the profit maximizing price and quantity. This means, as we pointed out in Chapter 7, that there is an underallocation of resources to the production of this good or service.

It is fairly evident then that if the government wishes to maximize the total value of output to society for a given amount of resources, it should set a price that corresponds to the intersection of the MC curve and the demand curve—P_c in Figure 8–9. At this point, price is equal to MC, so that value of the marginal unit is just equal to the value of goods given up to produce it.

Notice also that the socially optimum price, P_c, is somewhat less than the profit maximizing price, P_m, and the optimum quantity, Q_c, is greater than the profit maximizing quantity, Q_m. Although you might have noticed as well that the monopoly firm is still making a pure profit at the regulated price and quantity because price is still greater than ATC.

Because of this pure profit you might suggest that price be lowered still further to the point where ATC intersects the demand curve. But if this were done, we see that MC would be greater than price, indicating an overallocation of resources to this production activity. If competing firms were allowed to enter this industry, there would be a decrease in demand facing this firm and a gradual competing away of these pure profits. The government, however, in order to maintain the monopoly prohibits entry of other firms.

Does the monopoly, then, continue to reap pure profits? Probably not. The likely outcome of this situation would be an eventual bidding up of the value of the firm's assets pushing the ATC curve upward. For example, over the years the value of New York City taxi cab medallions, which represent an exclusive right to operate taxi cabs in New York City, has increased substantially. The original or past owners enjoyed a capital gain while new or future owners probably earn or will earn just a normal return to their labor and investment, taking into account the increased cost of operating a cab because of the interest charge (explicit or implicit) on the medallion.

In the case of government regulated monopolies, there are some people who argue that the "regulator" soon becomes the "regulatee." They argue that monopolies develop powerful lobbies to influence the decisions of the government agencies that are supposed to regulate them. We see some evidence of this when the government either raises or lowers prices in response to pressure from regulated firms or industries. It is possible to argue, therefore, that a regulated price is not greatly different than a profit maximizing price.

Moreover, we cannot be certain that a regulated price is always lower than the profit maximizing price. If new technology comes on the scene, lowering MC, downward adjustments in the regulated price probably lag behind the adjustments that would automatically take place if the monopoly purposely tries to maximize profits. We must remember that higher prices do not necessarily imply higher profits.

WHY MINIMIZE MONOPOLY?

We have seen that in some industries, mainly the public utilities, the government creates and maintains monopoly. However, in other industries the government attempts to discourage monopoly power and maintain an atmosphere of competition. Why? There are probably several reasons.

First, as we just discussed in the preceding section, any situation where price is greater than marginal cost results in a misallocation of resources, needlessly resulting in a smaller total value of output for society given the resources available. However, it is not likely that the general public or their elected representatives in the government have been greatly motivated by this reason. In general people have not become very concerned over a misallocation of resources because they are not able to envision the total value of output without the misallocation.

The general public does, however, have an idea of what is a reasonable or "just" level of profit. And it is assumed, probably correctly, that a firm which is able to monopolize an industry will reap excessive profits, resulting in an unjustifiable transfer of income from consumers to the owners of the monopoly. An atmosphere of competition is maintained, therefore, to keep profits down to what people consider a reasonable level.

A third reason for attempting to maintain competition is to encourage the adoption of new, cost reducing technology, or development of new and better products. Again if a firm has no competition there is little incentive to risk or develop anything new.

COLLUSION AND ANTITRUST

In some industries, particularly those characterized by oligopoly, there is a possibility for firms to collude with one another and agree not to compete. When a number of firms get together and act as one, we have what economists call a "cartel." It is as if there were just one firm in the market, i.e., a monopoly. Since the cartel would act as a monopoly, it would set a price higher than would exist if there were many firms competing in the market. This is illustrated in Figure 8–9, where the monopoly price, P_m, would be higher than the price that would exist under perfect competition, P_c.

The two main legal tools that the government uses to fight nonsanctioned monopoly or cartel are the Sherman Antitrust Act of 1890 and the Clayton Antitrust Act of 1914. The Sherman Act makes "restraint of trade" or any attempt to monopolize trade a misdemeanor, i.e., a criminal offense against the federal government. This means going to jail for being convicted of the crime.

The Clayton Act essentially duplicates the Sherman Act but does spell out in a bit more detail the various illegal activities that might eventually lead to monopoly or cartel. The intention of this act was to curb monopoly before it came into existence rather than to just punish it after the fact. The Federal Trade Commission (FTC), also set up in 1914, was given power to investigate "unfair" business practices and to take legal action if required.

In addition to government action against monopoly, or cartel, there is a market force acting as a continual deterrent. This is the temptation by colluding firms to cheat on one another. As shown in Figure 8–10, an industry that becomes a monopoly or cartel must reduce its output in order to raise price. Thus each individual firm that agrees to collude must agree to reduce its output in order for the scheme to work. But if each firm is maximizing profits by equating MR with MC before the collusion takes place, as is reasonable to expect, then after they agree to reduce quantity and raise price MR for each firm will be greater than MC as shown in Figure 8–10. Before collusion each firm maximizes profits by producing Q_0—that quantity that corresponds to the intersection of the MC and MR. During collusion each firm reduces output to Q_1. We cannot, however, illustrate the new higher price that will result from collusion on the diagrams in Figure 8–9 because these are demand curves facing each firm not the market demand. We can only assume that the new higher price will result in higher net profits for each firm else it would not pay to collude in the first place.

But the important point to note is that during collusion each firm is in a situation where MR is greater than MC. Thus it is in the interest of each individual firm to sell a few extra units of output "under the table." By doing so the firm can increase profits even more. But when all or most firms taking part in the collusion "cheat" in this manner, the market price must come down otherwise the additional output cannot be sold. Unless the group of colluders can impose a penalty on the "cheaters" there is a tendency for the collusive agreement to break down. And it is difficult to enforce any kind of penalty on a firm for refraining from an activity that is itself illegal.

FIGURE 8–10. The effect on individual firms of colluding to reduce quantity and raise price

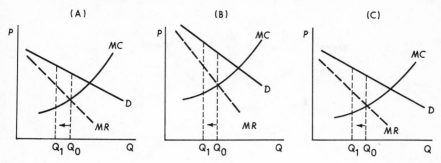

ADVERTISING

There is a wide range of activity that can be classified as advertising. The homemade "for sale" sign on an automobile, the "want ads" in the newspaper, roadside signs, and radio and TV commercials are all examples of advertising. Sometimes advertising is done by a buyer, such as "help-wanted" ads, although the majority is probably done by sellers.

Essentially advertising can be divided into two major types: (1) informational and (2) persuasive. Informational advertising, as the name implies, is intended to inform prospective customers about what is for sale, its characteristics, and its price. Some examples of informational advertising are the grocery store advertisements in the newspaper telling the prices of various items that can be bought at the particular store. Persuasive advertising, on the other hand, attempts to persuade people to buy one product over another. Most of the advertising we see on television or hear on radio is of the persuasive variety.

All advertising attempts to accomplish one objective: to increase the demand for the good or service being advertised. Of course, we must realize that advertising costs money. Thus when a firm or group of firms decides to advertise, we can only assume that the marginal revenue obtained by advertising is at least as great as the marginal cost (including advertising expense) of the extra units sold. The economic effects of advertising are illustrated in Figure 8–11; demand shifts upward and to the right, but ATC and MC also shift upward.

A great deal of disagreement exists over the merits of advertising. Most people, including economists, probably would agree, however, that informational advertising is beneficial. In order for consumers to maximize utility they must know what is for sale, something about the good or service being sold, and the selling price.

Much less agreement exists, though, about persuasive advertising. The advertising industry argues that advertising stimulates the economy by

FIGURE 8–11. The effects of advertising

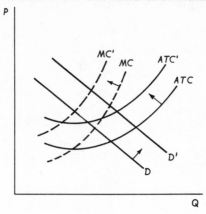

enticing people to spend. Others, particularly those who have recently experienced a rather nauseating commercial, argue that persuasive advertising is pure waste because of the effect of one firm's advertising is just to cancel out the advertising of other firms.

A truly objective appraisal of advertising, if such is possible, would likely rate it somewhere between these two extreme views. No doubt, advertising stimulates spending on the item being advertised, else it would not pay to advertise. But it is less clear if advertising really makes people spend a larger share of their income. Expenditures on advertising have increased greatly during the past three or four decades, but on the average people spend about the same proportion of their income today as they did 30 or 40 years ago. Nor is it clear that it is even desirable that people spend a larger share of their present income on consumer goods.

It has been suggested that the government ban advertising of the persuasive variety and allow only informational advertising. The problem, however, is to separate the two. One could argue, for example, that telling people that product A is superior to all competitors is really information advertising. It is likely that a ban on persuasive advertising also would result in much "waste" through lawyers' fees and court costs.

POLLUTION BY IMPERFECT COMPETITION

We discussed in the chapter on perfect competition the effect of pollution or social costs on the allocation of resources and prices. We should, of course, emphasize that this problem exists in the area of imperfect competition also. Undoubtedly a large share of the total waste material in the United States results from the production of firms that fall in the category of imperfect competition.

The same general analysis of social costs can be applied to the imperfectly competitive firm as we used for the firm in perfect competition. Recall that the existence of a social cost means that the true cost of producing a product is greater than the cost perceived by the firm. For example, the cost of getting rid of waste material exceeds the cost of the smoke stack or the sewer pipe.

The effect of social costs for an imperfectly competitive firm is illustrated in Figure 8–12. The lower MC curve represents the cost as perceived by the firm whereas MC' represents the true or full marginal cost of production. If the firm were made to bear the full costs, we see that quantity produced would decline from Q_0 to Q_1 and price would increase from P_0 to P_1.

FIGURE 8–12. The effect of pollution
control on the firm in
imperfect competition

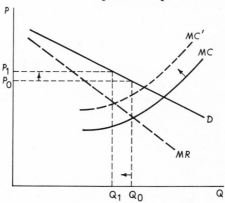

Again in this case we see that if the firm is made to bear a larger share of the costs of eliminating waste materials, there will be an inevitable increase in the price of the product produced. This is not to say that pollution control is undesirable; it only says that a clean environment is not a free good. It appears, though, that society is becoming more willing to pay the price of pollution control, especially people in the middle and upper income brackets.

MARGINAL COST AND SUPPLY

Throughout the discussion on imperfect competition we have deliberately avoided the use of the word supply. This is because an imperfectly competitive firm does not have a supply curve as such. Recall in the case of perfect competition that the firm's marginal cost curve is essentially its supply curve. The firm, faced with a given price, maximizing profits by producing up to the point where price equals marginal cost. The MC

curve, therefore, is the supply curve because it denotes the quantity that will be produced at a given price, or vice versa.

The marginal cost curve of an imperfectly competitive firm, however, is not its supply curve because for a given quantity the price charged will depend upon the demand curve facing the firm. Thus we cannot determine both price and quantity from the *MC* curve alone. We have to know both MC and demand in order to determine price and quantity for a firm operating in imperfect competition, as we have shown in this chapter's diagrams.

However, the same factors that shift the *MC* or supply curve of a perfectly competitive firm also shift the *MC* curve of a firm in imperfect competition. Moreover the result of a shift in *MC* is the same as a shift in supply. For example, a shift to the left, or an increase in *MC*, reduces quantity and increases price in imperfect competition which is the same as a decrease in supply in perfect competition. Remember from our discussion of product supply that an increase in costs is equivalent to a decrease in supply, and vice versa.

DEMAND FACING THE FIRM—A SUMMARY

It will be useful at this point to summarize and compare the demand curve facing each of the four types of firms we have studied. We began in Chapter 7 with the perfectly competitive firm which faces a perfectly elastic demand. Then in this chapter we looked at three types of im-

FIGURE 8–13. Summary of demand curves facing the firms in the four major types of market situations

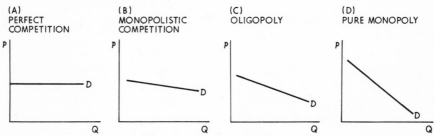

perfectly competitive firms: monopolistic competition, oiliopoly, and pure monopoly. Each of these firms faces a downward sloping demand. In general the smaller the number of firms and the more differentiated the product of each firm, the steeper or more inelastic the demand facing each firm. The demand curve facing the firm in each of the four market situations is illustrated in Figure 8–13.

As we pointed out at the beginning of this chapter, it is best to think of these four types of firms as a continuous distribution rather than four hard and fast categories. These categories are useful to the extent that they identify where in the distribution a given firm would be located.

Most firms in the U.S. economy would fall somewhere within the two extremes of perfect competition and pure monopoly. As a result, economists will often describe a firm by the degree of monopoly power it wields, instead of trying to decide if it is a monopolistically competitive firm or an oligopoly.

THE IMPERFECTLY COMPETITIVE BUYER

Thus far in this chapter we have been concerned exclusively with the selling side of the market. It is possible, although less common, to observe firms that would be classified as imperfectly competitive buyers. Imperfect competition on the buying side of the market results if there are a relatively small number of buyers each purchasing a significant share of the market.

The distinguishing characteristic of an imperfectly competitive buyer is that he faces an upward sloping supply curve. This means that the buyer has some control over the price he pays for the product. It also means, of course, that in order to purchase larger and larger amounts the buyer must pay a higher price.

It is rather difficult to find examples of buyers in the product market that would face an upward sloping supply curve. It is a bit easier to find examples of imperfect competition on the buying side in the labor market, however. One such example might be a "company" town where there is just one major employer of labor. We will defer further discussion of imperfect competition on the buying side, therefore, until the next chapter where we will study the labor market.

MAIN POINTS OF CHAPTER 8

1. Imperfect competition is defined as a market where each firm sells a differentiated product, supplies a significant share of the market, or both.

2. The imperfectly competitive firm faces a downward sloping demand curve which implies that the firm has some control over the price of its product.

3. Marginal revenue (MR) is the additional revenue obtained by producing and selling an extra unit of output.

4. The downward sloping demand curve implies that marginal revenue is less than price. MR is less than price for the firm in imperfect competition because additional units can be sold only if price is lowered,

and the lower price must apply to all units sold not just to the marginal units.

5. Monopolistic competition is characterized by a market in which there are many firms, each selling a small proportion of the market but each selling a slightly differentiated product. Retail trade is an example of monopolistic competition.

6. The firm in monopolistic competition is restricted to a price that is relatively close to its competitors. Each firm, however, attempting to maximize profits produces up to the point where *MC* is equal to *MR*.

7. If a substantial share of the firms in monopolistic competition are reaping pure profits there is a tendency for additional firms or resources to enter the industry resulting in a decrease in the demand facing each firm. There is also a tendency for the price of assets of profitable firms to be bid up, resulting in higher costs and lower profits for these firms.

8. An oligopoly is a market where there are a few firms each selling a substantial share of the market. An ologopoly may or may not sell a differentiated product. Oligopoly is common in heavy industry or nationally marketed products.

9. Products produced by oligopolies that have close substitutes must sell for about the same price as the substitutes. Each oligopoly, however, attempting to maximize profits produces up to the point where *MC* is equal to *MR*.

10. Because of the few number of firms the action of each firm in an oligopoly has a direct effect on its competitors. For example, an increase in costs and price for one firm results in an increase in demand and price charged by other firms.

11. The kinked demand curve is an attempt to explain the apparent inflexibility of prices charged by oligopolies. It is derived under the assumption that each firm tries to hold present customers or attract new ones.

12. Pure monopoly exists when there is just one firm providing a good or service, although relatively imperfect substitutes generally are available for monopoly produced products.

13. In order for a monopoly to persist for any length of time entry into the market must be blocked. The most effective method of blocking entry is by government issued licenses.

14. The U.S. post office and the public utilities provide the best examples of pure monopoly. The reason for creating monopoly is to avoid costly duplication of facilities, but it is becoming less clear that avoiding duplication outweighs the disadvantage of avoiding competition.

15. The socially optimum price and quantity for a public monopoly corresponds to the point where the *MC* curve intersects the demand curve. At this point *MC* will equal price. The profit maximizing output for a monopoly corresponds to the point where *MC* equals *MR*, the same as is true for monopolistic competition and oligopoly.

16. The existence of private monopoly or monopoly power results in a misallocation of resources because profit maximizing price is greater than marginal cost. Public condemnation of private monopoly, however, probably stems from the fear of excessive monopoly profits, hence a transfer of income from consumers to the owners of the monopoly.

17. The Clayton and Sherman Antitrust Acts provide the government with legislation to fight monopoly or "restraint of trade." The temptation of colluding firms to cheat on one another also provides a check on cartels or collusion.

18. The objective of advertising is to shift product demand to the right. However, advertising also increases costs so the additional sales from advertising must outweigh the additional expense, else it will not be undertaken.

19. The existence of pollution by firms in imperfect competition means the cost as viewed by the firm is less than the true or full costs of production. Pollution control by firms will have the inevitable result of increasing costs and prices of products.

20. The *MC* curve of an imperfectly competitive firm is not its supply curve as is true for the perfectly competitive firm. In order for the *MC* curve to be a supply curve it must show the quantity produced for a given price or vice versa. For imperfect competition demand and *MR* combine with *MC* to determine price and quantity.

21. Moving from perfect competition to pure monopoly the demand curve facing each firm becomes more inelastic.

22. The imperfectly competitive buyer faces a supply curve that is upward sloping. This is a relatively rare situation, occurring occasionally in the labor market.

QUESTIONS FOR THOUGHT AND DISCUSSION

1. "Perfectly competitive firms are small whereas imperfectly competitive firms are large." Is this a valid distinction? Comment.

2. The perfectly competitive firm is sometimes called a "price taker" while the imperfectly competitive firm is a "price maker." Can you explain why these terms might be used?

3. "The imperfectly competitive firm places a price tag on his product, therefore, it can charge any price it wishes." Comment.

4. Suppose by lowering the price of its gasoline from 34.9 to 33.9 cents per gallon, a station can sell 500 extra gallons per week. Can we infer from these figures that the marginal revenue of an extra gallon sold in this range of output is 33.9 cents. Why or why not?

5. Think of a monopolistically competitive firm in your neighborhood. Then explain why economists would consider it to be such.

6. A Standard Oil Company station at one location sells gasoline for 32.9 cents per gallon whereas another Standard Station one mile away on a busy intersection sells gasoline for 35.9 cents per gallon. How can this be explained? Aren't these stations selling the same product?

7. Explain the process of adjustment that would take place if the hamburger stands in a new suburban development are making substantial pure profits. Employ a diagram.

8. The fact that the list prices of new automobiles do not change over the year proves that oligopoly prices are inflexible. Comment.

9. Suppose General Motors decides to raise the price of its new cars because of a rise in labor costs. Explain the effect of this change in GM prices on the Ford Motor Company. Utilize diagrams.

10. Think of a pure monopoly in your area. What would be some substitutes for the product of this monopoly?

11. Suppose you are a public school superintendent. What arguments could you make for requiring children in your school district to attend your school?

12. Suppose you and two others are the only people selling new cars in your town or area. One of the others suggests that the three of you get together and decide on a minimum price for your cars. Discuss the possibilities of the three of you colluding and the problems you might encounter.

13. Suppose you are the manager of a pizza parlor in your neighborhood. What kind of reasoning would you go through in deciding whether or not to advertise?

14. Suppose the exhaust fan from the kitchen of your pizza parlor in Question 13 emitted a disagreeable odor. Illustrate with a diagram your MC of production and the true or full MC. Show what would happen if the city required you to take steps to stop polluting the air of the neighborhood.

CHAPTER
9
THE LABOR MARKET

Up to this point we have been concerned primarily with the market for consumer goods and services. In this and the next chapter we will study the market for the two primary factors of production: labor and capital. It is true, of course, that most production utilizes inputs in addition to labor and capital such as fuel, light and power, and raw materials of all kinds. But these latter inputs, often referred to as intermediate inputs, are themselves a product of some production activity. If we trace through the manufacture of these intermediate inputs we would find that all are derived ultimately from labor and capital. In years past when agriculture was the predominant industry, economists generally included land as a separate primary input; but now in most cases land is also thought of as capital.

LABOR AS A FACTOR OF PRODUCTION

Economists at times have been accused of being callous or insensitive to the feelings of human beings by treating labor as an input or factor of production. It is argued that such treatment dehumanizes labor making people equivalent to inanimate objects that are bought or sold.

As a matter of fact, economists are probably no more or less callous than any other group in society, with the possible exception of the clergy. Economists recognize that people are not bought and sold but their labor or services are (professional athletes may be an exception). And economists have found that economic principles can be brought to bear in analyzing past behavior of the market for human services (labor) and predicting future behavior. Moreover, as we shall see, the special attributes of labor such as the feelings of individuals are reflected in the labor market.

173

We should also be aware that there is a certain amount of capital embodied (no pun intended) in labor. This comes about because of the education and training that people receive. As we will see in Chapter 11, education or training of any kind can be thought of as an investment. It is an investment that results in the creation of human capital. In a modern society there is relatively little demand for a person who does not possess some human capital having only labor to sell. So in this sense workers have become capitalists.

The labor market, just as the product market, is made up of demanders and suppliers. And we will see that the price of labor (wages or salaries) is determined by the interaction of demand and supply. Society, or at least certain groups in society, may not like the wage that the market determines and as a result may attempt to change the wage. But let us first see how the market functions before we study attempts to modify it.

INPUT DEMAND: PERFECT COMPETITION IN THE PRODUCT MARKET

In our study of the labor market we will begin by deriving the demand for labor by a firm selling its product in a perfectly competitive market. As we saw in Chapter 7, this is the type of firm that faces a perfectly elastic demand curve for its product.

You might be surprised to learn that we have already constructed in Chapter 4 the basic foundation of the demand for labor: the marginal physical product (MPP) of labor. Recall that the MPP of labor is the additional output obtained from adding one more unit of labor, holding other inputs constant. Remember also that after some point the MPP of labor begins to decline. We referred to this phenomenon as the law of diminishing returns. In our discussion of labor demand we will only be concerned with the area of diminishing returns, i.e., the downward sloping portion of the curve representing MPP.

In order to derive the demand for labor we need only to assign a value to MPP. Keep in mind that MPP is given in physical units of the product. We used bushels of tomatoes in the example in Chapter 4. In order to determine the value of MPP we simply multiply the price of the product times MPP. For example, if the MPP for a certain input of labor is 7 bushels of tomatoes and the price of tomatoes is $3 per bushel, then the value of the marginal product (VMP) of this labor is $21.

The relationship between MPP and VMP is illustrated in Figure 9-1 (A) and (B). Both curves look exactly the same except the measure on the vertical axis for MPP is bushels for MPP and dollars for VMP.

The line or curve depicting VMP is downward sloping meaning that successive increments of the input, labor in this example, adds less and

FIGURE 9–1. Relationship between *MPP* and *VMP*

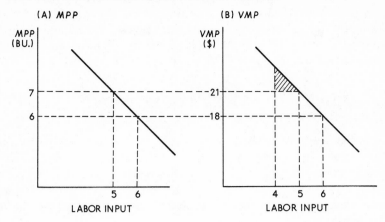

less to the total value of output. The downward sloping characteristic of the line is due entirely to the law of diminishing returns.

Now that we have derived *VMP* we are able to determine how many units of labor the firm will hire given the price of labor. Suppose for example that the price of labor is $21 per day, regardless of how many units the firm hires. Just to choose a number from Figure 9–1 (B), suppose the firm hires four units. At four units of labor, we see that the *VMP* of the last or fourth unit hired is somewhat greater than $21. In other words, if the firm spends $21 for an extra unit of labor, this labor will earn somewhat more than $21 for the firm. Anytime you can spend a dollar and receive more than one dollar in return, do it. Thus the firm would definitely want to hire the fourth unit.

But would the firm want to stop hiring at four units of labor? To answer this question, assume that the firm can hire some fraction of a unit, say an hour. We can see from Figure 9–1 (B) that adding an extra hour over the fourth unit also adds more to total revenue than to total cost, i.e., profits are increased. Thus as long as *VMP* is greater than the price of the input, the firm can add to total profits by hiring more of the input. And it will continue to add more of the input until its *VMP* comes down to the price of the input, five units in Figure 9–1 (B). If the firm had stopped at four units it would have foregone profits equal in value to the shaded triangle in Figure 9–1 (B).

Choosing another price (or wage), say $18, we see that the firm maximizes profits by hiring six units. Thus the *VMP* curve tells us how many units will be hired at a given price. But this is none other than a demand curve. It is a relationship between price and quantity demanded, just as is true for a demand curve for a product. The firm's *VMP* curve of an input is, therefore, the firm's demand curve for that input.

We can obtain an approximation of the market demand for an input summing all the individual firm demand curves. The technique for summing input demand is exactly the same as we used for summing product demand back in Figure 3–5. At each price, all the individual quantities are summed to obtained market demand.

INPUT DEMAND: IMPERFECT COMPETITION IN THE PRODUCT MARKET

Now that we have derived the demand for labor under perfect competition, it is a relatively easy task to derive labor demand under imperfect competition. The imperfectly competitive firm, you recall, faces a downward sloping demand curve for its product; and as a consequence, marginal revenue of an extra unit produced or sold is less than the price of this unit.

Because MR is less than price in this case we are not able to determine the value of the marginal product of an input by multiplying MPP by product price. The reason is that the price of the product must fall in order for the firm to sell any extra units produced. And this price reduction must apply to all units produced not just the marginal unit. So the value of the additional output obtained by adding an extra unit of labor is equal to MR times MPP. Economists refer to the product of MPP times MR as the marginal revenue product (MRP). Thus the demand curve for an input of a perfectly competitive firm is denoted by VMP and input demand of a firm in imperfect competition is known as MRP.

Because price equals marginal revenue for a perfectly competitive firm, there is really no difference in the method of calculating input demand for each type of firm. The abbreviations VMP and MRP are useful, however, to identify the type of market we are dealing with.

Since marginal revenue is less than price it is reasonable to expect that for a given level of input use, MRP would be less than VMP. This is illustrated in Figure 9–2 where we see that MRP declines at a faster rate than VMP.

It is a bit easier to understand why MRP declines faster than VMP if we keep in mind that VMP declines only because of the law of diminishing returns. On the other hand, MRP declines for two reasons: (1) the law of diminishing returns which is reflected in a declining MPP and (2) the decline in marginal revenue as larger quantities of the product are sold.

Although our concern in this chapter is primarily with labor we have phrased our discussion so that it can be applied to any input. And as we proceed we will see that from the standpoint of input demand there is little difference between labor and other inputs. The unique characteristics of the labor market are found mainly on the supply side. Let us now turn to the supply side of the labor market, beginning first with the labor-leisure choice.

FIGURE   9–2.   Comparing *VMP* and *MRP*

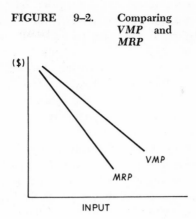

THE LABOR-LEISURE CHOICE

Each of us from the time we are old enough to have an influence on the way we spend our time must decide what proportion we spend working and what proportion we spend on leisure. This decision has a direct bearing on the supply of labor; the more time people are willing to work the greater the labor supply.

In our discussion of labor-leisure choice we will define labor as any activity that results in a wage or salary. This is not to say that pulling down good grades in school is leisure. To be sure, students probably work as hard if not harder than most "employed" people. But it will be better if we defer the discussion on schooling until Chapter 11 where we take up the economics of education.

Each person in the labor force must decide first if he or she will enter the labor force. If a person decides to enter the labor force, then the decision of how many hours to work must be made. Although the decisions to go to work and the type of work chosen depend on many factors such as health and capabilities of the person, self-esteem as well as the esteem of one's peers and family, the satisfaction that results from mastering a difficult task, etc., the econmic factor is generally present. Most of us have to earn a living. Moreover the wage or salary we obtain can be expected to influence our choice of work and how much we will work.

The effect of wages and salaries on our work decisions can be made a bit clearer if we think of leisure as a good. Like any other good, a certain amount of it brings us satisfaction. Since few of us are paid for our leisure time, the decision to spend some of our time at leisure means that we must forego a certain amount of income. In reality then, the price of an extra hour of leisure is the income we forego by not working this hour.

As is true for everything else we buy, price has an important bearing on the quantity we consume. If you recall from the discussion of Chapter 3 on product demand, consumers change their purchases of products with a change in prices because of the substitution and income effects. For example, if your wage increases, the price of your leisure increases. The substitution effect says that you will substitute other goods and services for leisure—you will work more. On the other hand, a higher wage also gives you a higher income which you may use in part to "buy" more leisure.

Thus the substitution effect pulls you toward more work and less leisure while the income affect enables you to "buy" more leisure. For a given individual it is impossible to predict which effect will prevail. At low levels of income, a raise in wages probably increases work and decrease leisure. At relatively high levels of income, a person can afford more leisure so he might work less.

SUPPLY OF LABOR

The supply of labor like the supply of a product denotes a relationship between price and quantity. From our discussion of the substitution and income effects on the labor-leisure choice we can reasonably expect hours worked to increase as wages increase, at least at relatively low

FIGURE 9-3. Wage response and a market supply of labor

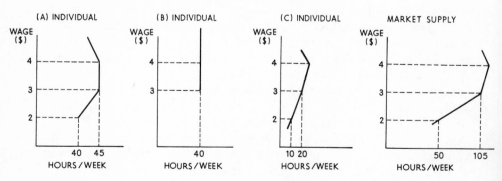

wage levels. As we move to higher wage levels, however, people can afford more leisure so we might expect less response to wage increases.

The changing response to wage increases is illustrated in Figure 9-3. Diagrams (A), (B), and (C) represent the supply of labor by three individuals. At $2 per hour, individual A is willing to supply 40 hours a week of labor. As the wage increases to $3 per hour, he increases his workweek to 45 hours. At $4 per hour he works the same amount, 45 hours, and at wages exceeding $4 he reduces the length of his workweek. In other words, at the $4 and over wage the income effect overrides the substitution effect.

Individual B, on the other hand, does not enter the labor force until wages rise to $3 per hour. Then in the range of wages considered, the workweek remains at 40 hours. Individual C will work 20 hours per week at the $3 wage but does not increase his hours worked very much as wages rise. These, of course, are just examples of what we might expect from different individuals. The first person might be the main "breadwinner" of a family, the second a housewife who decides to enter the labor market at a $3 wage, and the third a college student holding a part-time job.

If we assume, to keep the example simple, that these three individuals comprise the available supply of labor, then we can derive the market supply by adding together the quantity supplied at each price. At $2 per hour, individuals A and C supply 40 and 10 hours, respectively, making a total of 50 hours. At the $3 per hour wage level individual B is included in the labor force. Thus along with the slight increase in labor offered by individuals A and C, we obtain a total of 105 hours supplied.

We should take note that the market supply of labor can be more elastic than the supply of any or all individuals in the market. This is because of the entrance of people into the labor market as wages rise. The result is a greater response to wage increases for the market than is true for any given individual in the market.

We should also recognize, of course, that in any given area there are likely to be a number of labor markets. There is likely to be one for unskilled or semiskilled labor, others for the skilled trades, and still others for professional and managerial personnel. In general the more highly skilled the labor that is involved, the wider the market area. For example, the market for economists is considered to be nationwide or perhaps even international in scope.

WAGE DETERMINATION: PERFECT COMPETITION IN THE LABOR MARKET

In Chapters 6 and 7 we saw that prices of goods and services are determined in the market by the forces of demand and supply. We can apply these same principles to the market for labor.

We know that the market demand for labor consists of a summation of all the VMP and/or MRP curves of labor for all employers in that market. And as we pointed out in the preceding section, the market supply of labor is the summation of all the individual suppliers. The wage that is forthcoming in the market is a result of the interaction of the demand and supply for labor. The process of wage determination is illustrated in Figure 9–4 (A).

If the wage happened to be above the equilibrium, say W_1, there would

FIGURE 9–4. Wage determination: perfect competition in the labor market

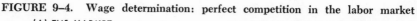
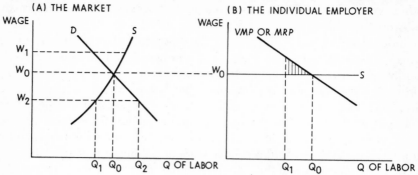

be more people willing to work than are demanded by prospective employers. As a result there will be a number of unemployed people willing to work at a wage lower than W_1. Knowing this, employers will reduce wages down to W_0 because they obviously would not want to pay more than what people are willing to work for. Of course, as wages come down to W_0 the quantity of labor supplied decreases and the quantity demanded increases. At W_0 these two quantities coincide so that everyone who is willing to work at this wage has employment.

If wages are lower than the equilibrium, say at W_2, employers would like to hire more labor than what people will supply. And you will note that at this low wage and relatively small employment, the VMP or MRP of labor for employers in the market is greater than the wage. Thus employers can increase profits by increasing wages to induce a larger quantity of labor to be offered in the market. As wages rise the quantity of labor offered increases and the quantity demanded decreases. The increase will continue until it reaches W_0. At this point the incentive for employers to pay higher wages to obtain more labor disappears.

If we assume that the market is in equilibrium with wage W_0 prevailing, then the perfectly competitive employer of labor faces a supply curve of labor as shown by S in Figure 9–4 (B). Such a supply curve implies that the individual employer cannot influence the wage he pays; he takes the wage as determined in the market. This situation exists if the firm hires a small share of the labor force in his community or area.

Even though the firm depicted in Figure 9–4 (B) is a perfectly competitive buyer of labor, as far as selling its product is concerned, it can be either a perfectly competitive or imperfectly competitive firm. This is why the firm's demand for labor is labeled VMP or MRP. It is considerably more common to observe perfect competition on the buying side of the labor market than to observe it on the selling side of the product market.

If the firm wishes to maximize profits it will hire labor up to the point where the wage (W_0) is equal to the firm's VMP or MRP. If it stopped short of this point, say Q_1, then the contributions of a marginal worker would be greater than the wage of this worker. Suppose that *VMP* or *MRP* is \$3 at Q_1 and the wage is \$2.50. By adding an extra hour of labor the firm pays out \$2.50 but receives \$3 in return. These two figures come closer and closer together as the firm continues to add labor but total profits continue to increase. If the firm stopped hiring at Q_1, it would forego profits equal in value to the shaded triangle which is shown in Figure 9–4 (B).

As we said the implication of a horizontal supply curve of labor facing a firm is that the firm has no control over the wage it pays and that if the firm lowers the wage slightly the quantity available to the firm falls to zero. But because labor is not strictly homogeneous as bushels of wheat or corn, the firm probably can get by with paying a slightly lower wage than the average of other employers in its vicinity.

Firms that pay a slightly lower wage, however, usually attract employees who are slightly less qualified or productive than the average. Also low wage firms tend to have a higher turnover of personnel, which adds to the cost of training or "breaking in" of employees. Thus it is not always in the interest of the employer to pay a lower than average wage. Firms that pay relatively high wages can be more selective in whom they hire and can avoid a high turnover of personnel.

At any rate, the perfectly elastic supply curve of labor facing the firm is more accurately interpreted as a range of wages around the average. For example, if the average wage is \$2.75 per hour for a given type of labor, an individual employer might pay anywhere from \$2.50 to \$3 per hour.

WAGE DETERMINATION: IMPERFECT COMPETITION IN THE LABOR MARKET

Although imperfect competition on the buying side of the labor market is less frequent than perfect competition, it is possible to observe cases where employers hire a fairly large share of the labor in an area. Some examples might be a "company" mining town in the West or a canning factory in a farming community.

A common characteristic of all imperfectly competitive employers is that they face an upward sloping supply curve of labor. An upward sloping supply curve of labor implies that the employer must pay a higher wage if he wishes to increase his labor force. Or if he wishes to reduce the number of people he employs, he can reduce the wage he pays.

An inevitable result of an upward sloping curve facing a firm is that the additional or marginal cost of adding more labor exceeds the wage of the extra workers. The reason for this phenomenon is that the firm must pay a higher wage to attract additional employees, and this higher wage must be paid to all employees.

Economists refer to the cost of adding additional labor as the marginal resource cost (MRC) of labor. At any level of labor hired, the MRC of labor is greater than the wage paid. Thus if we wish to represent this relationship on a diagram, the MRC curve would lie above the supply curve and would rise at a faster rate, as shown in Figure 9–5.

FIGURE 9–5. Wage determination: imperfect competition in the labor market

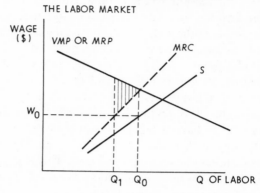

You will note that MRC on the buying side of the labor market is strictly analogous to MR on the selling side of the product market. Marginal revenue is less than price because to sell more the price reduction must apply to all units sold; MRC is greater than the wage because to hire more the higher wage must apply to all labor employed, not just the marginal workers.

If the firm wishes to maximize profits it will attempt to equate the MRC of its labor with labor's VMP or MRP and hire Q_0 of labor. If it stopped short of this point, say at Q_1, the contribution of a marginal unit of labor would exceed its cost. And as we saw in the preceding section, increasing the labor hired from Q_1 to Q_0 results in an addition to total profits equal in value to the shaded triangle in Figure 9–5.

We should take note also in Figure 9–5 that the wage paid by the imperfectly competitive employer of labor is equal to the W_0, the point on the supply curve corresponding to Q_0, the quantity of labor hired. At this quantity of labor, people are willing to work for W_0. Unlike the situation for a perfectly competitive employer, VMP or MRP is greater than the wage. This is not to say that the imperfectly competitive firm "exploits" labor. By attempting to maximize profits this type of firm is behaving in exactly the same manner as a perfectly competitive employer. The situation is different so the outcome is different.

In order to differentiate imperfect competition on the buying side of the market from the selling side, economists have labeled a market where there are few buyers as an oligopsony. This is in contrast to oligopoly which as you recall characterizes a situation of few sellers in a market. If there is only one buyer of labor, the firm would be referred to as a monopsony, in contrast to monopoly on the selling side.

This does not mean, however, that an oligopoly on the selling side results in oligopsony on the buying side or vice versa. The same is true of monopsony. For example, your local light and power company might have a virtual monpoly on the sale of electricity, but in all likelihood it is a perfectly competitive buyer of labor.

SHIFTS IN DEMAND FOR LABOR

So far in this chapter we have studied how wages are determined in the two kinds of labor markets. Now we will attempt to explain changes in wages and levels of employment. We saw in Chapter 6 that if a product market is in equilibrium, the only way a change in price can occur is by a change or shift in either demand and/or supply of the product. The very same thing is true for labor. Wages change in response to a change in demand (VMP or MRP), supply, or both.

Let us look first at changes or shifts in the demand for labor. Most of what we say about shifts in demand for labor can be applied to the demand for any other input as well. Recall from our discussion of the product market that an increase in demand occurs when it shifts upward and to the right, as shown by D_1 in Figure 9–6 (A), or MRP, or VMP, in Figure 9–6 (B). You will notice in this case that the equilibrium or profit maximizing wage will also increase. And as you might expect a decrease in

FIGURE 9–6.   Shifts in the demand for labor

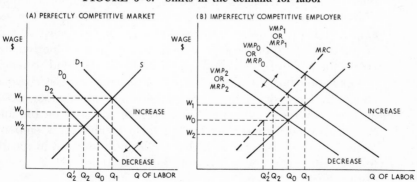

labor demand (VMP or MRP) will result in a decrease in wages as illustrated by D_2 or VMP_2 or MRP_2 in the diagrams in Figure 9–6.

Because VMP for a perfectly competitive buyer of labor is derived by multiplying MPP times product price, we would expect either a change in product price or a change in MPP of labor to shift the demand for labor. The same would be true for an imperfectly competitive buyer of labor because a change in price also results in a change in MR. We can conclude, therefore, that the demand for labor will shift in response to a change in product price or a change in the productivity of labor. The same would hold true for any input.

1. *Change in product price.* A rise in product price, of course, results in a higher VMP or MRP for a given level of input use. The opposite would be true for a decline in product price.
2. *Change in marginal physical product.* There are three major factors that can change or shift an input's MPP. These are:
   a) *Change in quantity of complementary inputs.* Economists define a complementary input as one that increases the MPP of a given input when the use of the complement is increased. Consider, for example, a man digging a hole with a spade. Give him a power shovel and his productivity or MPP will increase. Thus the power shovel would be considered a complement to labor. Also, raw materials of all kinds would be considered complements to labor. Without bricks, mortar, or lumber, for example, a construction worker would not be very productive.
   b) *Changes in quantity of substitute inputs.* Economists define a substitute input as one that decreases the MPP of a given input when the use of the substitute is increased. For example, the use of a second man on one spade would reduce the MPP of the first man because he could use it only part of the time.

      It is not obvious in a given production activity whether two inputs are complements or substitutes. Furthermore, this relationship can change at different levels or mixes of input use. For example, giving the power shovel to the two men and the spade will increase the MPP of the man who operates the machine but decrease the MPP of the second man if he just stands and watches.

      For some labor, therefore, capital or machines serve as complements, by increasing labor's productivity. For other labor, however, usually those with the lowest skills or seniority on the job, capital may be a substitute, forcing them to find other employment. It is this latter situation that we hear about most in regard to automation and unemployment. But let us defer our discussion of the effects of automation until later in the chapter.

c) *Changes in quality of the input itself.* This factor is especially important for labor. Through education and training people have become more productive, i.e., have increased their *MPP,* which in turn has resulted in an increased demand for their labor.

SHIFTS IN THE SUPPLY OF LABOR

In general the supply of labor tends to be more stable than labor demand. The overall supply of labor to the entire economy depends largely on the population. The more people there are, the more labor that will be supplied at a given wage. Thus the aggregate supply of labor in the United States has increased along with population.

The supply of labor facing a given industry or area would, of course, depend also on the population of the area. Although in this case the supply of labor can shift also in response to a change in wages in some other industry or area. Suppose for example, there is a sudden increase in the demand for labor as occurred in the recent oil discoveries in northern Alaska. The increase in wages for people to man the oil rigs attracts more labor to this occupation. But this in turn tends to reduce or shifts to the left the supply of labor to other nearby industries such as mining, trapping, or the service trades. You might find it useful to illustrate this situation with two supply-demand diagrams of your own, one for oil drilling, the second for the other industries that employ similar types of labor.

WAGES AND EMPLOYMENT CHANGES

As we know there has been a long-run upward trend in both wages and employment in the United States. We know also that because of our population growth and the increased participation of women in the labor force, the supply of labor has been increasing or shifting to the right. From this information we would have to conclude that the demand for labor has been shifting to the right more rapidly than the labor supply. Otherwise there could have been an increase in both wages and employment.

The two main factors shifting labor demand to the right, thus raising wages, have been (1) an increase in the use of complementary inputs, mainly capital, and (2) an increase in the quality of the labor force through education. Recall from the preceding section that these two factors increase the productivity or *MPP* of labor and thereby increase labor demand.

For individual geographic areas, industries, or firms, however, there are instances where we can observe a decrease in demand for labor. This can occur if there is a decrease in demand for the good or service produced. As a result the firms involved reduce the quantity of inputs used that are complementary to labor, mainly capital and raw materials. As a result there is a decline in labor's MPP and consequently a decline in labor demand, as shown in D_2 in Figure 9–6 (A) for example.

The logical thing to expect in this situation is a decline in wages and employment. If we were dealing with a nonhuman input, no doubt this would occur. But in the case of labor, it is rather unwise for a firm to immediately reduce wages of its employees in response to a decrease in its VMP or MRP of labor. An across-the-board wage cut affects all of a firm's employees and to say the least leaves employees rather unhappy. And disgruntled employees generally are not conducive to high labor productivity and profits. Moreover, if labor is represented by a union, the wage contract may forbid any decrease in wages.

Rather than reduce wages when there is a decline in demand for labor, most firms will choose to "lay off" more people, at least in the short run. A layoff only affects a relatively few of the firm's "marginal" employees, leaving the remainder virtually untouched. The people who are laid off may be disgruntled but they are not around to affect the firm's productivity anyway.

This situation is illustrated in Figure 9–6. In diagram (A), a decline in labor demand to D_2 would for a nonhuman input result in a wage decrease to W_2 and a decrease in quantity employed to Q_2. But in order to avoid an unhappy labor force, firms hold wages at the same level, W_0, but reduce employment back to Q_2'. At this point the wage still equals VMP so the firm continues to maximize profits. In the event of a prolonged layoff, however, when the affected workers are forced to take lower paying jobs in the community, the market wage will probably drift down to W_2. If and when this occurs, employers have an incentive to hire back some of those laid off.

The same thing occurs with an imperfectly competitive employer. Ordinarily the firm would reduce wages and employment to W_2 and Q_2, respectively. But to avoid immediate "wage grumbles," the firm leaves wages at W_0 and reduces employment to Q_2'. If the firm believes that it cannot lower wages below the going rate, then the MRC curve becomes a horizontal line at the level of the going wage extending from the vertical axis up to the supply curve. Thus at Q_2', the firm still equates VMP or MRP with MRC to maximize profits. Again in a period of prolonged and excessive unemployment when wages paid by perfectly competitive employers begin to decline, we would also expect some reduction in wages paid by imperfectly competitive employers. It is important to bear in mind as well that wages paid by both types of employers have to stay somewhat in line with each other, else workers have a strong incentive to change employers.

As individuals in the labor market, it is important for us to realize that we must contribute at least as much to the output of our employer as we are paid. For example, if we are paid $7,000 per year and produce only $6,000 per year of goods or services, the firm loses $1,000 per year on us. A firm that loses $1,000 per year on an employee is better off without the employee, so we could look forward to losing our job. This does not mean that employers are inhuman or heartless. A firm that pays more out than it takes in soon goes out of business.

The situation does not change if we work for a public agency even though the agency is not "profit minded." Here if we produce less than our wage taxpayers obtain less than what they pay for. Unless taxpayers or our fellow citizens wish to make a gift to us equal to the difference between our *VMP* and our wages, we will find our job in jeopardy. We might bemoan the fact that the world is so cruel but it is a fact no one can change, regardless of the economic system.

WAGE DIFFERENCES

We know, of course, that large differences exist between the wages or salaries of different people or groups. Sometimes these differences seem unjustified. The movie star or professional athlete may earn $100,000 per year working possibly six months, while the poor but honest laborer has to toil from dawn to dusk for a meager $4,000 per year. Why?

Wage differences can largely be explained by demand and supply. A person lucky enough to possess some scarce talent that is in relatively high demand, such as being able to throw a baseball or football exceedingly well, tends to enjoy a relatively high wage. Other talents such as being able to push or pull a lever on a machine all day that are in abundant supply relative to their demand will be less paid.

Some occupations require lengthy training periods which has the effect of reducing the supply from what it would otherwise be. The M.D., lawyer, or college professor who spends 8 to 10 years preparing for his profession must be compensated for the investment he has made in himself, else it would not pay to enter the profession.

It is possible to find occupations that require similar skills but pay different salaries. Consider the bank clerk and the construction worker. Because there are people who are willing to take a lower pay to work in pleasant surroundings, we find that bank clerks earn a lower wage than construction workers. In a sense the bank clerk takes part of his wage in better working conditions. As another example, following World War II teachers and college professors earned a salary substantially lower than could be obtained in alternative occupations. Yet many people willingly choose these professions. The satisfaction of doing a job they liked was sufficient to compensate them for the loss in salary.

AUTOMATION

Automation, the substitution of machines for human effort in a production activity, is a word that has become popular in recent years. However, the process of automation is not by any means new. In fact it probably began at the dawn of history when man discovered that by using wheels one individual could pull as much as two or three could carry. Automation as we think of it today probably began with the industrial revolution over 100 years ago. Although in recent years the computer has opened up more possibilities for automated production.

Is automation good or bad? Ask this question of wage earners and chances are many will say bad especially if it is a threat to their jobs. But we must ask, what would life be like if there had never been any automation? Most of us would be living in caves or tents, scratching a meager living from the soil with a few crude tools. Without the aid of machines man is a relatively unproductive creature. Obviously we that are living in the 20th century benefit a great deal from past automation or mechanization of production.

As we learned in the section on labor demand, machines or capital serve as a complement to some labor, shifting its *MPP* curve upwards and to the right. And as man's real output increases so does his wage and income. But as we learned, machines or capital can at the same time be a substitute for other people, reducing their *MPP* and eliminating their jobs.

It is this latter group of people who fear automation, and with good reason for relatively few people like to see their job disappear. But the picture may not be quite as dark as might first appear. Because automation represents a more productive or cheaper method of production, the supply of the final product will be shifted to the right.

As consumers respond to the lower price of the product by purchasing more of it, the firm or industry will, of course, purchase more raw materials which in turn will shift the *MPP* of the marginal workers to the right also. If the increase in output is sufficient to absorb the jobs eliminated by the automation, labor can end up in the happy situation of higher pay with a greater number of jobs.

We should be aware also that because of population growth and the expanding economy, most industries are increasing their output. The effect of automation in this case is for employers not to take on additional labor as they increase output. As you would expect this is not nearly as unpleasant to labor as losing jobs that were already in existence. A good illustration of this phenomenon exists in the United States where we observe growth in the service trades relative to manufacturing where automation has been more prevalent.

A common fear that prevails nowadays is that because of automation jobs will become more and more scarce. Some go as far as to say that people will have to reduce their workweek to 20 to 30 hours in order for everyone to be employed. But this fear will remain unfounded until everyone has reached a state of complete satisfaction. As long as some people desire to consume more goods or services than they now do, there is no reason why everyone who wants a job cannot be working. Knowing human nature, we should not expect to soon see the day when everyone is satisfied. We must keep in mind that it is not jobs that are scarce but people and resources to do these jobs.

DISCRIMINATION

It is very difficult, if not impossible, to assess the full effect of discrimination in the labor market unless we ourselves have been denied a job because of our race, creed, or color. The full effect goes much deeper than the loss of income. The feeling of frustration, hopelessness, and low self esteem can only be known by those discriminated against. Since this is a book on ecnoomics, however, we can only recognize that discrimination results in more than just economic harm.

In instances of discrimination there is a tendency to place the major blame on employers. Obviously, it is argued, employers who deny employment because of race, creed, or color are guilty of discrimination. But the problem usually goes a bit deeper than this. If the hiring of people from a minority group creates bitterness, strife, and the loss of productivity among workers already employed, no employer is going to be very eager to hire these people. In this situation the blame for discrimination must be shared by employees as well as the employer.

In addition, there can well be discrimination against the output of a firm that hires from a minority group. This situation can easily prevail in the services or retail trades. For example, if high and middle income whites do not want black men to come into their homes to repair appliances, few appliance stores will hire black repairmen. In this case the blame must fall also on customers.

Undoubtedly there would be much less descrimination in the United States, if it were more profitable, or at least less unprofitable, for employers to integrate their labor forces. Other employees and consumers can facilitate integration by not discriminating against employers who integrate their labor force, or perhaps even by discriminating against those who do not integrate.

Perhaps the most damaging of all discrimination occurs at the elementary and secondary levels of school. Since minority groups tend to live in poor neighborhoods and because schools obtain a large share of their financing from local taxes, the quality of instruction tends to be much lower among minority group children than among the children of high or middle income people.

The result, of course, is a poor preparation for the labor market or for further training. If minority people possess only minimum skills, hence a low marginal physical productivity, they can only qualify for low-paying jobs. Thus discrimination and poverty tends to perpetuate itself; poor schooling leads to low income, and low income results in poor schooling.

In addition to the low quality of schooling, young people from minority groups have terminated their schooling much sooner than young people from middle class neighborhoods. Since schooling is such an important prerequisite for a decent job in modern society, at first glance it appears that dropping out of high school or deciding not to attend a college or technical school is not very rational. A closer look, however, reveals that because of discrimination in the job market, it may indeed be rational not to invest in schooling. If the jobs that can be obtained with further schooling are not open to certain people, there is little incentive to train for them.

LABOR UNIONS

The primary objectives of labor unions are (1) to obtain higher salaries for their members and (2) to improve working conditions. In this section we will look primarily at the methods that unions use in attempting to raise wages together with the limitations of these methods.

From our discussion of wage determination, we know that wages are determined by forces of supply and demand similar to the determination of prices in the product market. It is reasonable to believe, that in order for unions to modify wages they must in some way modify or change the market for labor. There are three basic ways this can be done.

1. *Increase the demand for labor.* This method is probably the most desirable of all three but the most difficult. It is desirable because it results in both a higher wage and larger employment. This is illustrated in Figure 9–6, diagrams (A) and (B). It is difficult because in general unions do not have much influence over the demand for labor.

One means of increasing labor demand is by increasing the demand for the final product. In years past unions utilized advertising urging consumers to buy "union-made" products. But as more and more industries became unionized, it became more difficult to distinguish "union" from "nonunion" products.

In recent years unions have been quite active in discouraging imports of foreign made products by lobbying for protective tariffs or quotas on imports. The success of this kind of program is difficult to gauge because limiting imports has the effect of in turn limiting our exports. If we do not buy from other nations, they understandably limit their purchases from us. As a result there is a decrease in the export demand of union-made products.

Increasing the productivity of labor (*MPP*) will, as we saw, also increase the demand for labor. As a result unions have attempted to improve working conditions and shorten the workweek so as to maximize each man's potential. Unions also have encouraged education and have been active in apprenticeship programs. Although, as we will see shortly, apprenticeship programs have been a more effective device for limiting the supply of labor.

Unions also have attempted to increase or at least maintain the demand for labor by negotiating over job description. For example, a certain job may call for the services of men from two or more unions, each doing a specific part of the job. For example, in building a house, the carpenters dare not infringe on any job the electricians or painters are supposed to do.

Related to this is the practice of "featherbedding" which is an attempt by unions to create or maintain a job that employers claim is not really necessary. The railroad fireman provides a good example. In the days of steam locomotives, this job was of course necessary. With the coming of diesel and electric power railroads argue that the fireman is now redundant and that union insistence that this job remain constitutes "featherbedding."

Any kind of make-work scheme on the part of unions cannot be very successful, however, because it invariably results in higher than necessary production costs. As consumers substitute other goods and services that are cheaper for the higher priced union-made products, the demand for union labor will decline so the union loses in the long run.

2. *Reduce the supply of labor.* By in large unions have been more successful in raising wages by limiting the supply of labor than by increasing demand. This is particularly true among the so-called craft unions that represent skilled tradesmen. The prime vehicle for limiting entry into the profession or trade is by controlling entry into the training or apprenticeship program.

In most skilled trades or professions it is virtually impossible for an individual to find employment without a certificate or license bearing witness of successful completion of the training program. Because the power to issue licenses is generally in the hands of the trade or profession itself, it is not difficult to understand why they are generally in short supply.

Shifting the supply of labor back and to the left from what it would be with free entry into the profession increases wages and reduces the number of people employed. Trade unions and professional associations such as the American Medical Association (AMA) have utilized this technique with a high degree of success because the outcome (higher wages and less employment) does not, at least in the short run, harm established members of the trade or profession. Their wages are high and they never have to fear unemployment.

The people that are harmed by this technique are those that could obtain higher incomes had they been allowed to enter the profession, and the general public who end up paying more for services rendered. If wages and the cost of services become excessively high, however, public opinion may result in some governmental pressure to allow more freedom of entry. We are witnessing an example of this in the building trades at the present time. Also substitute products will begin to show up, as evidenced by "mobile homes" or factory-built housing, which results in a decrease in demand for the services of skilled building tradesmen from what it would otherwise be.

3. *Bargain for a union wage.* This technique is utilized by unions representing unskilled or semiskilled workers—the teamsters, the steel workers, the auto workers, etc. These are often referred to as the industrial unions as opposed to the craft unions that we just discussed. As opposed to the craft unions who limit membership, the industrial union's goal is to bring all workers in the industry into union membership.

The wisdom of this policy becomes clear when we remember that because the jobs represented by industrial unions require little or no training, there is always a large pool of substitute labor that can easily step in if union labor becomes more costly than nonunion labor.

In addition, the success of industrial unions hinges on the condition that all firms in the industry employ union members. For if unionized firms paid a higher wage, hence incurred higher costs, the lower priced products of the nonunionized firms would soon take over the market.

In bargaining for a union wage, unions attempt to obtain a higher wage for their members than would be determined in a free market. As we explained earlier in this chapter, this wage corresponds to the intersection of labor's demand and supply in a perfectly competitive market, as is illustrated in Figure 9–7 (A) by W_0. The free market wage in an imperfectly competitive labor market is denoted in Figure 9-7 (B) by W_0. The union wage is denoted by W_u in both diagrams.

FIGURE 9–7. Union wages in the labor market

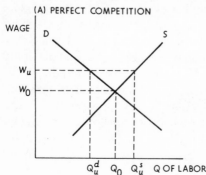

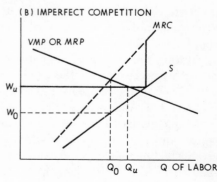

Looking first at perfect competition you will note that the imposition of the union wage reduces the quantity of labor employed in the market from Q_0 to $Q_u{}^d$. In order for employers to pay the higher wage they must reduce employment until labor's *VMP* or *MRP* rises to the level of the wage. If they did not cut back on personnel, the wage of the marginal workers would exceed the value of what they produce.

The resulting decline in employment serves as a check on the union's bargaining power, however. Naturally unions like to see a small amount of unemployment along with higher wages. Moreover, unions traditionally have not enjoyed a large, loyal membership during periods of high unemployment.

You will notice also in Figure 9–7 (A) that the quantity of labor seeking employment in the union wage industry increases from Q_0 to $Q_u{}^s$, resulting in an unemployed fringe equal to the distance between $Q_u{}^d$ and $Q_u{}^s$. Essentially these represent the waiting list of hopeful employees.

The outcome of a union wage in an imperfectly competitive labor market, illustrated in Figure 9–7 (B), is a bit surprising. You will note that in a free market the imperfectly competitive buyer of labor pays W_0 and hires Q_0. But when the union comes in and bargains for a wage, say W_u, the employer increases employment up to Q_u. Thus workers benefit in two ways: their wages are higher and their employment has increased.

This situation occurs because the union wage nullifies the firm's original *MRC* curve. The reason is that at wage W_u, the firm can hire any quantity of labor it wishes at this wage without having to pay more for additional workers. The firm's *MRC* curve under a union wage, therefore, consists of the solid line beginning at W_u on the vertical axis, running out to the supply curve and then extending up to join the original *MRC* curve of the firm.

We should be aware, however, that this situation exists only if the union wage is set somewhere between the original free market wage, W_0, and the point where the firm's original *MRC* intersects the *VMP* or *MRP* curve. If the union wage is higher than this intersection, quantity will decline with increases in the wage.

Considerable disagreement exists among economists over the influence of unions, particularly industrial unions, on wages. Some argue that their influence is obvious, we continually observe negotiated wage increases in unionized industries. Others argue that the normal forces of supply and demand would result in comparable wage increases.

This latter group even argues that unions may actuallay retard wage increases by long-term contracts. Without long-term contracts employers might be more willing to raise wages a bit sooner. Also inflation may "eat up" the wage increase before it becomes time to negotiate a new contract. Cost-of-living clauses have been used to avoid this problem, however.

One thing we can be sure of, however, is that if unions have succeeded in raising wages in unionized trades or industries, the resulting reduction in employment in these occupations has increased the supply of labor to other nonunion trades or industries. For example, if trade unions have increased wages in the skilled trades by limiting entry, as is quite reasonable to believe, wages are lower than would otherwise be the case in the unskilled and semiskilled occupations.

MAIN POINTS OF CHAPTER 9

1. The labor market is primarily concerned with the demand and supply of the services of individuals. The special attributes of labor are reflected in the market.

2. The demand for labor, or any input, by a perfectly competitive firm in the product market is equal to the input's VMP curve. Value of the marginal product (VMP) is equal to MPP times product price.

3. The demand for labor, or any input, by an imperfectly competitive firm in the product market is equal to the input's MRP curve. Marginal revenue product (MRP) is equal to MPP times marginal revenue.

4. Leisure can be thought of as a good. The more leisure we demand, the less labor we supply. The price of an extra hour of leisure is the income foregone by decreasing labor one hour.

5. The amount of leisure demanded is influenced by the substitution and income effects. At higher wages leisure becomes more expensive so we substitute labor for leisure. But offsetting this is the income effect. At higher wages we can afford to buy more leisure.

6. If the income effect more than offsets the substitution effect, the supply of labor will be "backward bending" meaning that less labor will be supplied at higher wages.

7. In a perfectly competitive labor market wages are determined by the interaction of labor demand and supply. An employer will be a perfectly competitive buyer of labor if he hires a small percent of the labor force in his vicinity.

8. Although a perfectly competitive employer faces a perfectly elastic supply curve of, labor, he may have some leeway in the wage he pays because labor is not homogeneous.

9. The perfectly competitive employer hires workers up to the point where the wage is equal to the VMP or MRP of an additional worker. To stop short of this point would involve an unnecessary loss of profits.

10. Imperfect competition in the labor market occurs if each employer hires a large share of the labor in a vicinity. The imperfectly competitive employer maximizes profits by hiring labor up to the point where labor's VMP or MRP is equal to the MRC of labor.

11. The demand for labor, or any input, shifts if there is a change in product price or the *MPP* of labor.

12. An increase in the use of a complementary input increases the *MPP* of labor, whereas an increase in the use of a substitute input decreases the *MPP* of labor.

13. The supply of labor shifts if there is a change in population or in the wages paid in other labor markets. In a given labor market the supply of labor will decrease if there is an increase in wages in alternative employment.

14. The long-run trend towards increasing wages and employment implies that the demand for labor has been increasing more rapidly than the labor supply.

15. In the short run, a decrease in demand for labor by a given firm or industry tends to result in layoffs rather than a reduction in wages.

16. Wage differences between occupations occur because of differences in demand and supply conditions.

17. Automation, a new term for an old process, results in higher wages for labor. Jobs need not be eliminated if the increase in output offsets the decrease in demand for labor. In an expanding economy the substitution of machines for labor generally takes place by not replacing employees who leave.

18. The end to discrimination in the labor market can be facilitated by making integration more profitable. Employers may be forced to discriminate if their present employees and customers also discriminate. The low level and quality of education among minority groups also perpetuates discrimination.

19. Labor unions attempt to raise wages of their members by (1) increasing demand, (2) decreasing supply, and (3) bargaining for a union wage. All involve certain drawbacks, although the second, decreasing labor supply, likely has been the most successful.

20. Economists disagree over the success of unions in raising wages. If unions have succeeded in raising wages in some occupations, the inevitable result, however, is a reduction in wages of other occupations from what they would otherwise be.

QUESTIONS FOR THOUGHT AND DISCUSSION

1. It is said that labor and capital are the two primary inputs or factors of production. Consider the production of automobiles. Do all inputs used by the auto makers fall under the categories of labor and capital? Explain.

2. Explain the relationship between *MPP* and *VMP*, also between *MPP* and *MRP*.

3. Differentiate between *VMP* and *MRP*.

4. Two of your friends are having an argument. One argues that raising wages increases the quantity of labor supplied. The other argues that it does the opposite. Can you resolve this argument?

5. Suppose you are the owner of a firm that hires a small percent of the labor force in your area. Explain how you would go about deciding what wage to pay your employees and how many you would hire. Utilize diagrams in your explanation. (Assume you are an imperfectly competitive seller of your product.)

6. Suppose you are the owner of a firm that hires a large percent of the labor force in your area. Explain how you would go about deciding what wage to pay your employees and how many you would hire. Utilize diagrams in your explanation. (Assume you are an imperfectly competitive seller of your product.)

7. Two of your friends are having another argument. One argues that capital is a complement to labor because it makes labor more productive. The other argues that capital is a substitute for labor because less labor is required to do the job when capital is employed. Can you resolve this argument?

8. Suppose you are the owner of a firm that employs a unionized labor force. Suddenly there is a sharp reduction in the demand for your product. Explain using diagrams what effect this would have on your demand for labor, wages, and employment. (Assume you are a perfectly competitive employer of labor and that you sell your product in an imperfectly competitive market.)

9. "Movie stars are paid more than they are worth, while laborers are paid less than they are worth." Comment.

10. "In the future when we have completely automated factories, jobs will be scarce and will have to be rationed out to those you need to work the most." Comment.

11. "Employers have the power to end discrimination immediately if they just wanted to." Comment.

12. In what jobs, industries, or areas would you expect to see the most rapid progress in eliminating discrimination?

13. Suppose you are a leader of a craft union representing skilled tradesmen. How would you go about obtaining higher wages for your members? What would be your limitations?

14. Suppose you are the leader of an industrial union representing semiskilled, "blue-collar" workers. How would you go about obtaining higher wages for your members? What would be your limitations?

CHAPTER
10
THE CAPITAL MARKET

THE CONCEPT OF CAPITAL

In the context of business or economics, the word capital has taken on two slightly different meanings. The businessman may think of capital as cash or money to carry on a business, as in "working capital." The economist, however, generally defines capital as durable or long-lasting inputs such as machinery, tools, buildings, land, etc. Of course the quantity of capital employed is generally measured in terms of monetary value.

We separate the study of capital from labor because of a number of differences between these two inputs. The first, and most obvious, difference is that capital is an inanimate, nonliving input devoid of feelings or preferences. Although the owners of capital are concerned about the wage or return that capital receives, they do not particularly care about its working conditions, the length of its workweek, or whether it is employed in a prestigious occupation. Thus many of the factors that are important for labor need not concern us in our discussion of capital.

A second difference is that capital is generally purchased for use over a relatively long period of time. For example, you may purchase a building this year that will go on producing for you the remainder of your lifetime. Labor, or other inputs such as raw materials, are purchased for immediate or current use only. Granted there may be an understanding between employer and employee over the length of time, they will associate, but unlike capital, the employer of labor does not generally pay the employee a lump sum for all future services. We will see shortly that this difference is quite important.

A third difference between capital and labor is that the purchase of capital may involve an expenditure well in advance of the date it begins to contribute to output. Economists refer to this time interval between the expenditure and the beginning of flow of output as the "gestation period." This time interval becomes important for capital such as buildings or heavy equipment.

THE COST OF CAPITAL

What does capital cost? At first glance the answer to this question may appear obvious. Surely, you might respond, the cost of capital is what buyers pay the people who produce it. But the answer is not quite this simple. Let us return briefly to our tomato production example. Suppose you purchase a $1,000 garden tractor to increase output. Would the $1,000 you spent be considered an expense of this year's production?

It would seem a bit unreasonable to require this year's output to carry the entire $1,000 outlay. After all the tractor will still be available next year. But at the same time, it seems reasonable to charge at least part of the $1,000 towards current production. If we agree to this, then we have at least bracketed this year's cost of the $1,000 capital item to somewhere between $1,000 and zero. Clearly $1,000 is too much and zero is too little.

It would be reasonable to charge this year's production with at least the amount that the garden tractor had depreciated in value. Suppose during the year the tractor's market value declined to $700. If we desired, we could sell the tractor for $700 after using it the first year. Thus the depreciation cost of this capital item for the current year would be $300.

Aside from the normal operating expense such as gasoline and oil, would the $300 be the total cost of this capital item for the current year? Not quite. Where did we obtain the $1,000 to buy the tractor? If we borrowed it from a bank we are required to pay interest on the loan. Suppose it is 10 percent per year. At this interest rate we would have to pay the bank $100 per year for the use of their money. Adding up the depreciation plus interest we obtain $400 as the cost of this capital item for the current year.

We should not conclude from this example, however, that the interest charge is only included when capital is purchased with borrowed funds. It would be equally necessary to include an interest charge if our own funds were used to make the purchase. Because in this case we would have to forego the interest income of the $1,000 that we could have obtained had we not purchased the garden tractor.

If the $1,000 were our own funds, however, the interest charge probably would not be quite as high as would be the case if we had borrowed the money. The reason is that we as individuals lend money at "wholesale" but borrow at "retail." Banks and other lending institutions which serve to channel funds of individual lenders into a central location and then screen and loan to borrowers must be paid for their services. The difference between the interest we obtain on savings and the interest paid for a loan constitutes the payment for these services.

To summarize briefly, the cost of capital for a given period consists of two components: (1) depreciation and (2) interest. We will discuss the techniques of estimating depreciation later in the chapter. For now it is just necessary to keep in mind that depreciation is an important component of capital's cost during a given year.

THE MARGINAL PRODUCT OF CAPITAL

The use of capital in any kind of production, of course, results in an increase in the output of goods or services. If we wished to follow the technique we established for labor, we could measure capital's contribution to output by its marginal physical product (MPP). Recall that the MPP of labor is the additional output obtained by adding one more unit of labor. Similarly the MPP of capital is the additional output obtained by adding one more unit of capital.

The fact that capital's contribution to output is spread over more years than just the year of its purchase, however, makes it necessary when deciding whether or not to purchase the capital to alter our decision technique slightly. For example, suppose the addition of the $1,000 garden tractor increases our tomato output by 250 bushels the first year. If the price of tomatoes were $2 per bushel the VMP of the garden tractor would be $500.

At first it may appear that the purchase of the tractor was a bad decision. We spent $1,000 but took in only $500. But we must keep in mind that the tractor will continue to increase output for several years to come. Thus it would be wrong to compare capital's VMP for a production period with the price of the capital item. Essentially, this is what we did with labor; we compared labor's hourly VMP with its wage.

The decision to buy a capital item should be based instead on a comparison of its annual VMP (or MRP if the firm sells in imperfect competition) with its depreciation plus interest expense. In the garden tractor example, we estimated that the annual depreciation plus interest amounted to $400. Now if we compare the annual VMP of $500 with the $400 expense, it becomes clear that the decision to purchase the tractor was correct. Anytime we can spend $400 and receive $500 in return, we should do it.

THE RATE OF RETURN ON CAPITAL

An alternative method of gauging the profitability of capital is to express its contribution as an annual rate of return. The rate of return on capital is the amount that each dollar earns each year after subtracting all expenses except the interest charge. It is commonly expressed as a percentage figure. For example, a 10 percent rate of return means that each dollar invested in a capital input earns 10 cents per year. You have probably recognized that the rate of return on capital is essentially the same idea as the rate of return on your savings account in the bank.

Because most capital depreciates, and as a result earns less and less as years go by, it is somewhat more complicated to compute a rate of return on an item of capital than it is on a dollar in a savings account. As long as you keep the dollar in your account it goes on earning the stipulated rate of return.

Let us, therefore, begin by considering a capital item that does not tend to depreciate—land. In fact, during recent history land has generally gone up in value, or appreciated. But to keep the example simple, suppose we purchase a small plot of land for $1,000 and expect it to remain at this price. Also suppose that we can collect $100 per year for as long as we want by renting this land to a tomato grower. We are assuming here that the renter will maintain the land's fertility so there is no depreciation.

The rate of return on capital that goes on earning a return for all time to come is computed as follows:

$$r = \frac{\text{Annual return}}{\text{Capital value}}$$

In our example the rate of return would be

$$r = \frac{\$100}{\$1,000} = 0.10 = 10 \text{ percent}$$

CAPITALIZED VALUE

By manipulating this formula slightly we can derive another formula that is very useful for deciding the maximum price we could afford to pay for a piece of property. To make the formula more manageable let us abbreviate, letting R represent the annual return and K the capital value. Now we have

$$r = \frac{R}{K}, \text{ or } K \times r = R, \text{ or } K = \frac{R}{r}$$

The resulting formula $K = R/r$ tells us how much a piece of property is worth if we know its annual return and the interest charge. Suppose in order to purchase this plot of land we took out a $1,000 loan at 8 percent. Utilizing this formula we find:

$$K = \frac{\$100}{0.08} = \$1,250$$

If we were assured of an annual $100 net return on this land and the money to buy it cost 8 percent per year, we could have paid as much as $1,250 for the land. Economists refer to the K in this formula, or the $1,250 in this example, as the "capitalized value" of the property. In a competitive market prospective buyers would tend to bid the price of the property up to this amount. And sellers, knowing this, will be prone to set the selling price at the capitalized value. If we are able to buy a piece of property for $1,000 that has a capitalized value of $1,250 we, of course, have made a good deal for ourselves.

We should note also from this formula that for a given annual return (R), the capitalized value (K) will vary inversely to the size of the interest rate (r). If the interest rate we had to pay on our loan were 10 percent, K would have been $1,000. A lower interest rate such as 5 percent results in a capitalized value of $2,000.

Although the relationship between the interest rate and the capitalized value is an algebraic phenomenon—the larger the denominator, the smaller the quotient, and vice versa—it has an underlying economic rationale. At a relatively high interest rate, say 10 percent, the income that will be forthcoming many years in the future is more expensive to obtain than if the interest rate were lower. For at high interest rates we are required to pay more for the distant income either in terms of an interest charge on borrowed funds or foregone interest from our own funds, hence we cannot pay as high an initial price for the capital.

CASH FLOW ANALYSIS

Most capital that we might consider purchasing such as buildings or equipment would not be expected to yield a stream of returns into infinity, however. As years go by capital generally becomes less productive and its maintenance costs rise. As a result the stream of net returns may exhibit a downward trend, eventually coming to an end when it no longer pays to keep the capital item.

As you might expect it is somewhat more difficult to compute a rate of return to a capital item in this more common but realistic situation. To facilitate computation of capital's rate of return, economists have devised a technique called "cash flow analysis." As the name implies this technique involves comparing the cash outflow of a capital item, i.e., its purchase price, with the inflow of cash that results from the use of the item.

We can use the garden tractor purchase also to illustrate this technique. Suppose we denote as year 0, the time we purchase the tractor. The first step is to assess, as best we can, the contribution of the tractor to our total production and sales of tomatoes during the years we expect to own it. One way to do this is to estimate our total sales during these years without the tractor and then estimate our total sales, less the added expense such as gasoline, repairs, etc., with the tractor. The difference between these two sets of figures gives us the net inflow of cash that results from owning the tractor. Our figures might look something like the following:

	Year 0	Year 1	Year 2	Year 3	Year 4	Year 5
Cash outflow	−$1,000	–	–	–	–	–
Gross cash inflow.....	–	+$350	+$400	+$450	+$475	+$600
Less added expense....	–	−$100	−$125	−$150	−$200	−$300
Net cash inflow...	−$1,000	+$250	+$275	+$300	+$275	+$300

It is reasonable to assume that the tractor does not begin to pay off at once. Suppose the first payoff comes about one year after we buy it, call this year 1. Also assume that we expect to use the tractor for five years. The gross cash inflow figures essentially represent the tractor's *VMP* for each year, except for the last year where gross cash inflow also includes the selling price of the tractor.

The added expense figures denote the expenses related to owning the tractor. They include the normal operating expense of fuel, oil, repairs as well as the cost of any additional labor that is incurred by operating the tractor. This figure should also include the implicit cost of any additional hours of our own labor utilized. Notice that the added expense figures become larger as the years go by. The main reason for this is the larger amount of repairs that we can expect as the tractor grows older.

The additional expense figures, however, do not include the depreciation expense or a charge for interest on the $1,000. The depreciation is taken into account in the gross cash inflow figure for year 5, the year we expect to sell the tractor. The $600 gross cash inflow figure for year 5 includes both the extra value of production, say $400, and the selling price of the tractor, $200 in this example. The total depreciation over the five-year period of $800 is therefore reflected in the reduced gross cash inflow in year 5. If there had been no depreciation, the gross cash inflow would have been $1,400 in year 5. Probably the main advantage of cash flow analysis is that we do not have to be concerned with the pattern of depreciation of a capital item. Also the interest charge will be taken account of when we calculate a rate of return on this investment.

Assuming that we are fairly confident in the accuracy of our estimates of the added income and expense connected with the tractor, we still are faced with the question, should we or should we not buy the tractor? If we add up the net cash inflows over the five-year period we see that the $1,000 investment in the tractor enables us to take in a total of $1,500.

DISCOUNTING FUTURE RETURNS

Before we become too optimistic about this investment, however, we should keep in mind that positive net cash inflows are not available to us until future years. And as we know a dollar that we obtain, say next year, is not as valuable to us as a dollar of income at the present. For we could always loan out or invest the present dollar at a positive rate of interest, enabling us to obtain something more than one dollar a year from now.

How much is one dollar of income forthcoming a year from now worth at the present? In order to answer this question, we must specify the rate of interest that we could obtain by lending the dollar, call it r. The formula for discounting one dollar of future income to the present is given by $1/(1 + r)^n$. The n represents the number of years in the future the income is forthcoming. For example, if r is 5 percent, or 0.05, then one dollar forthcoming one year from now is worth $1/(1.05)$ or 95 cents at the present. Economists would refer to this 95 cents as the discounted present value of one dollar, one year in the future. Notice that if the interest rate increases, the discounted present value declines. At an interest rate of 0.10, the discounted present value of one dollar one year from now declines to 91 cents.

By using this discounting formula we can determine the present value of the future returns of the garden tractor. Let us suppose that the market rate of interest is 10 percent. The present value of the returns in year 1 is $250/1.10 or $227 approximately. In year 2 it would be $275/(1.10)^2 or $227, etc. The discounted present value in year 0 of the net cash inflows from years 1 through 5 is shown below:

Year 1	Year 2	Year 3	Year 4	Year 5	Total
$227 +	$227 +	$226 +	$188 +	$248 =	$1,116

It is interesting to note that the $1,500 total return from the five year's net cash inflows is only worth $1,116 at its discounted present value, assuming a 10 percent interest rate. We would, of course, still consider the garden tractor to be a good investment, the $1,000 buys $1,116 of present value. But we would not greet the prospect with quite as much enthusiasm as we might have first thought after seeing the $1,500 nondiscounted return.

This does not mean, however, that the nondiscounted $1,500 return to the $1,000 investment would always be acceptable. Suppose the interest rate we had to pay increased to 15 percent, or alternatively we have another use for our funds that would return 15 percent. Discounting the same $1,500 stream of returns back to year 0 using a 15 percent results in a discounted present value of only $978. Here we find that the present value of the $1,500 is only worth $978. Now the tractor would not be an acceptable investment. This illustrates the importance of the interest rate in making investment decisions. The higher the interest rate, the less will future returns be worth. As you might have recognized the discounted present value is essentially the same thing as the capitalized value discussed earlier. The term "capitalized value" is generally used in reference to capital that does not depreciate or is nonreproducible.

INTERNAL RATE OF RETURN

Although comparing the discounted present value of the stream of returns with the cost of the capital item is a perfectly acceptable method of judging an investment, economists frequently use another criterion called the "internal rate of return." The internal rate of return is defined as that rate of interest which makes the discounted present value of the stream of returns equal to the cost of the investment.

In the garden tractor example, we saw that a 10 percent rate of interest discounted the $1,500 stream of returns down to a present value of $1,116. Thus the internal rate of return is slightly larger than 10 percent. On the other hand, the 15 percent rate was slightly too high; the present value of the $1,500 was reduced to $978. Thus we can conclude that the internal rate of return on the garden tractor is somewhere between 10 and 15 percent.

The only way that we can compute an internal rate of return is by trying alternative interest rates until we find one that makes the discounted present value equal to the cost of the capital item. In the garden tractor example, it turns out to be about 14 percent. Using a 14 percent discount rate, the $1,500 stream of returns reduces down to $1,004 in year 0. Thus the internal rate of return is just a shade over 14 percent, but it generally does not pay to strive for greater accuracy than this.

Sometimes the purchase or construction of capital will involve more than one year to complete, such as investment in reforestation, or in education. In order to measure costs correctly in this case we should accumulate each annual expenditure up to the point where the investment begins to pay off. The formula for cumulating past investment is $(1 + r)^n$ where n in this case is the number of years between the expenditure and the beginning of the pay off or net cash inflow.

For example, if r is 0.10 and if $1,000 is spent two years before any payoff is forthcoming, the cumulated cost is $1,000 (1 + 0.10)^2$ or $1,000 \times (1.21)$ which equals $1,211. We accumulate in order to take account of the interest charge on money invested. At any rate, the internal rate of return in this case is that rate of interest which makes the cumulated expenditure equal to the discounted future returns. We will make use of the cumulating procedure in the next chapter where we evaluate the returns to investment in education.

The meaning of this 14 percent internal rate of return is that the $1,000 investment pays off at the rate of 14 percent per year, or $140 per year, during the five-year payoff period. If you paid, or could have earned, 10 percent on the $1,000, you would reap a 4 percent, or $40 per year, pure profit.

Although the $140 per year net income from this investment may seem like a trifling, we must remember that $1,000 is also a fairly small investment. It does not require a very large business these days to have $100,000 or more invested. And if you obtain 14 percent on $100,000, your yearly earnings from capital are $14,000. If you borrowed the entire $100,000 for 10 percent, your pure profit per year is $4,000. Remember this is in addition to your labor income.

Most of the rich and super rich have gotten to be so by the income from capital. Moreover, most of these people, at least when they started out, utilized borrowed funds. Earning 14 percent on one million dollars, returns $140,000 per year. Even if you pay 10 percent for this money, you still clear $40,000 per year letting the capital work for you. Few people, except the top professional athletes, movie stars, and the highest paid executives, can obtain an income over $25,000 to $30,000 per year without supplemental earnings from capital. Thus if you strive for a relatively high standard of living in the future, it is never too early to set aside part of your income for investment purposes.

Of course, we must realize too that ownership of capital does not guarantee a high income. For example, if you borrow $100,000 at 10 percent and the capital that is purchased with the money only pays off at 5 percent, you lose $5,000 per year. When playing with stakes this high, it is important to assess rather carefully the anticipated rate of return. Thus the internal rate of return technique that we just discussed is a very useful and important tool for investors.

To summarize briefly, we have discussed so far three ways to assess the profitability of an investment: (1) comparing the annual VMP or MRP of capital with its annual depreciation plus interest expense, (2) comparing the capitalized value or discounted present value of the stream of future returns with its purchase price, and (3) comparing the internal rate of return with the interest rate on borrowed funds or on our own funds.

DEMAND FOR INVESTMENT FUNDS

Most business firms or investors face an assortment of different investment opportunities. The firm, for example, has to decide whether it pays to buy additional machinery or equipment, add on or build a new facility, or invest in some other business such as an apartment house. Moreover, these opportunities are continually changing. For example, building a new facility might promise a high return at one point in time, but if conditions change, such as a new competitor setting up business nearby, the anticipated rate of return can be substantially reduced.

Because of the assortment of investment opportunities it is useful to be able to rank them according to their anticipated rate of return. For example, in our tomato-growing endeavor, we might estimate that $100 spent on garden tools (hoes, rakes, etc.) would pay off at a 20 percent rate of return. Adding additional capital such as the $1,000 garden tractor may yield a 14 percent rate of return. Perhaps another $1,000 invested in irrigation equipment (pump, pipes, sprinklers, etc.) might be estimated to yield 8 percent, etc.

A convenient way to express such a ranking of investment opportunities is by a diagram. Using the figures from this example we plot the internal rate of return on the vertical axis and the cumulative amount invested on the horizontal axis. To simplify the example, let us assume that there is a continuous array of investment opportunities which enable us to connect the points and draw a continuous downward sloping line as in Figure 10–1.

Faced with these investment opportunities we now must decide which ones to accept and which to reject. In order to make this decision, we need to know the interest rate that would have to be paid on borrowed funds, or that could be obtained on our own funds. Let us suppose this is 8 percent. If so then we would want to invest in those opportunities that yield 8 percent or above. In the example depicted by Figure 10–1, the total investment for the year would be $2,100.

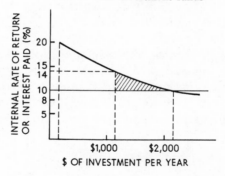

FIGURE 10–1. Cumulative ranking of investments or demand for investment funds

Stopping short of this amount, say at $1,100, would reduce profits by the value of the shaded area in Figure 10–1. Say we invest $1,101 instead of $1,100. We pay 8 cents per year on this extra dollar of investment and it returns 14 cents per year, so in net it adds 6 cents to our total profits (or it reduces our losses by 6 cents if we are operating in the red). Continuing to add extra dollars of investment will continue to increase profits, or reduce losses, until we reach the $2,100 point. Increasing the investment beyond $2,100, however, would reduce profits because the interest rate of return on this capital would be less than the interest charge on it.

You might have noticed by now that the curve representing the cumulative ranking of investment opportunities is, in reality, a demand curve for investment funds. At any given interest rate an investor maximizes profits, or minimizes losses, by investing the amount that corresponds to this point on the curve. In Figure 10–1, for example, a higher interest charge, say 14 percent, would reduce the quantity of funds demanded down to $1,100. Conversely, at a lower interest rate, there is a greater quantity of funds demanded.

You might have noticed also that there is a close similarity between Figure 10–1 and the demand for labor. Recall that the labor demand curve is given by the curve representing labor's *VMP* or *MRP*. At a given wage the employer maximizes profits by hiring up to the point where the wage is equal to labor's *VMP* or *MRP*, as the case may be. The same is true for capital; the investor maximizes profits by investing up to the point where the interest charge is equal to the internal rate of return of the marginal dollar invested.

Although the investment demand in Figure 10–1 is for an individual, we can visualize an industry or market demand as well. The market demand for investment funds is obtained by summing at each interest rate the investment demand of all the firms in the market.

One aspect of the capital market that you might find a bit puzzling is that even though additional capital is put into place each year, the internal rate of return on the marginal dollar invested does not appear to be declining. You might reasonably expect it to as each firm moves further down its investment demand curve. In fact, many people including some economists have feared a gradual "drying up" of investment opportunities as the stock of capital grows larger.

What appears to be occurring, however, is a continual surfacing of new investment opportunities that hitherto had not been thought of or imagined. For example, in the past 10 years a large amount of investment has taken place in computers and data processing equipment. New areas of investment that seem to be surfacing now are pollution control equipment and new capital for factory construction of housing. Of course, there is always some investment capital to replace that which is worn out. Those who have the talent for predicting the high payoff investment of the future generally are well rewarded for their efforts. Capital invested in the "ground floor" so to speak can yield several hundred percent per year for the first few years until additional capital can move in to compete the product price down. The usual procedure seems to be for a small investment to strike a successful venture, begin to pay off handsomely, and other investors seeing this, begin moving in to "get a piece of the action." One must remember, though, that the failure rate for completely new ventures tends to be high, so these tend not to be the best place to invest one's "lunch money."

SHIFTS IN DEMAND FOR INVESTMENT FUNDS

In our discussion of product demand and again in that for labor demand, we saw that shifts in demand are important considerations in these markets. This is equally true for investment demand in the capital market. An increase, or a shift to the right in investment demand, means that business firms are willing to increase the amount invested at each level of interest rate, as shown in Figure 10–2. A decrease, of course, has the opposite meaning.

FIGURE 10–2. Shifts in demand for investment funds

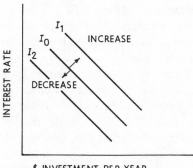

$ INVESTMENT PER YEAR

Probably the major cause of shifts in investment demand is a change in expectations of future business conditions. If businessmen become more optimistic of future sales and profits, they will be more willing to purchase additional capital or at least replace the old. That is, investment demand will shift to the right or increase. By the same token, there is little incentive to purchase additional capital if sales and profits are expected to decline in the future. This situation would be reflected by a shift to the left of investment demand.

Expectations of future business conditions are especially important for investment decisions because capital pays off over a long period of time. Even in the example of the relatively short-lived garden tractor investment, we had to predict the additional sales five years in advance. If we had been more pessimistic about future production and prices of tomatoes the stream of returns from the $1,000 investment would have been lower, and we might have decided not to purchase the tractor after all. Moreover, the longer we attempt to predict into the future, the less sure we can be about our predictions.

SUPPLY OF INVESTMENT FUNDS

In most cases firms do not have the cash on hand to purchase an item of capital, at least something that represents a sizable outlay. Consequently, at least part of the purchase price of much capital is financed by funds borrowed from lending institutions, mainly commercial banks and savings and loan associations. The issue of bonds is another way of borrowing funds, although this method is utilized mainly by large firms and governments.

One rather significant difference between the capital and labor market is that the small, perfectly competitive buyer in the capital market probably does not face a perfectly horizontal, or elastic, supply of funds. Recall that in the labor market the perfectly competitive employer can hire or lay off people without affecting the wage he pays, i.e., he faces a perfectly elastic supply of labor.

The perfectly competitive borrower of funds, on the other hand, can be expected to face an upward sloping supply curve of funds. The reason is risk. The larger amount that a firm borrows, the larger its proportion of debt to equity, which in turn increases the risk taken on by the lender.

For example, in the garden tractor case, if we had borrowed only $250 of the $1,000 purchase price, the bank would not be greatly concerned about being repaid because the tractor would sell for substantially more than this if the venture failed in its early years. But if we had borrowed say $900, the sale price of the tractor may not cover the loan, so the bank would not be so sure of being paid back. To compensate for the additional risk, the bank would require a somewhat higher rate of interest before it would be willing to make the larger loan.

In extremely risky ventures the bank may refuse to make the loan because the interest rate it could legally charge would not be high enough to compensate for the risk. If the prospective borrower is still determined to make the investment he would have to seek other sources of funds; a finance company, relatives, or as a last resort a "loan shark."

THE STOCK MARKET

In addition to borrowing, a second major method of acquiring funds for capital is to sell stock. In recent decades this has proved to be the most effective method of acquiring a large amount of capital. Virtually 100 percent of the large firms in the country today are corporations which are just firms owned by stockholders. Although it is by no means necessary to be an industrial giant to finance the purchase of capital by selling stock. There are many family corporations where the stockholders are limited to family members.

In order to sell stock, a firm must obtain a charter from the state in which it chooses to set up headquarters. In years past the charter would specify rather narrowly the type of activity and area in which a corporation could operate. The state of New Jersey, being an exception, allowed a less restrictive charter which is why it became a popular place for corporations to be from. Nowadays, however, most states require only vague statements of purpose and area of operation.

Once a firm becomes a corporation and sells stock its stockholders become the owners of the firm. Thus capital acquired through the sale of stock is equity capital. This is in contrast to capital acquired by selling bonds which is debt capital.

At the time of its sale each stock certificate carries a face value. The exact amount is largely up to the discretion of the issuing firm. Let us suppose we wished to raise $1,000 to finance our garden tractor. After receiving our charter we issue 100 stock certificates at $10 each. If these were "preferred stock" we would be required to specify the annual dividend; if they were "common stocks" we would not be required to specify.

The fact that each certificate carries a face value of $10 would not guarantee that the 100 shares would raise $1,000, however. If prospective buyers of the stock were unsure of our chances for success, they might not be willing to pay the $10 price. If we were able to obtain only $8, for example, the remaining $200 would have to be raised by our own funds or by borrowing.

At any rate the price of our stock would closely reflect the stock market's evaluation of our earning and growth potential. If we were fortunate enough to enjoy a profitable year and paid a good dividend, the value of our stocks would likely rise and there would be no legal restriction on how far up they could go; the determining factor would be the economic evaluation of our firm by the people buying and selling in the stock market.

This is not to say that the "psychology" of the market is not important. For if people believe that our firm will be successful, this is enough to bid the stock price higher. Essentially the price of a stock is determined by the forces of supply and demand. Fluctuations in stock prices are due primarily to shifts in demand. A good report or rumor is enough to shift the demand for a stock to the right and increase its price.

Over the long run, however, a stock probably will not exhibit a sustained increase in price unless the firm's assets also increase in value. A successful firm accomplishes this by "plowing back" profits into the firm. In recent years there has been a growing tendency for firms to pay modest dividends, say a 3 or 4 percent return to the stockholders, but strive for a more rapid growth of the value of their stocks. These have come to be known as "growth stocks."

Stockholders have shown a preference for growth stocks because of favorable tax treatment they obtain. For example, if you are in the 30 percent income tax bracket and receive $100 in dividends you pay $30 in income taxes. But if the stock you own increases in value by $100 and you sell the stock you pay only $15 in taxes. This is because the increase in value of capital, which is known as "capital gains," is taxed at only one half the rate of ordinary income. Moreover the tax does not have to be paid until you actually sell the stock, so by owning growth stocks you can postpone paying your income tax as well as having it reduced by a half. Small wonder that growth stocks have become popular.

Unfortunately there is no secret formula for choosing stocks that will quickly double or triple in value so that we can turn our modest savings into fortunes. Although success in the stock market can never be assured, it does help to know as much as possible about the firm you are buying into. Is the firm producing a good or service that will enjoy a substantial increase in demand? Is the management competent and progressive? These are a couple of important questions that bear upon the future value of stock. Purchasing stocks by hunch or "hot tip" is akin to playing the "slots" in Las Vegas or betting on the horses. It is possible to be lucky but the odds are against you.

DEPRECIATION

As we mentioned earlier in the chapter it is not logical to charge the entire purchase price of a capital item that lasts over a number of years against production in the year it is purchased. Rather it is necessary to assess the amount that the capital item declines in value during each year. We refer to this annual decline in value as depreciation and must add it to the annual interest charge to obtain the annual cost of capital.

We include this section mainly to call attention to the various patterns of depreciation that are possible for a given item of capital. For example, does the item decline in value more the first year of use than the last, or vice versa.

It will be easier to see why we observe different patterns of depreciation if we first point out why capital depreciates. There are two basic reasons: (1) the wearing out or using up of the item and (2) obsolescence. The current market value of a piece of equipment or a building is a reflection of its expected contribution to future output. Naturally the older an item becomes the fewer years of productive life that remains. Moreover, the annual net *VMP* of the item also can be expected to decline as more time is taken for repairs or maintenance.

In our age of change and new technology, capital also becomes obsolete. If something new comes on the market that reduces production costs or increases efficiency, the demand for the old capital will decline, hence its price will fall. Thus the depreciation of capital depends not only on its own productivity but also on the productivity of the new capital being produced. Because of this it is difficult, if not impossible, to predict in advance how fast an item will become obsolete. Nor is it easy or even useful to attempt to separate how much of an item's depreciation is due to wearing out and how much is due to obsolescence; both have the same effect.

Because it is necessary to estimate depreciation for income tax purposes all firms must make an estimate of its amount. Also it is required that once a certain pattern of depreciation is selected for a capital item, the same pattern must be followed for as long as the item is kept.

Two widely used methods of estimating depreciation are (1) the straight-line method and (2) the constant percentage method. The resulting decline in value of the item being depreciated for each of these methods is illustrated in Figure 10–3. The straight-line method amounts to decreasing the value of the capital by a constant number of dollars each year. For example, if we were depreciating our $1,000 garden tractor by the straight-line method over a period of five years, we would assess $200 per year as depreciation.

If we employ the constant percentage method we would multiply each year's market value by a constant percentage. For example, if we depreciate the garden tractor 30 percent per year, the first year's depreciation would be $300, the second year's $210 ($700 × 0.30), the third year's $147, etc. You might notice that under this method the annual deprecation is higher when the item is new, resulting in a lower depreciated value during its early years of use.

You might notice also that with this method the item does not depreciate to zero. After five years its depreciated value under the constant percentage depreciation is $168. In fact, under this method the depreciated value never completely reaches zero, although it comes close.

FIGURE 10–3. The straight-line and constant percentage patterns of depreciation of the $1,000 garden tractor

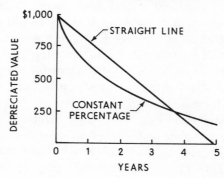

The method of depreciation chosen and the length of time involved depends, of course, on the item to be depreciated. The constant percentage method would seem to be a bit more realistic for most items since depreciation usually is higher the first few years of ownership. Automobiles, for example, tend to depreciate about 20 percent of their current market value each year. So if you buy a $3,000 car, it depreciates $600 the first year, $480 the second, etc. The fact that the constant percentage method does not result in a zero depreciation value also is realistic since most capital retains some scrap value.

MAIN POINTS OF CHAPTER 10

1. Capital as used in the context of this chapter refers to durable or long lasting inputs such as machines, buildings, land, etc., rather than cash or money.

2. The annual cost of capital is made up of two components: (1) depreciation and (2) the interest charge.

3. The marginal product of capital is the additional output obtained by adding one more unit of capital.

4. One method of gauging the profitability of an investment is to determine whether or not capital's annual *VMP* or *MRP* is greater than its annual depreciation plus interest charge.

5. The rate of return on capital is the amount of net income that each dollar invested earns each year. For example, a 6 percent rate of return means that each dollar earns 6 cents per year.

6. The capitalized value of nondepreciable capital is obtained by dividing the annual dollar return by the interest rate.

7. Cash-flow analysis is a technique used to compare the cash outflow of a capital item, i.e., its purchase price, with the additional net cash inflows or net returns resulting from the use of the item.

8. The discounted present value of one dollar to be received n years in the future is equal to $1/(1 + r)^n$ where r is the rate of interest.

9. A second method of assessing the profitability of an investment is to compare the purchase price of the capital with its capitalized value or the discounted present value of its stream of future returns.

10. The internal rate of return on a capital item is that rate of interest which makes the discounted present value of the stream of returns equal to the purchase price or total cost of the capital.

11. The third method of determining the profitability of a capital item is to compare its internal rate of return with the rate of interest that has to be paid on borrowed funds or that can be earned on equity funds.

12. To maximize profits a firm should invest in capital until the internal rate of return on the marginal dollar invested is equal to the interest rate.

13. The demand curve for investment funds is given by the curve showing the relationship between the internal rate of return and the cumulative amount invested.

14. The demand for investment funds shifts mainly in response to a change in investor expectations of future business conditions.

15. The supply curve of borrowed funds facing an individual borrower can be expected to be upward sloping because the larger the loan, the greater the debt-equity ratio, hence the greater the risk for the lender.

16. For large firms the principal method of raising funds to purchase capital is through the sale of stock certificates. The value of a firm's stock depends largely on the stock market's assessment of the earning ability and future growth of the firm.

17. Capital depreciates for two reasons: (1) wearing out and (2) obsolescence. Two common methods of estimating depreciation are the straight-line method and the constant percentage method.

QUESTIONS FOR THOUGHT AND DISCUSSION

1. "Society would be better off without capital because it corrupts mankind by placing too much emphasis on wealth." Comment.

2. Suppose you consider purchasing a new typewriter for $100 that you would use for four years of college. How would you estimate the annual cost of this typewriter?

3. How would you estimate the value of the marginal product of this typewriter? (Hint: If you hired someone to type your papers, how much would it cost per year?)

4. How would you determine the discounted present value of the stream of returns to this typewriter? Do you think it would be a worthwhile investment? Why?

5. Suppose a rich uncle leaves you a plot of ground in a downtown area that is rented out as a parking lot for $1,000 per year. How would you determine the capitalized value of this land? If someone offered you $10,000 for it would you accept? Why?

6. Referring back to the typewriter in Questions 2, 3, and 4, how would you utilize cash flow analysis to estimate the internal rate of return to the typewriter.

7. Using the two methods of depreciation discussed, straight line and constant percent, compute the annual depreciation for the typewriter.

CHAPTER
11
THE ECONOMICS
OF EDUCATION

THE CONCEPT OF HUMAN CAPITAL

In our discussion of the capital market in Chapter 10, we defined capital as durable or long-lasting inputs, such as buildings and equipment, that contribute to the production of goods and services. We were reminded too that capital inputs are expensive items and that the present value of their stream of returns must be greater than their purchase price in order for them to yield a net positive contribution to total output.

In recent years there has been a growing awareness that the acquisition of knowledge and skills by human beings also results in the creation of capital—human capital.[1] At the same time there has been a reluctance on the part of some educators to regard education and training as a kind of capital formation. Their rationale is similar to those who have argued that labor, the services of human beings, should not be treated as an input of production subject to economic analysis. After all, is it not dehumanizing to think of boys and girls learning to read and write, or of young men and women acquiring a knowldege of mathematics, history, economics, etc., as a process that results in the formation of capital? Surely the psychological and sociological aspects of human beings must be considered.

Again, as we pointed out at the beginning of the labor market chapter, there is no reason why economists who work in the area of labor eco-

---

[1] For a comprehensive review of the literature in this field see, T. W. Schultz, *The Economic Value of Education* (New York and London: Columbia University Press, 1963).

215

nomics or human capital need to be less "human" than anyone else. Indeed the separation of the study of the labor market or the economics of education allows us to take into account the uniqueness of people as compared to nonhuman inputs such as machines, tools, raw materials, etc. Thus the mere fact that we identify human capital as a separate field of study denotes its uniqueness.

Keeping in mind the special characteristics of human beings, there are still a number of similarities between nonhuman capital and human capital or the existence of skills or knowledge acquired through education or training. First, both kinds of capital, human and nonhuman, enhance the productive capacity of society. Man without tools and without knowledge is a very unproductive creature.

Moreover even a cursory knowledge of history will impress upon us that human capital must exist before nonhuman capital can be produced. For example, the wheel came into being when man learned that a round object rolling along the ground encountered less friction and took less power to move than a flat object being dragged. Since that time we could point to innumerable examples of new knowledge leading to the production of new nonhuman capital.

A second similarity between the two kinds of capital is that they both pay off over a long period of time. Indeed the stream of returns to education for most people covers 30 to 40 or more years. We will discuss shortly the kind of returns that human capital provides. For the moment, though, it is sufficient that we become aware of the consequences of this long payoff period. First, it precipitates a great deal of uncertainty. There is an uncertainty about whether there will be any payoff at all. Growing up in the "shadow of the bomb" and with the prospect of military duty ahead, many young people have grown pessimistic, to say the least, about the future.

There is uncertainty also with regard to job opportunities in the future. Students are faced with the nagging question of whether the job that is being prepared for will even exist 10 to 20 years hence. Or whether the skills and knowledge that are acquired will be sufficient to handle the job in the future.

Moreover, at the high school or undergraduate level of training, it is virtually impossible to predict what kind of employment will be forthcoming. Furthermore a person's job can be expected to change several times during a lifetime. As a result it is important that training, particularly at the college level, be of the kind that facilitates learning new jobs and adjusting to new environments.

Another consequence of the long payoff is the need to discount future returns, as we did in the garden tractor example of the last chapter. For instance, one dollar forthcoming 40 years from now discounted back at a 6 percent interest rate is worth less than 10 cents today. With the demands of the present, such as car, clothes, and travel, upon a young person's re-sources, the decision to invest now for a payoff far into the future is indeed difficult.

We mentioned also in Chapter 10 that some nonhuman capital requires a lengthy building period. The formation of human capital is similar in this respect, although this period is generally a good deal longer for human capital. Eight years is about the least and runs up to 18 or 20 years of schooling for people who obtain the Ph.D. or other professional degrees. We will see later in the chapter that this long gestation or building period coupled with the long payoff period makes the discounting factor especially important in the case of human capital.

Still another similarity between the two kinds of capital is that both tend to depreciate. The ultimate depreciation for human capital, of course, is growing old and passing from the scene. But there is a more immediate depreciation that begins the minute after we learn something new—forgetting. Educators tell us that a large part of what we learn is forgotten in a relatively short time. How much do you recall of a book you read or a course you took last year or even last quarter or semester?

Depreciation of human capital occurs also because of obsolescence. Each year new knowledge is being produced that reduces the value of old knowledge. Skills such as the ability to repair a steam locomotive or to fly a propeller-driven aircraft are no longer in demand because of new knowledge and technology that has come on the scene. Because of obsolescence it is necessary for most of us to continue learning throughout our lifetimes. This is particularly true for people in the professions or skilled trades. A college professor who wants to keep abreast of new knowledge in his field, for example, probably should spend about 20 to 25 percent of his time learning.

HUMAN CAPITAL FORMATION

The major part of all human capital is the result of formal schooling provided by elementary schools, high schools, trade and vocational schools, and colleges and universities. Not all schooling, of course, needs to be of this type. A good deal of learning takes place on the job either through apprenticeship programs or through learning by doing.

In addition, some learning takes place by individual study, although the self-made man that we all admire, Abraham Lincoln, for example, always has been a rare case. In spite of the criticism levied against the traditional student-teacher arrangement in learning, it is the rare individual who can master a field or body of knowledge by himself. Most of us require someone who can tell us what is important or what to study. In fact, this may be the most valuable function of a teacher.

Of course, different teachers have different ideas of what is important.

But the ability to identify and teach the important material just might be the crucial characteristic of a "good" teacher; a teacher who allocates the time of his students to material that he considers important but in fact turns out to be trivial cannot be "good" no matter how lucid or entertaining he might be. The ability to foresee and identify the important, high payoff material seems to be a scarce talent, however.

PERSONAL RETURNS TO EDUCATION

Let us now look at education in somewhat more detail. What does an individual obtain from education? Essentailly there are two components to the return to education: (1) investment and (2) consumption. The investment component of the returns to education refer to the future years of increased earning power that can be obtained with additional years of schooling.

The increased earning power that accompanies additional schooling comes largely from one or both of two factors: (1) an increase in the productive capacity of the individual and (2) the ability to produce new goods or services that are valued more highly by society.

The contribution of education to increased productivity appears to stem, at least in part, from an increased ability to organize and use resources efficiently, including the very scarce resource, time. Surely no one appreciates the importance of time more than the student. With two or three exams coming up and a term paper to finish, the student is forced to make each minute count. The experience gained in allocating time efficiently is perhaps one of the most important attributes of a college education, at least from the standpoint of productivity of the individual.

Increased education also enhances productivity by enabling the individual to more readily identify new technology and to use it effectively. Education is particularly important with regard to technology that requires new or different skills. The more highly educated person seems to posses a greater capacity for self-teaching and adapting to new situations.

The effect of education on the kinds of goods and services produced is demonstrated clearly by comparing output of a modern, highly educated society with that of a traditional society. The traditional society's choice of goods and services tends to be limited to a rather narrow array of low quality items, most of which are considered necessities.

On the other hand, the output of the more highly educated society is of a higher quality and much more diverse in nature. The world would be a dull place for the educated man if greater education only resulted in greater output of the traditional necessities such as food, clothing, and shelter. Thus the monetary rewards of additional education stem at least in part from the increased ability to conceive of and produce new and different goods and services that are demanded by a more productive society.

Of course, when considering the monetary rewards of increased education, it is always possible to point out exceptions: self-made men with an eighth-grade education who have built up fortunes in the business world, or high school dropouts who made it big in show business.

But if we look at large numbers of people, we find that high school graduates, on the average, earn more than people with an eighth-grade education, and people with college training earn more than high school graduates. Thus, an individual who does not achieve a high school or college education is not necessarily doomed to a life of poverty, but the chances that he will remain poor are substantially higher than if he would have gotten the schooling.

For most people the returns to additional education exceed the investment component, i.e., the monetary value of increased earnings over a lifetime. The consumption or nonmonetary returns to education include: (1) the immediate utility or satisfaction that a person receives during the time of his schooling and (2) the long-run stream of increased satisfaction that accrues to a person during his lifetime because of the educational experience.

Although few students think fondly of exams or assignments, most derive some satisfaction from being in an educational environment. The friends that are made, the dances and parties, the dates, the sporting events, the good books that are read, etc., all provide immediate satisfaction that is not measured in monetary terms.

But the nonmonetary rewards to schooling are not limited to the immediate time spent in school. Many friendships that begin in school endure over a lifetime. Many girls acquire a husband, and many fellows find a wife during their school years. It would seem also that education enhances the quality of life by facilitating an awareness and greater understanding of the world around us. Our lives are less ruled by superstition and fear and more by rational thought and deliberate choice.

Although as yet we do not have adequate quantitative measures of happiness, psychological studies seem to indicate that people with more education are on the average happier and find greater fulfillment in life than those with less education. Perhaps education is even more important than money in finding that elusive and nebulous thing called happiness.

At any rate, it is fairly certain that individuals obtain more from education than just the monetary rewards as reflected by a higher income. One can think of these nonmonetary rewards to education as a consumption good. It provides utility hence people are willing to pay a positive price for it. It appears also that education is a superior good; as incomes rise the demand for education also rises.

It is reasonable to believe, also, that as incomes continue to rise, the nonmonetary rewards to education will grow in importance relative to the monetary returns. Young people will come to school more to enrich their lives than to "make a bundle." We see more and more evidence of this phenomenon particularly among young people from middle and upper income families.

If in fact education is becoming more a consumption good, then we might expect, as well, that students will demand more voice in the courses that are offered. If courses are taught primarily to increase earning power, the professional in the field, i.e., the professor, wins hands down as far as knowing what to teach. But when it comes to offering courses more for consumption or nonmonetary purposes, it must be admitted that the student has a better idea of what "turns him on" than the professor or school administrators.

This does not imply, however, that courses need be less scholarly or the thinking less rigorous than is now the case. But we would expect to see greater emphasis placed on the relevance of the course and interest of the student. With the increased emphasis on the consumption component of education we might expect to see also a decreased emphasis on grades. If the student is not particularly concerned with the effect of courses on his earning capacity, there is less incentive to master the fine points of the course for an "A" or "B."

The fact that we are observing a trend in this direction is evidence that the monetary return to an education is becoming slightly less important. However, the monetary return, no doubt, still represents the major reason for attending college, and even more so for graduate or professional school attendance.

PUBLIC RETURNS TO EDUCATION

Thus far we have considered only the returns accruing to the individual. But society as a whole also benefits when its populace enjoys a high level of education. Perhaps most important is the greater political stability that accompanies a more highly educated public. Also the chances of a tyrant gaining power are less if people know and are concerned about social political structure of society.

It is not likely that Hitler could have gained power in Germany if a substantial share of the German people had been liberal arts graduates. Nor will the repressive or dictitorial types of governments that exist today be able to keep as tight a grip on their people as more and more rise to higher levels of education. Educated people demand self-determination and the right to think for themselves. A great deal of bloodshed may have to occur before repressed people will be able to gain this right, however. Small wonder that repressive types of governments attempt to keep such a tight grip on education and information flowing into their countries.

Education also helps to reduce the "social overhead" expenditures of a country. It is well known that a lack of education and vocational opportunities leads to poverty and crime. It is perhaps unfortunate that we have tried to combat the symptoms of inadequate education by increasing expenditures on welfare, the police, and other law enforcement agencies rather than investing more of this money at the root of the problem.

Even at the level of the individual there is a public return to education. This benefit stems from the fact that most people prefer to live in a community where there are good schools, an abundance of community activities for young and old, and a neighborhood feeling of goodwill and trust among people rather than fear and suspicion. Observe the level of education in communities with the above characteristics and there can be little doubt about the role that education plays in making a community a better place to live.

PERSONAL COSTS OF EDUCATION

Needless to say, education is not a free good. Indeed, it is becoming more expensive each year as every student and parent is well aware. It will be useful at this point, therefore, to itemize the major costs that a student or his parents bear for education. These include:

1. Foregone earnings.
2. Tuition.
3. Books and supplies.

It is a temptation not to include foregone earnings (the money you could be earning if you were not in school) as part of the cost of an education because it is not paid by check or cash. But we must admit that a person who decides to go to work after high school gives up a college or technical school education. Thus it is just as logical to argue that a person who decides to go to school gives up full-time employment earnings during these years.

In more developed countries of the world, foregone earnings are negligible for the elementary and junior high school student but begin to loom large as the student finishes high school and enters college or some other kind of advanced training. In the poor countries where educational attainment is very low and children enter the labor force at a relative young age, foregone earnings become relatively important even in the lower grades.

Although the average student may not feel the pinch of foregone earnings as much as the out-of-pocket costs of tuition, books, etc., it is necessary just the same to take this money into account when deciding how far to go in school. If we reflect for a moment on the relatively modest salary that a high school graduate can obtain the first few years out of school, say five to six thousand dollars per year, it becomes clear that even a modest amount of income foregone becomes relatively large when viewed as a cost.

The foregone earnings expense can be reduced substantially, however, by taking part-time employment while attending school. For example, if you could be earning $5,500 per year on a full-time job were you not in school, but you work part time for $2,000 per year, your foregone earnings are reduced to $3,500 per year. Of course, the further one goes in school, the higher are the earnings foregone for additional schooling.

In addition, it should be kept in mind that time spent on a part-time job means less time for studies, so it is wise for the students to reduce their class loads somewhat if hours worked becomes substantial. Students who work 30 to 40 hours per week while trying to maintain a full load of courses come face to face with the concept of opportunity cost the hard way.

Any scholarships or financial aid received by students also would be deducted from foregone earnings. In the example above, a $500 scholarship would further reduce earnings foregone down to $3,000 per year.

The other two cost components, tuition and books, supplies, etc., are familiar enough to us, so we need not go into detail here. Except we should keep in mind that tuition generally does not cover the full educational costs of colleges and universities. We will consider this part of the cost in the next section.

One cost item that is conspicuous by its absence is board and room. Surely, you might argue, a student who pays $1,000 during the school year for a room and meals at the college dormitory should include this amount as a logical part of college costs. But we must bear in mind that everyone has to be somewhere so if the student did not pay the $1,000 for the purposes of going to college he would have to pay as much or more to live wherever he worked. Thus the cost items listed above only include the extra costs involved with attending college as opposed to doing something else. We measure costs in this manner so we can compare them with the extra income that is obtained by furthering our education.

PUBLIC COSTS OF EDUCATION

Let us now look at the costs of education from the viewpoint of the total society. All of the private costs that we considered in the previous section would, of course, be a part of the total educational cost that society must bear. The operation of schools and colleges financed in part by tuition, the production of books, supplies, etc., and the loss of earnings during school years all involve a using up of real resources that could have been used to produce something else had they not been used to produce education.

In the majority of our educational institutions, however, tuition does not come close to covering the cost of operating the schools. In the public elementary and high schools, tuition is zero so the entire cost is borne by the taxpayers. In colleges and universities tuition varies a great deal; some city or community colleges set tuition at zero or close to it while the more exclusive private schools try to cover a larger share of their operating costs by tuition. Although even most of the high tuition private schools must rely on endowments and grants to make ends meet.

A good case can be made, however, for public support of educational institutions. In a large part, the people who purchase the services provided by these institutions (students) in general have zero or very low incomes. The young child obviously could not earn his way through elementary school. Even in more advanced schooling the student has had little chance to save or to earn even enough to pay for the services he purchases.

One alternative to public payment of tuition, therefore, is for parents or families to foot the bill. For wealthy or high-income people this is sometimes done, but for the majority of people, particularly young parents, the cost would be prohibitive. Their children would in turn be doomed to a life of poverty because they could not afford to buy the means of escape—education.

A second alternative to public support of education is for students to borrow. But this alternative has not enjoyed much popularity even among students in professional or graduate schools, to say nothing of high school or elementary school students. In fact, students seem more reluctant to go into debt for schooling than for an automobile. It is not clear why.

Perhaps it is the uncertainty of the future. The automobile provides immediate and certain utility, whereas the payoff to education is both uncertain and far off. Also no student relishes the thought of paying off a substantial loan during the first few years out of college. These are the years of his lowest income and greatest demand for consumer goods— housing, furniture, automobile, young children to care for, etc. At any rate, it appears that many students are not eager to borrow for an education even though the rate of return on this investment may be higher than the rate of interest they have to pay on their loans.

But lending agencies also have not been especially eager to promote educational loans as compared to making auto loans, for example. No doubt, risk is a prime consideration for the lender also. If a person who borrows for an automobile defaults on his payments, the lender can always repossess the car. But if a person who borrows for an education de-faults, it is not possible to reposses the person. True there are devices such as the wage garnishment, but these generally involve extra legal expense and trouble.

It appears, therefore, that if society desires its young people to achieve a high level of schooling, then it must be willing to use public tax funds to finance education. Essentially this means that the out-of-pocket costs of education are paid later in life when a person is better able to afford them.

MEASURING MONETARY RETURNS TO EDUCATION

Although the returns to education are reflected in more than just mon-etary rewards, it is helpful to obtain measures of both the costs and re-turns to investment in human capital or education. For if education turns out to be a good investment strictly from a monetary point of view, then we can be sure it is an even better investment when nonmonetary returns are considered. Let us look first at the monetary returns to education.

The figures in Table 11-1 provide an indication of the monetary value of various levels of education. These figures are the median incomes of male persons (all races) for the year 1968 classified by age and educa-tion, published by the U.S. Department of Commerce, Bureau of Census.

It is interesting to note some differences in the income streams of peo-ple with different levels of education. Most obvious, of course, is the in-creased size of income as education increases. Secondly, note that a per-son with an eighth-grade or even a high school education cannot look forward to as large an increase in his income as he grows older as he could if he were a college graduate. People with relatively less schooling tend to reach their peak income years during the 35–54 age span whereas college graduates and people with postgraduate work by in large con-tinue to enjoy increased incomes until they retire. Of course, with overall economic growth occurring, there has been a tendency, in the United

TABLE 11-1. Median incomes of full-time employed males by age and education, 1968

Level of School Completed	Age Span			
	25–34	35–44	45–54	55–64
Eighth grade................	$ 5,994	$ 6,702	$ 6,815	$ 6,787
High school.................	7,762	8,826	8,686	8,194
One to three years over high school.................	8,409	10,076	10,009	9,400
Four years college............	10,132	12,596	12,910	13,063
One or more years postgraduate work...........	10,538	13,508	14,401	14,634

Source: U.S. Department of Commerce, *Current Population Reports*, Series P-60, No. 66, December, 1969, table 41.

TABLE 11–2.   Income differentials for various levels of education ($ per year)

Differences in Educational Level	Age Span			
	25–34	35–44	45–54	55–64
High school over 8th grade...................	$1,768	$2,124	$1,871	$1,407
One to three years college over high school.............	647	1,250	1,323	1,206
Four years college over high school.............	2,370	3,770	4,224	4,869
One or more years post-graduate over college.........	406	912	1,500	1,571

Source: Computed from table 11–1.

States at least, for everyone to enjoy income growth. But people with more education tend to enjoy more income growth than people with less education.

In order to use these figures to calculate the monetary returns of achieving a given level of education, we must compute the differential in earnings between the various levels of schooling. For example, the monetary value of a high school over an eighth-grade education during the 25–34 age span is $7,762–$5,994, or $1,768 per year. During the 35–44 age span it is $2,124 per year, etc. These income differentials are presented in Table 11–2.

Assuming a 40-year working life, we can obtain a rough idea of the extra income that a person can expect by completing a given level of schooling. For example, during the 10-year 25–34 age span a person can expect to earn about $17,680 more by completing high school than by stopping at the eighth grade. Total lifetime earnings differentials for various levels of schooling are presented in Table 11–3.

Bear in mind that the figures in Table 11–3 are additions to income because of additional years of schooling, not total income. For example, the total lifetime income of a high school graduate is in the neighborhood of $334,680, as obtained from Table 11–1, whereas lifetime earnings of a college graduate is $487,010.

There are some interesting differences to note in these differentials. Notice that by investing in four years of high school, total lifetime earnings increases by $71,700. But observe that by investing in four years of

TABLE 11–3.   Total lifetime earnings differentials for various levels of education

Differences in Educational Level	Dollars
High school over eighth grade.......................	$ 71,700
One to three years college over high school............	44,260
Four years college over high school..................	152,330
One or more years postgraduate over college..........	43,890

college the extra income over high school increases to $152,330, or just about double the payoff to the four high school years.

But we do not have sufficient information yet to evaluate the payoff to different levels of schooling. We must consider two additional factors: (1) the cost of the schooling and (2) the present value of future income. Let us consider costs first.

MEASURING COSTS OF EDUCATION

Recall that the three major cost components of education are (1) foregone earnings (less earnings from part-time work, scholarships, and financial aid); (2) tuition; and (3) books and supplies. Since a four-year college education represents substantial costs, particularly in terms of foregone earnings, let us consider this investment as an example.

To obtain a measure of foregone earnings while attending college we need to estimate what a person could earn on a first job immediately out of high school. Unfortunately the figures in Table 11–1 do not help us a great deal here. The $7,762 median earnings figure for the 25–34 age span would be more representative of a person with a high school education who has worked about 10 years rather than a new graduate.

Instead let us assume that a new high school graduate could earn about $5,500 per year for the first two years out of school and $6,000 per year for the next two years. Also let us assume first that while attending college the student does not hold down a part-time job during the school year but earns $1,200 on a summer job. His net foregone earnings would be $4,300 per year for the first two years of college and $4,800 annually for the last two years.

Let us assume also that the student pays resident tuition at a large state university, say $500 per year. This figure would increase up to around $2,000 to $2,500 or more per year at the more exclusive private schools, of course. But in some cases private school tuition also includes a charge for board and room so this amount should be subtracted.

Books, supplies, etc., may seem expensive when they are purchased, but they actually constitute a relatively minor part of total costs. Choosing a rather liberal figure of $250 per year would include most students. We summarize these three cost items for the four years of college in Table 11–4.

Table 11–4.   Summary of costs for a four-year college education

	Freshman	Sophomore	Junior	Senior
°Foregone earnings..........	$4,300	$4,300	$4,800	$4,800
Tuition	500	500	500	500
Books and supplies..........	250	250	250	250
Total.................	$5,050	$5,050	$5,550	$5,550

°Assuming a $1,200 per year summer job.

The figures in Table 11–4 impress upon us the importance of foregone earnings in the total cost of a college education. In this example they comprise about 85 percent of the total costs. And the further one goes in school the larger foregone earnings become. This undoubtedly explains why students become more and more anxious to join the labor force the closer they approach the end of their schooling. Some, particularly Ph.D. students, leave school before they are finished hoping to complete their requirements on the job. Some never do.

If we add up the total costs of four years of college we obtain in this example $21,200. It is unlikely that most college students realize how much they invest in themselves during their college years. Comparing this $21,200 cost figure with the $152,330 additional income figures from Table 11–3, would, however, make it appear that the expensive investment is well worth the cost. But before we become too optimistic, we should remember that the $152,330 additional income is spread out over an entire lifetime. One dollar forthcoming 30 to 40 years from now is not worth much at the present. We need to, therefore, compute the present value of this extra income stream just as we did in the garden tractor example. In the process we can estimate the internal rate of return to a college education. First let us set up the problem in terms of cash flow analysis as we did with the garden tractor in the preceding chapter.

CASH FLOW ANALYSIS APPLIED TO EDUCATION

In the context of cash flow analysis we can view the costs of going to school (Table 11–4) as the cash outflow and the added income over a high school education as the cash inflow. The configuration of these cash flows for a college education is illustrated in Figure 11–1.

The net cash outflow increases slightly after the first two years because of the increased earning potential of people with two extra years of schooling. The level of cash inflows is illustrated in a stepwise fashion because of the age groupings given by the census data on earnings (Table

FIGURE 11–1. Cash outflows and inflows from investment in a college education

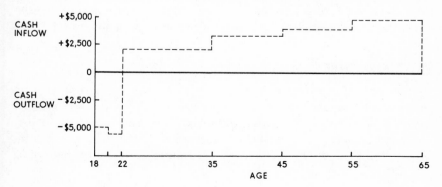

11–1). Although it would be more realistic to show earnings differentials rising in a smooth line, the stepwise procedure will not alter the results greatly. We assume a 43-year working life starting at age 22 and extending up to age 65.

INTERNAL RATE OF RETURN
TO A COLLEGE EDUCATION

We know from our discussion of investment in the previous chapter that we must discount the streams of cash inflows back to the present in order to compare them with the cost of the investment. Recall also that the internal rate of return to an investment is equal to that rate of interest that makes the discounted present value of the stream of returns equal to the cost of the investment.

For an investment that takes place over a number of years, such as education, it is necessary also to accumulate each annual cash outflow, multiplying it by $(1 + r)^n$ where n represents the number of years back from the beginning of returns that the expenditure was made. To discount a return back to the present, you recall, we divide by $1/(1 + r)^n$ where n in this case is the number of years in the future that the return is forthcoming.

Choosing a reasonable rate of interest, 10 percent, the four years of expenditure for a college education accumulates to a total of $26,910 if we take each year up to the point where the investment starts paying off (age 22 in this example). If we discount each of the 43 years of returns back to age 22 by an interest rate of 10 percent, we obtain a cumulative figure of $27,860. Thus the internal rate of return to investment in a four-year college education appears to be just slightly over 10 percent.

In view of the fact that the total undiscounted extra earnings of a college education over that of a high school education came out to be over 152 thousand dollars, or over seven times the $21,200 unaccumulated expenditure, we might have expected the internal rate of return to be somewhat higher. But we must remember that with a 10 percent rate of discount the extra $4,869 forthcoming at age 65 is only worth about $97 at age 22. It is not surprising then that young people do not consider the extra earnings forthcoming much later in life to be very important.

PART-TIME EMPLOYMENT

Because earnings foregone represent such an important part of the cost of a college education, let us next consider the case where the student holds down a part-time job during the school year. Choosing some plausible figures, suppose as a freshman the student earns $100 per month, $150 per month as a sophomore, and $200 per month during his junior and senior years. These earnings could be obtained if the student worked about 10 to 15 hours per week during his first two years and 15 to 20 hours per week during his junior and senior years, which is not uncommon.

If we assume that other costs remain the same, as shown in Table 11–4, we can obtain the revised costs by subtracting the above part-time earnings from these figures, obtaining:

Freshman: $5,050 − $ 900 = $4,150
Sophomore: 5,050 − 1,350 = 3,700
Junior: 5,550 − 1,800 = 3,750
Senior: 5,550 − 1,800 = 3,750

Adding up these figures for the four years, we obtain a total cost of $15,350 compared to the $21,200 when the student did not work during the school year. Assuming the same stream of returns and following the same procedure as before where we accumulate the 4 years of costs up to the end of the senior year and discount the 43 years of returns back to this point, we obtain approximately a 13 percent internal rate of return. At this rate of discount accumulated costs add up to $21,208 and discounted future returns total $20,561. Thus the internal rate of return to a four-year college education with $5,850 part-time earnings is just slightly less than 13 percent.

Although it cannot be disputed that part-time earnings are very important to a college student during his time in college, it is a bit surprising to find that they do not drastically alter the rate of returns to a college education. Granted, of course, 13 percent is better than 10 percent. But even with substantial part-time earnings, foregone earnings still constitute the largest part of the cost of attending college.

One additional problem we have not considered in regard to part-time employment is its effect on the quality of education, both in terms of nonmonetary returns and future earning power; or its effect on the time required to finish the degree. We have assumed the same monetary returns and the same four years of time in college in the above calculations. However, virtually no quantitative information exists on the effect of part-time employment during college. Does it hamper a person's future earning power or enhance it? Also how much if any does it delay a student's graduation date?

It is a fairly safe assumption that part-time employment during college reduces somewhat the nonmonetary returns that college life brings. There is less time for social life and few memories later in life of parties, friends, etc. Much more research needs to be done on the "costs" of part-time employment during college. Something has to be given up; what is it and what is it worth?

THE COLLEGE DROPOUT

Of course not all students who enter colleges and universities come out with a four-year bachelor's degree or equivalent. For example in 1960, 930,000 freshman enrolled in U.S. institutions of higher learning. Four years later, in 1964, roughly 502,000 received a bachelor's degree or equivalent.[2] Thus of all students entering college, almost one half drop out somewhere along the way.

Part of the gap between freshman enrollment and the number of bachelor's degrees granted four years later is taken up by junior college students who decide to terminate their studies with the two-year degree. Moreover, enrollment in junior colleges has increased substantially in recent years. In 1960 for example, there were 454,000 students in junior colleges whereas in 1965 this figure almost doubled to 845,000.[3] Part of these students, of course, transfer to four-year institutions and obtain a bachelor's degree.

At any rate, because almost half of all college students either stop at the two-year degree or drop out of four-year institutions, it is important that we know something of the return to this schooling.

Let us take as an example, a student who invests in two years of college. Let us assume also that the annual cost of attending college during these two years is equal to the freshman and sophomore year costs shown in Table 11–4: $5,050 for each year.

Tables 11–1 and 11–2 provide an indication of the monetary returns to investment in one to three additional years of schooling beyond high school. Let us assume that these figures are representative of the earnings forthcoming from two years of college. As shown in Table 11–3, the total lifetime earnings differential for one–three years of college is about $44,000.

But in order to correctly evaluate the two-year college investment, as opposed to four years, we must both consider costs and discount the future returns back to their beginning. If we use a 10 percent rate of interest to accumulate the two years of costs and discount the 45 years of returns, we obtain $11,665 for the costs and only $7,372 for the returns. Hence the internal rate of return to two years of college is somewhat less than 10 percent. It turns out that the discounted returns just about equals the accumulated costs when a 7 percent rate of interest is used. Thus the internal rate of return to two years of college as opposed to stopping at high school is about 7 percent. Although this is a bit more than one can obtain from a savings account, it isn't spectacular.

Of course, the two-year student also can work part time, so we should compute the rate of return in this situation too. Let us assume in this case

[2] *Statistical Abstract,* 1967, pp. 133–39.
[3] *Ibid.,* p. 133.

that the student earns $900 during the first year of college (in addition to the $1,200 summer job) and $1,350 the second year, resulting in total costs of $4,150 and $3,700, respectively for these two years. Accumulating these two years of costs and discounting the 45 years of returns (assuming the same returns as the previous case), we obtain an internal rate of return of about 9 percent.

SUMMARY OF RETURNS TO INVESTMENT IN EDUCATION

We have covered a variety of different situations so it will be useful to summarize the rates of return we obtained. These are presented in Table 11–5.

Table 11–5. Summary of internal rates of return to investment in a college education

	Rate of Return (Percent)
Four-year degree, full-time school	10
Four-year degree, part-time earnings	13
Two-years college, full-time school	7
Two-years college, part-time earnings	9

We should keep in mind that these figures represent the private rate of return to a college education. Because society pays a substantial share of the cost of operating most colleges and universities, the public return would be somewhat lower. With relative low rates of return to one to three years of college, we might at least raise the question of whether it is wise for society to encourage the entry of students who will likely drop out after one or two years of college. Perhaps the technical institute or trade school is a more profitable alternative both for these individual students and for society. Of course, it is very difficult to predict in advance which students will be successful and complete the four-year program.

RETURNS TO THE CO-ED

In our discussion of the monetary returns to education we have assumed that the person works 40 years or more. But we know that most girls who attend college do not remain in the labor force all their lives. Most get married shortly after college and settle down to raise a family. Thus if we were to estimate the monetary returns to a college education for women it would be somewhat less than for men.

This is not to say, though, that college is a bad investment for girls. Strictly from a personal point of view, a college educated girl will likely enjoy more purchasing power during her life simply because she will more likely marry a college educated man. The girl who attends college to obtain her MRS. degree undoubtedly knows this very well. Of course, even without the higher future income, a girl buys some security with college because if forced to enter the labor force later in life she is better prepared. In addition, the consumption or nonmonetary returns of a college education both to herself and her husband can justify the cost.

FUTURE RETURNS TO EDUCATION

In estimating the returns to education we, of course, have to use data that show the present income differences between groups with different educational levels, high school versus college for instance. But it is reasonable to ask, can a person who invests in education today expect these differentials to continue into the future?

Basically the wages or earnings of people with various levels of education depend largely on the supply and demand for people with various degrees of skills. If, for example, demand for people with a four-year college degree is growing more rapidly than the supply of people with this training, their earnings will rise. Moreover, if the demand for college trained people is increasing faster than the demand for high school graduates, the income differential for college over high school will increase.

Although no one can predict with certainty what the future will bring, we might be able to obtain some idea of future income differentials by looking at the long-run trends in these figures. In Table 11–6 we present differences in mean income for various levels of education for selected years.

The most striking thing about the figures in Table 11–6 is the long-run upward trend in income differentials that result from more schooling. It appears, therefore, that the demand for people with higher skills is increasing faster than the demand for people with less skills. From these trends we might conclude that present investment in education will likely pay off at a high rate in the future than our current data would indicate.

TABLE 11–6. Mean annual income differentials for selected years by years of school completed

	1949	1956	1961	1965
High school over eighth grade	$ 955	$1,552	$1,740	$2,236
Four years high school over one–three years high school	558	816	785	994
One–three years college over high school	639	814	1,402	1,234
Four years college over high school	2,395	2,694	3,871	3,924
Four years college over one–three years college	1,756	1,880	2,469	2,690

Source: *Statistical Abstract*, 1967, p. 117.

ADDITIONAL CONSIDERATIONS

In order to keep the analysis as simple as possible, we have throughout the discussion on the returns to education neglected to mention a number of factors that could affect the outcome. One important consideration is taxes, particularly income taxes. Of course, our calculations have been based upon differences in income rather than absolute levels so there is a tendency for taxes to cancel out because everyone regardless of the amount of schooling they have must pay them.

However, to the extent that tax rates are higher for higher income people, there will be a slight reduction in the private returns to education if income taxes were first deducted from everyone's income. The social returns to education are, of course, not affected by taxes because society can still enjoy the increased output due to education.

A second consideration is the innate ability of people. It has been argued that the procedure we have used to estimate the returns to education results in an overestimate of the returns to education alone. For it is argued that the more capable people obtain more education and as a result part of what we attribute to education is in fact a return to superior innate intelligence. Granted this is to some extent true. But we must bear in mind as well that education opens doors to occupations that are otherwise closed regardless of one's innate intelligence. Education in a sense enables one to exploit his capabilities to a much greater extent.

A third consideration is a difference in nonmonetary rewards relating to jobs that require more education. As a rule an increase in the amount of education results in an increase in job satisfaction as well as income. Jobs available to people with relatively little education tend to be menial and routine in character and do not pay off much in terms of personal satisfaction.

Also there is less security in less skilled types of work. In times of high unemployment, it is usually the unskilled workers that are first to be laid off and last to be hired. And increased job security has some psychological benefits as well as the advantage of a more certain income. One doesn't have to be as concerned about whether his family will be provided for in the future.

MAIN POINTS OF CHAPTER 11

1. Economists have come to regard the skills and knowledge acquired through education as human capital.
2. A number of similarities exist between human and nonhuman capital: (1) both contribute to the real output of society, (2) both pay off over a long period of time, (3) both require a building period, and (4) both tend to depreciate.

3. Most human capital formation takes place as the result of formal schooling. A very critical role of the teacher is to point out the important, high payoff material to be learned.

4. The returns to education for the individual consist of two components: (1) monetary and (2) nonmonetary. Monetary returns refer to the increased earning power that results from additional education, nonmonetary returns refer to the utility that students derive out of being in school and the increased satisfaction that life brings because of the educational experience.

5. Society as a whole also gains when more people attain higher levels of education by such things as greater stability of government, less chance of a dictitorial or repressive form of government gaining power, less expenditure on crime, welfare programs, etc., and the creation of more pleasing communities in which people can live.

6. The cost of education for the individual includes three main items: (1) foregone earnings, (2) tuition, and (3) books and supplies. Foregone earnings is by far the largest cost. Board and room is not included because it must be paid regardless of what one does; it does not represent a special cost of going to school.

7. There is a temptation not to include foregone earnings as a cost of education. But giving up earnings from a full-time job to attend school is in the same category as giving up an education to go to work.

8. The public cost of education that is borne by society is for most education greater than the cost to the individual because tuition generally does not cover the full cost of building and operating schools.

9. Income data collected by the U.S. Bureau of Census reveal that additional education results in higher incomes at every age level.

10. Monetary returns to education are measured by the differences in earnings of people with different educational achievement.

11. In order to correctly evaluate the payoff to investment in education it is necessary to accumulate costs and discount future returns by an interest charge.

12. Choosing plausible cost figures and using the U.S. Census data on income by educational level, we can compute an internal rate of return to investment in education. The internal rate of return is that interest rate which makes the accumulated costs equal to the discounted returns.

13. The internal rate of return to a college education for a student who attends school full time during the school year but earns $1,200 during the summer is approximately 10 percent. The rate of return increases to about 13 percent if the student holds down a part-time job during the school year because of the reduced foregone earnings cost.

14. About one half of all college students who enter the freshman year do not graduate with a bachelor's degree. The rate of return to investment in two years of college is substantially lower than four years; 7 percent for a full-time student without part-time earnings and 9 percent with part-time earnings during the school year.

15. Over the past 20 years the income differential for additional years of schooling has been increasing, indicating that the demand for people with higher skills has been increasing more than the demand for people with less skills. From this we might conclude that our current figures understate the future returns to present education.

QUESTIONS FOR THOUGHT AND DISCUSSION

1. Economists view a college education as an investment in human capital. Do you view your education as something that produces capital? Explain why or why not.

2. List the monetary and nonmonetary returns that you expect to receive from a college education. Would you attend if there were no monetary returns? If so, how many years?

3. If you attend college primarily for its monetary returns, would you demand a different curriculum than if you came primarily for its nonmonetary returns? Explain.

4. Can grades be viewed both as a monetary and nonmonetary return? Explain.

5. Do you believe that a democratic organization of society is related to the amount and kind of education obtained by the people? Explain.

6. Which would you most likely do, borrow $2,500 for a new car or $2,500 to pay tuition? Why?

7. Is the cost of a college education in anyway related to the job opportunities open to high school graduates? Explain.

8. What kind of work would you likely be doing and what salary would you likely obtain were you not in college?

9. Estimate, as close as you can, the cost of four years of college for yourself. What kind of job and what salary do you expect to receive when leaving or graduating from college?

10. Compare the two salary estimates you have made in Questions 8 and 9. How much, if any, extra do you expect to earn by attending college? Compare this to your cost estimates in Question 9. Set up a "cash flow" diagram of your costs and returns of a college education. You need not attempt to compute an internal rate of return unless you have access to a calculator or computer.

11. "Education is free if schools are financed through public tax funds rather than through privately paid tuition fees." Comment.

12. Would you expect the private return to a college education to exceed the public return? Explain.

13. What effect does part-time employment have on (1) the costs and (2) the returns to a college education?

14. In Table 11–2 it shows that the college dropout, after an average of two years in college, can expect only about one fourth as large an increase in salary over high school than the college graduate. Why do you suppose this is the case?

CHAPTER
12
THE ECONOMICS OF RESEARCH AND NEW TECHNOLOGY

THE PRODUCTION OF NEW KNOWLEDGE

We saw in the previous chapter that the process of education, the transfer of knowledge from books and teachers into the minds of students, is akin to an investment involving both a cost and a return. In this chapter we shall probe a bit deeper into this process, seeking an understanding of the production of knowledge itself. Unless knowledge exists so that there is something to teach the process of education cannot take place.

At the beginning of history the stock of knowledge that existed in the minds of men was indeed small as measured by today's standards. Hunting and fishing skills and the ability to transform nature's bounty into food, clothing, and shelter were about the sum total of knowledge that existed.

Then somewhere along the way man acquired the ability to communicate by sound. Although we now take this skill for granted, somewhat like animals or birds take their instincts for granted, a little reflection will impress upon us the tremendous advance in knowledge that the introduction of verbal skills represented. Every object, action, or thought became associated with a sound. Moreover, there had to be a common acceptance, at least within an area or tribe of the meaning of sounds produced by a human's vocal cords. Anyone who has studied a foreign language appreciates the difficulty of learning correct sounds and the advance in knowledge that this skill represents.

We need not belabor the importance of verbal skills in perpetuating and building up the stock of knowledge. With these skills it becomes possible to pass on from one generation to the next important bits of information that otherwise would have to be relearned anew by trial and error. Equally important, of course, was the introduction of written languages which are even more efficient in the transfer and acquisition of knowledge than verbal sounds.

A common characteristic of knowledge that was produced during the dawning of history and even throughout the middle ages is that most of it came into being as a result of a "happy accident." In other words, knowledge came as a by-product of everyday activities. In the process of sustaining himself, man learned new things about plants, animals, and the environment. And this new information helped man to be more proficient in his activities.

RESEARCH AS A PRODUCTION ACTIVITY

Little by little in the course of history it became apparent that the full-time pursuit of knowledge by certain people in society resulted in a much greater output per unit of effort than occurred when knowledge came as a by-product of daily activities. Obviously people with special talents toward discovery or production of new knowledge could accomplish more if freed from other tasks. People such as Galileo, Newton, Edison, Franklin, and Einstein hardly could have accomplished their feats had they been required to toil as full-time farmers or shopkeepers.

Beginning then as a by-product of daily activities, gradually emerging as the domain of a select few, the production of new knowledge through research has become established as a full-fledged industry. Moreover, in the United States during recent years research has become one of the country's most rapidly growing industries. In 1955 the resources devoted to research and development (R&D) in the United States amounted to about $6 billion; by 1965 this figure had grown to over $23 billion per year.[1]

We refer to research as an industry because it has much in common with more traditional types of production. Essentially research is a production activity. Inputs consist mainly of scientists and engineers, laboratories and testing facilities; output consists of new knowledge. The same concepts we employed in our discussion of producer choice and product supply, such as marginal and average product, marginal and average costs, diminishing returns, and economies of scale, apply also to the production of new knowledge.

---

[1] *Statistical Abstract*, 1967, p. 537.

At the same time there are some unique characteristics of research that we ought to mention. First, there is the difficulty of measuring output. Knowledge, as you know, does not come in easy to measure units as bushels, pounds or dollars. Economists have found ways of measuring knowledge indirectly, however, but let us postpone until later in the chapter our discussion of this problem.

A second unique characteristic of research is that there is reason to believe that research may not be subject to the law of diminishing returns. Recall that the law of diminishing returns refers to a situation where the addition of a variable input to one or more fixed inputs after a point results in a diminished marginal physical product to the variable input. It is conceivable to view scientists and their supporting personnel and facilities as the variable input and nature's secrets or the potential stock of knowledge as the fixed input in the production of new knowledge, i.e., research.

Will the addition of more scientists result in a diminishing and eventually a zero marginal product of scientific research? If nature's secrets or the potential stock of knowledge were finite, then we would reasonably expect diminishing returns to set in at some point. But if all knowledge, both known and unknown, is infinite, then research need not be subject to the law of diminishing returns.

In other words, as we acquire more knowledge will it become more or less difficult to add to the stock of knowledge. One would argue yes if one believes that the potential stock of knowledge is finite and that we already have discovered nature's most accessible secrets. On the other hand, it can be argued that knowledge, like the universe, is boundless and that previously discovered knowledge only scratches the surface and allows us to be even more productive in our future quest.

Unfortunately we will not likely be able to measure the limits of knowledge, at least within the confines of our finite lives here on earth. No one will be able to say, "we have now discovered all the knowledge there is to be known; nothing else remains to be discovered." When we consider that no two people who have lived or are living on earth are exactly the same, or that no two snowflakes have exactly the same form, we begin to appreciate the boundlessness of nature.

We should be aware, also, that knowledge is more than having information or facts. In large part it is the ability to know what to do with information. Prehistoric man, for example, knew that fire was hot and that water moved swiftly in rivers but did not know that these phenomena could be transformed into sources of power. Even today the libraries filled with information do us little good unless we can apply the information.

It will be useful to probe a bit deeper into the activity we call research. Actually research encompasses a fairly wide array of endeavor ranging from what scientists call basic research to the more applied and developmental types of activity.

BASIC RESEARCH

We can think of basic research as activity concerned strictly with unlocking the secrets of nature without having a preconceived idea of how the knowledge might be used. This does not imply, though, that the output of basic research is of little use. Indeed some of the most useful research results have come out of basic research.

A relatively small proportion of all research and development funds are spent on basic research, however. In 1965 basic research totaled $2.9 billion or about 12 percent of all research and development expenditures.[2] It is not difficult to understand why basic research has remained relatively small. An industrial firm invests in research for the purpose of increasing profits. If the firm has virtually no guarantee that the research results can be applied to the firm's operation, as is true for basic research, it has little incentive to pay for this research. Some of the large firms allow their scientists a relatively small amount of free time for basic research, but this is mainly a fringe benefit for the scientists.

As a consequence most basic research is carried on by colleges and universities or the federal government. But even here there has been a reluctance to "turn scientists loose." In part this might be due to a fear by the public that the funds would be squandered on scientists' pet projects with little chance for any payoff to society. Also basic research is a very risky business. Perhaps 1 project out of 10 really adds something significant to the fund of knowledge.

This is not to say, however, that the high degree of risk associated with basic research necessarily implies a low return to this research. The 1 or 2 successfull projects out of 10 can well pay for the failures. From the standpoint of risk, research is much like drilling for oil. In oil exploration roughly 1 well out of 10 produces a significant find. But as a rule the gushers more than pay for the dry holes.

APPLIED RESEARCH

As the name implies applied research is concerned with solving a particular problem or finding out a specific unknown. For example, the problem might be finding a way to reduce air pollution caused by automobiles, or a way to curb noise of jet engines.

As a rule both industry and public institutions have been more willing to finance applied research as opposed to basic research. Understandably

---

[2] *Ibid.,* p. 537.

the business firm is more certain that a return will be forthcoming if the research is centered on a problem of concern to the firm. Much the same holds true for publicly sponsored research. Society feels somewhat more certain that it is getting its money's worth from research if scientists work on a recognized problem.

DEVELOPMENT

The activity referred to as development is almost the exclusive domain of the large industrial firm or the federal government. Development activities include such things as building prototypes of new products and testing them before their introduction on the market. However, it is rather difficult to separate development from applied research. In a sense development is a kind of applied research because it is directed at finding out the unknown of a product or production technique. In fact most industrial research is lumped together in one category and called R&D (research and development).

There is some difficulty even in distinguishing between the basic and applied categories. For instance an applied research project can bring forth unexpected knowledge totally unrelated to the problem at hand. In this sense applied research has the same characteristics as basic research. It is best, therefore, to view these three categories of research as a continium ranging from pure basic research to the applied which in turn leads into the development type of activity on the other end of the scale.

RESEARCH BY INDUSTRIAL FIRMS (R&D)

As mentioned, research done by industrial firms tends to be concentrated towards the applied and development types of activity. The overall motivation for a firm to carry on R&D is to improve its profit position. Research and development can increase profits for the firm by (1) the development of new or improved products which has the effect of increasing the demand for the firm's products, or by (2) the development of new cost reducing techniques of production which reduce average and marginal cost for the firm. The production of new or improved products resulting from R&D is illustrated in Figure 12–1, diagrams (A) and (B).

Diagram (A) illustrates the situation for an imperfectly competitive firm before it undertakes the development of a new or improved product. If the R&D program is successful and a new product is developed, the demand facing the firm shifts to the right shown by D_1 in Figure 12–1 (B). As an example, this might depict a petroleum company that has developed a new additive for its gasoline which results in better gas mileage. Understandably the demand for the company's product shifts to the right as customers switch from brands that do not contain the additive.

FIGURE 12–1. The effect of new and improved products resulting from R&D

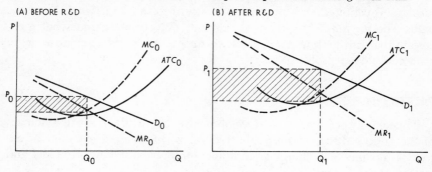

We must keep in mind, though, that R&D is a costly activity. Hence the R&D program will have the effect also of increasing the firm's average total cost and marginal cost from what they would otherwise be. Thus ATC_1 and MC_1 in diagram (B) of Figure 12–1 are drawn in slightly higher than their original position in diagram (A). In this particular example total profits, depicted by the shaded areas, are higher after the R&D than before, indicating that the additional revenue brought in by the increase in product demand more than offsets the additional cost of the R&D.

The second possibility for increasing profits through R&D is to reduce production costs through the discovery and adoption of new cost reducing techniques. For example, a petroleum company might develop a new, more efficient method of refining crude oil. This would have the effect of shifting ATC and MC down and to the right as illustrated in Figure 12–2. Here we assume that the product remains the same so that the demand and marginal revenue curves are the same in both diagrams.

FIGURE 12–2. The effect of new cost reducing techniques resulting from R&D

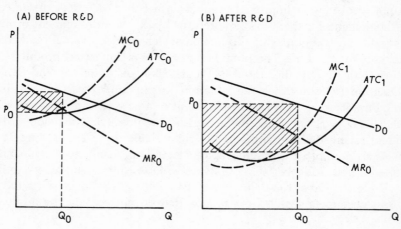

In this example we have assumed also that the cost saving obtained through the new techniques was more than enough to offset the increase in costs brought on by the R&D. Total profits, denoted by the shaded areas in Figure 12-2, therefore, increase as a result of the increased R&D expenditure.

RETURNS TO INDUSTRIAL R&D

Conceptually, the decision on whether or not to do R&D is rather straightforward; do it as long as expected revenue increases more than expected costs. But in actual decision-making situation, the main problem is to assess the returns to R&D. The firm has no guarantee, of course, that demand will shift right or costs shift down.

The usual procedure for a firm is to begin with a rather modest R&D program, perhaps hiring an engineer to spend full time thinking up new ways of doing things. If total revenue increases more than his salary and expenses, the firm may add another R&D person, etc. In other words, decisions to do or not to do R&D tend to be of a marginal nature. Because of the substantial increase in R&D during recent years, we can only infer that most firms have found it very profitable, hence they are doing more.

The decision by a firm to engage in R&D may be motivated as well by the desire to simply maintain a profit position. If other firms in the industry are investing in R&D to create new or improved products, or to lower production costs, the firm that does not keep up soon will find itself with few customers or excessively high costs and eventually will be forced out of business. Although even in this context the effects of R&D still can be illustrated by Figures 12-1 and 12-2. Profits after R&D are higher than they would otherwise be.

In deciding whether or not to engage in R&D the overriding consideration by the firm must be whether or not it will be possible to capture a return to its investment. If the new knowledge that is produced by R&D is readily available to competing firms, the firm that originally produced the knowledge will not be able to gain any special advantage.

For example, the petroleum firm that develops a new gasoline additive will naturally guard its secret very closely. For if other firms should find it out and duplicate the additive, they could gain all of its advantages without paying any of the cost. No doubt this explains why some firms find it profitable to employ industrial spies.

One alternative for the firm or individual who discovers or develops something new is to take out a patent with the U.S. government patent office. Patent laws forbid the duplication of the patented item or process by other firms or individuals for a period of 17 years. Without these laws or protection, it is argued, there would be little incentive to invest in R&D.

In reality, however, patent laws probably have not offered the protection that one might first suppose. Although a patented item cannot be duplicated exactly, in many cases a close substitute can be developed by making a few minor changes. Patenting certain products or processes, then, may actually hasten their discovery and adoption by competing firms. For this reason it is not unusual for firms to deliberately not patent something they have developed; rather they try to keep it a secret.

The decision whether or not to take out a patent depends mainly on the nature of the product or process. If it is something that is relatively easy to keep secret such as an additive or minute ingredient, it might be best not to patent. But if it is something like a machine or gadget that will be widely used then patenting provides some protection, although rarely complete protection, against copying by other firms.

Another important factor that bears upon whether or not a firm will invest in R&D is the absolute size of the firm. Understandably it will not pay for a small firm to engage in any sizable R&D effort. Consider, for example, our tomato-growing endeavor. Even if we were assured that no one would copy our research results, it would not pay us to spend several thousand dollars, attempting to increase tomato yields. Even if we could double the yield of each tomato plant, the return would be small compared to the conceivable cost of doing so.

On the other hand, a very large firm, Standard Oil, for example, can afford to spend a great deal on something that may improve its product only a small amount, say one penny per gallon. But if we multiply this penny per gallon by the millions of gallons of gasoline the company sells each year, we are able to see why it pays for the firm to engage in substantial R&D. In general the larger the firm, the more profitable it is to invest in research and development, for a given increase in demand or decrease in costs.

Thus far we have considered only the private returns, i.e., extra profits, of industrial R&D. But we should keep in mind that R&D can still be a good investment from the point of view of society even if it does not provide higher profits for the firm doing the R&D. What generally happens is that the extra profits coming from a new product or a new technique of production are eventually eroded away as more and more firms copy the product or technique.

But the fact that the individual firm's extra profits from R&D eventually disappear does not mean that society's benefits from R&D disappear also. Society continues to enjoy a return from R&D long after its profits are eroded away because of the resulting new or improved products that continue to be consumed and/or the reduced costs brought about by new technology. In other words, R&D makes it possible for society to obtain a greater value of output from its limited resources. Economists refer to this benefit as a "social return."

PUBLICLY SPONSORED RESEARCH

As we know, an industrial firm will not choose to invest in research unless it has a reasonable assurance that it will add to profits. Also the relatively small firm will not engage in research because the expense is too great to be borne by the relatively small output. However, it is recognized that society can benefit greatly from research that may not be profitable for an individual firm, or from research that affects the output of industries made up of firms too small to do their own research such as agriculture. For this reason the federal and state governments either sponsor or carry on research in their own laboratories or institutions.

Most publicly sponsored research is done in colleges and universities. Because of the risk involved and the small chance of capturing a profit on the knowledge produced, much of the country's so-called basic research is done in these institutions. Also, with the exception of market research on individual products, most economic research is done in institutions of higher learning. This is true as well for the humanities and other social sciences.

The decisions on what kind and how much of public research should be done are even more difficult than for industrial research. The decision-making process is slow, cumbersome, and often based on very inadequate information. Someone, of course, must make these decisions regardless of the information available. The basic decisions are made by society's elected representatives in the state and federal governments. They must decide how much of the taxpayer's money is to be devoted to research. Usually the amount that is allocated to research for a current year is based on what was allocated the year before plus a little extra for new problems, increasing expenses, and the like.

Once the funds reach the research institutions, more decisions are required to further allocate the money. How much goes to physics, how much to chemistry, economics, agriculture, etc.? Again the current allocation is made mainly on the basis of past allocation. Marginal changes come about with changes in personnel, or with the emergence or recognition of new and pressing problems such as pollution.

Ideally public research allocation should be made on the basis of the highest payoff to the research. But the main problem is to identify and measure the returns to public research. Let us consider this problem next.

RETURNS TO PUBLIC RESEARCH

Like education the returns to public research can be classified into an investment and consumption component. In the consumption area, society is willing to pay something to gain information about itself or about the universe even though this knowledge may not lead to an increase in value of real output of society. For example, society has been willing to pay a sizable amount to develop a means of getting to the moon and back. Society also considers it worthwhile to find out more about origin of man, and about his behavior both past and present. Even though knowledge of this sort may not add to the monetary value of real output, it does add to the utility of society.

Aside from the space program, most public research is aimed at increasing the value of output of society, i.e., an investment or monetary return. People value good health or the avoidance of the "grim reaper" before their time, hence they are willing to pay for medical research. Society places a value also on a clean environment, so it supports research on ways of achieving this goal without giving up the goods and services that contribute to the pollution.

Most of the basic research that is carried on, such as the work in physics, chemistry, biology, mathematics, etc., may not be aimed at a specific problem but it is anticipated that the knowledge produced will somehow have a monetary value.

Measuring the monetary value of public research is indeed a difficult problem. Not much headway has been made so far and a great deal of work remains to be done in this area. Until some quantitative measures can be found, decisions to allocate public research will have to be made from purely subjective criteria or historical precedence, neither of which guarantees that society is getting the most for its money.

AGRICULTURAL RESEARCH

We include a separate discussion of agricultural research for two reasons: first it is an area where some progress has been made in estimating returns; and secondly, there seems to be widespread misunderstanding about who benefits from this research.

The major outcome of agricultural research is to increase the productive capacity of farmers. These include new, higher yielding crop varieties, breeding and disease control advances making livestock and poultry more efficient converters of feed, completely new inputs such as herbicides and pesticides, and new and improved management practices for farmers.

As we pointed out in the chapter on product supply the effect of new technology is to increase, or shift to the right, the supply curve of individual producers and the industry, as shown in Figure 12–3. For a given price producers are willing to put more on the market, or will sell a given amount for a lower price.

The increase in productive efficiency, hence the increase in product supply, brought about by agricultural research in effect increases the total value of agricultural output for a given amount of resources. In other words, by producing knowledge and new, more productive inputs society obtains more output from its scarce resources. The annual value of this additional output to society is illustrated in Figure 12–3 by the shaded area lying between S_0 and S_1 bounded on the top by the demand for agricultural products.

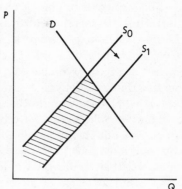

FIGURE 12–3. Illustrating the effect of agriculture research and the resulting new technology that shifts agricultural supply

Supply curve S_0 in Figure 12–3 represents what the supply of agricultural output would be without the new technology. By measuring the increase in productive efficiency of agriculture, economists have been able to determine the location of S_1 for a given year. The difference between these two curves, therefore, represents the value of output attributable to agricultural research.

By comparing the annual expenditure on research with the value of extra output attributable to research, economists have been able to obtain estimates of its social internal rate of return. The procedure used is essentialy the same as we used to compute the rate of return to education. In this case the cash outflows consist of expenditures on agricultural research (both industrial and public) and the cash inflows consist of the value of additional output obtained as a result of agricultural research (value of the shaded area in Figure 12–3).

Estimates of the internal rate of return to all agricultural research that has been done in the United States appear to be in the range of 18 to 20 percent.[3] Note that this rate of return is substantially higher than the returns we obtained for education. There is evidence also that the rate of return to recent investment in agricultural research is substantially higher than the return to this research that was done three or four decades ago.[4]

---

[3] Willis L. Peterson, "The Returns to Investment in Agricultural Research in the United States," University of Minnesota, Staff Paper P69–5, April, 1969, p. 31.
[4] Ibid.

To those that consider agricultural research as something that benefits farmers primarily, the increase in the rate of return to agricultural research might come as a bit of a surprise. After all, the farm population has declined from about 32 million people in 1920 to about 10 million people at the present. During this period the farm population as a percent of total population declined from about 30 percent to 5 percent.

This brings us to our second major point. The long-run beneficiaries of agricultural research tend to be consumers of farm products rather than farmers. Of course, farmers benefit as consumers along with everyone else. Consumers benefit from agricultural research because the resulting increase in productive efficiency shifts the supply of agricultural products to the right, thereby increasing food output and reducing food prices below what they would otherwise be.

Many people, particularly housewives, would argue, though, that food prices are not cheap, judging from the prices in supermarkets these days. But one must look at the real cost of food—the proportion of a country's resources that are devoted to food production. At the present time Americans spend less than 20 percent of their income on food and beverages. Contrast this to Nigeria, for example, where food accounts for 70 percent of a family's budget.[5]

Even in the United States at the turn of the century, people spent almost 40 percent of their income on food. A nation with a relative unproductive agricultural sector must devote a relatively large share of its resources to food production. As agricultural productivity increases, more and more people leave agriculture to produce other things that make life more interesting and enjoyable. If 70 to 80 percent of a nation's population are required to produce food, people cannot produce modern conveniences such as reasonably priced automobiles, adequate medical care, the host of labor saving appliances, etc., that make life more enjoyable. Life might have been simpler in the "good old days" when most people were farmers, but few people today would accept the inconveniences that our forefathers had to contend with.

This is not to say that agricultural research can take sole credit for economic development. Other knowledge is required as well to produce the variety of modern goods and services that raise the standard of living. But as developing nations are learning, little progress can be made without technological advance in agriculture.

SOCIAL COSTS OF NEW TECHNOLOGY

There is a growing concern in the United States and other highly developed nations that the total or true cost of research that produces new

---

[5] Marguerite Burk, *Consumption Economics: A Multidisciplinary Approach* (New York: John Wiley & Sons, Inc., 1968), p. 41.

knowledge and technology may exceed the expenditures for research. One of the concerns is the movement of people between occupations and areas. If new technology makes a job obsolete, what is the social cost of having the person who held this job move to another occupation in another location?

It is fairly easy to measure moving costs, but there are other things to consider. People who move must leave family, friends, and familiar ways of living for the unknown. Some find moving an exciting experience, others dread it. The largest case in point is the huge rural to urban migration that has taken place in the United States. Most would agree that the increased concentration of population in urban areas has contributed to many present day problems: air and water pollution, congestion of transportation systems and of housing, and the tension and unrest are some examples.

Without the new technology would these problems disappear? Perhaps some. But we must remember also that other problems plagued mankind in years past. Consider the disease, isolation, long hours of drudgery both in the home and on the job, ignorance, etc., that our forefathers had to contend with. Even pollution existed in those days. Imagine the smell in the cities when vehicles were horse drawn, or the smoke and soot that came forth when coal was the main source of heat and power. Indeed some of the worst pollution in the world today exists in countries that have experienced relatively little advance in technology. When dealing with present-day problems we tend to visualize things as we would like to see them, not as they existed in years past.

MAIN POINTS OF CHAPTER 12

1. The introduction of a spoken and written language early in history represented a significant advance in knowledge for mankind.

2. From the dawning of history through the middle ages new knowledge came mainly as a by-product of everyday activities.

3. During the course of history man learned that output of knowledge could be increased if certain people devoted full time to its production. Today the production of knowledge is a large and growing industry expending billions of dollars per year in the United States alone.

4. We can think of research as a production activity where inputs consist of such things as scientists and engineers, laboratories, and testing facilities, and output consists of new knowledge.

5. Unlike more traditional types of production, we cannot be sure that the production of new knowledge is subject to the law of diminishing returns. If the potential stock of knowledge is infinite there is no reason why diminishing returns must set in.

6. Knowledge is more than having information or facts; in large part it is the ability to know what to do with information.

7. Basic research is concerned with unlocking the secrets of nature without having a preconceived idea of how the knowledge might be used.

8. Applied research is concerned with solving a particular problem or finding out a specific unknown.

9. Development is an extension of applied research concerned with finding out the unknown about new products or production techniques and testing them before their introduction on the market.

10. Industrial firms are motivated to carry on R&D by the prospect of increased profits. Research and development can increase profits by (1) the introduction of new and improved products which shifts the demand facing the firm to the right, or (2) the development of new, cost reducing techniques of production, which shifts the firm's cost curves down and to the right.

11. The type of research carried on by a firm will be governed by its ability to capture a return to the research.

12. Patent laws are intended to help firms or individuals capture a return from new products or techniques. The ability of competitors to develop close substitutes for patented items limit their protection, however.

13. In general it does not pay a small firm to engage in organized R&D because the cost cannot be spread across a large enough output.

14. Even though the private profits from R&D may decline or be nonexistent, its expenditure can still be a good investment for society because R&D makes it possible for society to obtain a greater value of output from its limited resources.

15. Because society can benefit greatly from research that is not profitable for individual firms, the federal and state governments sponsor or carry on research of their own. Most public research is done in colleges and universities.

16. The allocation of public research is a difficult problem because knowledge does not come in easy to measure units as bushels, pounds, or dollars.

17. The value to society of agricultural research has been estimated by measuring the value of the increased output brought about by the increase in productive efficiency of farmers.

18. Contrary to popular belief the main benefits of agricultural research flow to consumers rather than to farmers. As agriculture becomes more productive, a larger share of a nation's resources are devoted to the production of things other than food.

19. There has been a growing awareness in recent years of problems associated with new technology. What is often overlooked, however, is the quality of life that existed in years past and the problems that confronted people before the advent of modern technology.

QUESTIONS FOR THOUGHT AND DISCUSSION

1. Letting your imagination run free, try to visualize how the ability to communicate orally and then by writing affected the growth of knowledge in prehistoric times.

2. In what ways is the production of knowledge similar to more traditional types of production, and in what ways does it differ?

3. Would you argue that the production of knowledge is subject to the law of diminishing returns? Why or why not?

4. Suppose you are the owner of a small manufacturing company. How could you decide whether or not to spend something on R&D, and if so how would you decide what to spend it on?

5. Suppose you are just hired as the director of R&D for a large auto maker with a $1,000,000 budget for the coming year. What are some of the possible kinds of research you could do? How would you go about deciding how to allocate this $1,000,000.

6. Does industrial R&D benefit anyone besides the firms who do the R&D? If so, how?

7. Why has society decided to pay for a substantial share of the nation's research by public tax funds?

8. If publicly sponsored research does not yield a profit to anyone, how can its returns be measured?

9. Suppose you are in charge of allocating research funds in a large university. How would you go about allocating these funds?

10. "Because the number of farmers in the United States is declining, the government should also decrease publicly sponsored agricultural research." Comment.

11. Knowing what you do about the relationship between price elasticity of demand and total revenue (Chapter 3), what effect would you suppose agricultural research has on total revenue going to farmers as a group if the demand for food is highly inelastic? Illustrate with a supply-demand diagram.

INDEX

253

This book has been set in 10 and 9 point Caledonia, leaded 2 points. Chapter numbers are in 14 and 30 point Bodoni Bold and chapter titles are in 18 point Bodoni Bold. The size of the type page is 27 by 45½ picas.

11-401

DATE DUE

GAYLORD			PRINTED IN U.S.A.

38067